Europeanisation of Public Policy in Southern Europe

Large or small, old EU member or new, and even EU member state or not – political economies across Southern Europe have been increasingly but distinctively 'Europeanised'. In political, public and scholarly debates on processes of Europeanisation, Southern Europe invariably features as *the* area of concern. These concerns have been all the more heightened when the current sovereign debt crisis disproportionately hit this 'flaky fringe'.

This volume systematically investigates the dynamics of Europeanisation in the 'Southern Periphery' by tracing the domestic constellations of ideas, interests and institutions over the course of the 2000s which came to a close with the crisis. Bringing together a multidisciplinary team of leading specialists, the volume focuses on the political economy of public policy reform in Greece, Italy, Malta, Portugal, Spain and Turkey. In order to allow for cross-case comparisons, these original country studies follow a common template framed by what the Editors call the 'Europeanisation as research programme'. The volume casts empirical light on the causes of the crisis in these cases as well as the past legacies conditioning their responses to the crisis. Its conclusions point to variegated patterns of Europeanisation in different policy areas across Southern Europe.

This volume will be of interest to students and scholars of European integration, European political economy, European public policy and comparative politics as well as specialists of Southern Europe.

This book was previously published as a special issue of *South European Society and Politics*.

Canan Balkır is Jean Monnet Chair in European Economic Integration and Head of Department of EU Studies at Graduate School of Social Sciences Dokuz Eylul University.

H. Tolga Bolukbasi is Assistant Professor of Political Science and Public Administration at Bilkent University.

Ebru Ertugal is currently Visiting Researcher at Bilkent University.

South European Society and Politics series

Series editors:
Susannah Verney, University of Athens, Greece
Anna Bosco, University of Trieste, Italy

The parallel regime transitions of the 1970s, when Southern Europe was the vanguard of the 'third wave' of democratisation, the impact of EU membership and Europeanisation and more recently, the region's central role in the eurozone crisis have all made Southern Europe a distinctive area of interest for social science scholars. The *South European Society and Politics* book series promotes new empirical research into the domestic politics and society of South European states. The series, open to a broad range of social science approaches, offers comparative thematic volumes covering the region as a whole and on occasion, innovative single-country studies. Its geographical scope includes both 'old' and 'new' Southern Europe, defined as Italy, Greece, Portugal, Spain, Cyprus, Malta and Turkey.

Titles in the series:

Europeanisation of Public Policy in Southern Europe
Comparative Political Economy from the 2000s to the Crisis
Edited by Canan Balkır, H. Tolga Bolukbasi and Ebru Ertugal

Transformations of the Radical Left in Southern Europe
Bringing Society Back In?
Edited by Myrto Tsakatika and Marco Lisi

Elections in Hard Times: Southern Europe 2010–11
Edited by Anna Bosco and Susannah Verney

Voters and Parties in the Spanish Political Space
Edited by Ignacio Sánchez-Cuenca and Elias Dinas

Previously published in the journal *South European Society and Politics*

Europeanization and the Southern Periphery
Edited by Kevin Featherstone and George Kazamias

Who Governs Southern Europe?
Edited by Pedro Tavares de Almeida, Nancy Bermeo and António Costa Pinto

Spain and Portugal in the European Union
The First Fifteen Years
Edited by Paul Christopher Manuel and Sebastián Royo

Mobilising Politics and Society?
The EU Convention's Impact on Southern Europe
Edited by Sonia Lucarelli and Claudio Radaelli

Reinventing Democracy
Grassroots Movements in Portugal
Edited by João Arriscado Nunes and Boaventura de Sousa Santos

When Greeks think about Turks
The View from Anthropology
Edited by Dimitrios Theodossopoulos

Party Change in Southern Europe
Edited by Anna Bosco and Leonardo Morlino

The South European Right in the 21st Century
Italy, France and Spain
Edited by Jocelyn A. J. Evans

Spain's 'Second Transition'?
The Socialist government of José Luis Rodríguez Zapatero
Edited by Bonnie N. Field

Dealing with the Legacy of Authoritarianism
The "Politics of the Past" in Southern European Democracies
Edited by António Costa Pinto and Leonardo Morlino

Perspectives of National Elites on European Citizenship
A South European View
Edited by Nicolò Conti, Maurizio Cotta and Pedro Tavares de Almeida

Euroscepticism in Southern Europe
A Diachronic Perspective
Edited by Susannah Verney

Turkey and the EU: Accession and Reform
Edited by Gamze Avci and Ali Çarkoğlu

Europeanisation of Public Policy in Southern Europe

Comparative Political Economy from the 2000s to the Crisis

Edited by
Canan Balkır, H. Tolga Bolukbasi and Ebru Ertugal

Routledge
Taylor & Francis Group
LONDON AND NEW YORK

First published 2014
by Routledge
2 Park Square, Milton Park, Abingdon, Oxon, OX14 4RN, UK

and by Routledge
711 Third Avenue, New York, NY 10017, USA

Routledge is an imprint of the Taylor & Francis Group, an informa business

British Library Cataloguing in Publication Data
A catalogue record for this book is available from the British Library

ISBN 13: 978-0-415-74293-1

Typeset in Garamond
by Taylor & Francis Books

Publisher's Note
The publisher accepts responsibility for any inconsistencies that may have arisen during the conversion of this book from journal articles to book chapters, namely the possible inclusion of journal terminology.

Contents

Citation Information ix
Notes on Contributors xi
Acknowledgements xii

1. Europeanisation and Dynamics of Continuity and Change: Domestic Political Economies in the 'Southern Periphery'
Canan Balkir, H. Tolga Bolukbasi and Ebru Ertugal 1

2. Europeanisation, Independent Bodies and the Empowerment of Technocracy: The Case of the Greek Auditing Oversight Body
Spyros Blavoukos, Constantinos Caramanis and Emmanouil Dedoulis 17

3. The Europeanisation of Macroeconomic Policies and Financial Regulation in Italy
Lucia Quaglia 35

4. All Hands on Deck! How Europeanised Is the Maltese Labour Market?
Rose Marie Azzopardi 53

5. Portugal in the European Union: The Limits of Convergence
Sebastián Royo 73

6. Spain's Catch up with the EU Core: The Implausible Quest of a 'Flying Pig'?
Luis Moreno 93

7. Europeanisation of Employment Policy in Turkey: Tracing Domestic Change through Institutions, Ideas and Interests
H. Tolga Bolukbasi and Ebru Ertugal 113

8. Europeanisation in the 'Southern Periphery': Comparative Research Findings on the EU's Impact on Domestic Political Economies
Canan Balkir, H. Tolga Bolukbasi and Ebru Ertugal 133

Index 155

Citation Information

The chapters in this book were originally published in *South European Society and Politics*, volume 18, issue 2 (June 2013). When citing this material, please use the original page numbering for each article, as follows:

Chapter 1
Europeanisation and Dynamics of Continuity and Change: Domestic Political Economies in the 'Southern Periphery'
Canan Balkir, H. Tolga Bolukbasi and Ebru Ertugal
South European Society and Politics, volume 18, issue 2 (June 2013)
pp. 121–138

Chapter 2
Europeanisation, Independent Bodies and the Empowerment of Technocracy: The Case of the Greek Auditing Oversight Body
Spyros Blavoukos, Constantinos Caramanis and Emmanouil Dedoulis
South European Society and Politics, volume 18, issue 2 (June 2013)
pp. 139–158

Chapter 3
The Europeanisation of Macroeconomic Policies and Financial Regulation in Italy
Lucia Quaglia
South European Society and Politics, volume 18, issue 2 (June 2013)
pp. 159–176

Chapter 4
All Hands on Deck! How Europeanised Is the Maltese Labour Market?
Rose Marie Azzopardi
South European Society and Politics, volume 18, issue 2 (June 2013)
pp. 177–196

Chapter 5
Portugal in the European Union: The Limits of Convergence
Sebastián Royo
South European Society and Politics, volume 18, issue 2 (June 2013)
pp. 197–216

Chapter 6
Spain's Catch up with the EU Core: The Implausible Quest of a 'Flying Pig'?
Luis Moreno
South European Society and Politics, volume 18, issue 2 (June 2013)
pp. 217–238

Chapter 7
Europeanisation of Employment Policy in Turkey: Tracing Domestic Change through Institutions, Ideas and Interests
H. Tolga Bolukbasi and Ebru Ertugal
South European Society and Politics, volume 18, issue 2 (June 2013)
pp. 237–258

Chapter 8
Europeanisation in the 'Southern Periphery': Comparative Research Findings on the EU's Impact on Domestic Political Economies
Canan Balkir, H. Tolga Bolukbasi and Ebru Ertugal
South European Society and Politics, volume 18, issue 2 (June 2013)
pp. 259–280

Please direct any queries you may have about the citations to
clsuk.permissions@cengage.com

Notes on Contributors

Canan Balkır is Jean Monnet Chair in European Economic Integration and Head of Department of EU Studies at Graduate School of Social Sciences, Dokuz Eylul University.

Spyros Blavoukos is a Lecturer in the Department of International and European Economic Studies at the Athens University of Economics and Business.

H. Tolga Bolukbasi is Assistant Professor in the Department of Political Science and Public Administration at Bilkent University.

Constantinos Caramanis is an Associate Professor in the Department of Business Administration, Athens University of Economics and Business.

Emmanouil Dedouils is a Lecturer in the Department of Business Administration, Athens University of Economics and Business.

Ebru Ertugal is a Visiting Researcher in the Department of Political Science and Public Administration at Bilkent University.

Lucia Quaglia is Professor of Political Science at the University of York.

Rose Marie Azzopardi is a Lecturer in International Economics at the University of Malta.

Sebastián Royo is Vice-Provost and Professor of Government at Suffolk University in Boston, and Director of the Suffolk University Madrid Campus.

Luis Moreno is Research Professor at the Spanish National Research Council (CSIC) in Madrid (IPP-CCHS) (www.ipp.csic.es).

Acknowledgements

The papers in this volume were presented at a workshop in October 2010 hosted by the Department of EU Studies at Dokuz Eylul University, Izmir. The workshop was generously funded by the Delegation of the European Union to Turkey and the Municipality of Konak (Izmir). We would like to thank especially Mr. Tibor Varadi, Deputy Head of EU Delegation to Turkey, Ms. Selda Paydak, Press and Information Manager at the EU Delegation to Turkey, Dr. Hakan Tartan, Mayor of Konak Municipality and Ms. Serpil Güngör, Vice Mayor of Konak Municipality. We are grateful to the contributors to this volume since they have meticulously followed the very detailed template (which is presented in the introductory article) in drafting the case studies. Each of the papers submitted was subject to double-blind peer review. We would like to thank our referees who put so much effort into making the volume better. Special thanks go to Timur Kaymaz for his able editorial assistance. We would like to thank Susannah Verney and Anna Bosco for their encouragement, support, patience and extremely efficient handling of the entire process without which the volume would not have come about. Last but not least, we would like to share with our readers our gratitude to Kevin Featherstone and George Kazamias for the inspirational and pioneering special issue on 'Europeanisation and the Southern Periphery' they had put together more than a decade ago. While our Izmir workshop was intended as a retrospective on that special issue, we hoped to contribute to the debate especially on the impact of the EU on domestic political economies in the wake of the Great Recession. We look forward to the continuation of this fascinating research on Europeanisation in/of the 'Southern periphery'.

Canan Balkir, H. Tolga Bolukbasi and Ebru Ertugal
Izmir and Ankara, August 2012

Europeanisation and Dynamics of Continuity and Change: Domestic Political Economies in the 'Southern Periphery'

Canan Balkir, H. Tolga Bolukbasi and Ebru Ertugal

This article provides the framework for some case studies on the dynamics of Europeanisation in South European political economies. It summarises the key features of the common template each case study adopts. Following a discussion on political economy as it is conceptualised in this volume titled "Europeanisation and the Southern Periphery' in Retrospect: Another Decade of Dynamism, Asymmetry, and Fragmentation?', the article elaborates the defining attributes of the Europeanisation research programme by focusing on its theoretical core, research design and method of conceptualising and operationalising domestic continuity and change centring on the troika of 'ideas', 'interests' and 'institutions' in unpacking the dynamics therein. It concludes by providing a summary of the contributions to this volume.

This volume presents six case studies exploring dynamics of Europeanisation in South European political economies by tracing changes in the constellation of ideas, interests and institutions. It is inspired by an earlier volume edited by Kevin Featherstone and George Kazamias titled 'Europeanisation and the Southern Periphery' which appeared as a special issue of *South European Society and Politics* more than a decade ago. While it builds on some of the insights of this earlier special issue (as will be clear in direct references below), it hopes to reflect the theoretical refinements in what we term the 'Europeanisation research programme' (Bolukbasi, Ertugal & Ozcurumez 2010 and see below). It also aims to provide a fresh empirical look into how the European Union

(EU) shapes the unfolding substantive developments across Europe's 'Southern Periphery', in particular in the domestic political economies of Southern Europe in the first decade after the publication of the original special issue by Featherstone and Kazamias (2000). It surveys the dynamics of continuity and change in domestic political economies by focusing on particular public policy areas in six case studies on Greece, Italy, Malta, Portugal, Spain and Turkey.[1]

The contributions in the present volume are designed as case studies within the Europeanisation research programme. To that end, each case study follows what we view to be the epistemological core of this research programme by relying on its common conceptual tools and the research design template. They address a set of key questions stemming from this research programme: What are the EU's key formal and informal rules, procedures, frames of reference, mechanisms and governance structures that may potentially bring about change at the domestic level? How can we portray the direction, extent and dimensions of domestic change (as well as continuity) in Southern European political economies over the course of the last decade? Once we have a picture of outcomes in different policy and governance domains at the domestic level, what are the different manifestations of Europeanisation in different public policy areas? How are the respective constellations of ideas, interests and institutions representing these domains evolving? How does the EU play a role in the evolution of these constellations over time?

In the rest of this framing article we discuss the key features of the common template each country case study has adopted by elaborating the main elements of research design and key conceptual threads. We, first, delineate the substantive scope of the volume by briefly discussing what we understand from the term 'political economy' as conceptualised in the comparative political economy literature and how this literature typically focuses on domestic public policies. In terms of its geographical scope, the volume focuses on differentiated processes of transformation across three clusters of countries in Southern Europe classified according to their actual or potential timing of accession. Second, we review what we consider to be the defining attributes of the Europeanisation research programme. Here we summarise the theoretical core (new institutionalism), the particular mode of designing research and the method of conceptualising and operationalising domestic continuity and change which is increasingly characterising new generations of empirical studies relying on the Europeanisation research programme. Third, we summarise our research strategy of using the troika of 'ideas', 'interests' and 'institutions' that comparative political economists rely on in unpacking the dynamics of continuity and change in Southern European political economies and the role that the EU plays in these processes. We survey how comparative political economists generally use ideas, interests and institutions as alternative explanatory principles representing different research programmes. Then we briefly describe our strategy of analysing the interplay of these categories in explaining the extent to which different public policy domains in the six Southern European political economies have been Europeanised. Finally, we conclude by providing a summary of the contributions of this volume.

Substantive and Geographical Scope: Domestic Political Economies of Southern Europe

In terms of its substantive scope, this volume explores the dynamics of Europeanisation in the domestic political economies of Southern Europe. While the scope of the earlier special issue by Featherstone and Kazamias (2000) was wider, focusing on institutional adaptation within government, transformation of structural power of domestic actors, adjustment of domestic macroeconomic policy regimes, changes in domestic party systems, redefinitions of national identity and foreign policy interests, this volume explores a narrower dimension of Europeanisation centring on the adjustment processes, or lack thereof, in selected public policy and governance domains in domestic political economies. Thus 'the domains where the effects of Europeanisation are supposed to materialise' (i.e. 'the objects of Europeanisation') are traced at the level of public policy and governance (Radaelli 2003, p. 35 and 30). We felt that a concentrated focus on continuity and change in domestic political economies would produce a rich set of findings amenable for comparisons across Southern European political economies through studying specific public policy areas.

While there does not exist a generally accepted definition of 'political economy', in our analyses we follow the conventional understanding of the term in the comparative political economy literature. A leading exponent of this literature summarises the conventional understanding by claiming that any domestic political economy 'consists of several institutions, such as those governing finance, labour-management relations, corporate governance, labour markets, and more' (Campbell 2010, p. 91). As another leading figure in the literature puts it, these institutional structures, which represent the interdependent pillars of the architecture of any domestic political economy, encompass 'organisational relations among economic actors, the policy regimes supporting those relationships, and the international regimes underpinning them' (Hall, forthcoming, p. 1). These institutional matrices are generally conceptualised as nationally specific while showing similarities across diverse varieties existing within capitalism, broadly defined.

In our accounts, we also subscribe to the view that comparative political economy is indeed an exercise in comparative public policy. As a classic review article puts it: 'much of what passes for comparative political economy ... remains an exercise in comparative public policy in the sense that the dependent variable is government policy (some kind of economic policy) and variations on the dependent variable are explained by governmental institutions or processes' (Pontusson 1995, p. 120). In this spirit, therefore, the case studies in this volume focus on various public policy domains representing different pillars of the domestic political economic architectures in exploring the extent to which South European political economies are Europeanised. It should be added that these case studies are authored by political scientists/political economists who carry out their assessments with an explicit emphasis on the qualifying adjective of 'political economy', i.e. on the 'political'.[2]

In terms of its geographical scope, in studying the impact of the EU in processes of continuity and change in different public policy areas the volume focuses on political economies of Southern Europe for a number of reasons. Although the existing literature on Europeanisation is showing signs of maturity, breeding a rich and variegated set of findings, this literature has disproportionately focused on 'older' member states of northwestern Europe and more recently on new member states of Central and Eastern Europe. With the exception of Italy (and, to a lesser extent, Spain), South European countries (especially the new Southern member states and candidate countries for accession to the EU) have received less attention. In addition to this gap in the geographical focus of the Europeanisation literature, there are substantive and theoretical reasons that justify a focus on Southern Europe as a region. When they focus on Southern European countries, scholars in the Europeanisation literature implicitly have come to take these as 'most likely' cases, expecting a high degree of EU impact. Summarising the developments in the region, Featherstone and Kazamias (2000, p. 2) identified the region as the EU 'periphery' where 'the challenge of "Europeanisation" can be expected to be set more starkly'.[3] In fact, the authors (2000, p. 3) emphasised that processes of Europeanisation in Southern Europe are central to the dynamics of transformation in this region. Accordingly, they concluded that Europeanisation itself 'represents a process of major structural transformation within the region; indeed, perhaps it is *the prime focus of change* that these states have in common'.

Aside from the Featherstone and Kazamias special issue that was the inspiration for the present volume, more recently, in another special issue of *South European Society and Politics*, on the financial crisis, Verney (2009, p. 3) referred to popular concerns over how Southern Europe was seen as the 'Achilles heel' not only in the processes of Europeanisation but also in the European integration project in general. It seems that even a decade after the original assessment of Featherstone and Kazamias (2000), Southern Europe is still capturing popular intellect as a region that does not quite fit the European model. Categorically characterised by a series of 'misfits' between their domestic structures and those of the EU in the academic, practitioner and public debates, Southern Europe is still assumed to be facing intense 'adaptational pressures' in processes of Europeanisation. These qualities render the members of this 'flaky fringe' (Verney 2009) as ideal test cases whereby the impact of Europeanisation is generally presumed to be potentially strong, ex ante.

Although the existing literature hints at differentiated mechanisms of the impact of the EU in different categories of states, we still do not have a full-fledged, differentiated examination of the intra-regional variations in 'Europeanisation'. Therefore, this volume aims to study the differentiated processes of transformation across three clusters of countries in Southern Europe, classified according to their actual or potential timing of accession: 'old' member states (Italy, Portugal, Spain and Greece), a 'new' member state (Malta) and a candidate country (Turkey). These three clusters constitute ideal cases for testing the often suggested but rarely systematically verified impact of 'differentiated Europeanisation' within a broader area of Southern Europe.

In addition to studying the differentiated impact of the EU across different clusters within the region, this volume also aims to evaluate the empirical validity of the more implicit proposition that Southern Europe—as a regional category—continues to be characterised by categorically quintessential misfits, ever inviting adaptational pressures.

Europeanisation as a Research Programme

Europeanisation emerged as a research field starting from the mid-1990s and has quickly become well established in EU integration studies in particular and in political science in general. While the definition of Europeanisation differed across the early works on the issue, it has conventionally come to be conceptualised *tout court* as the impact of the EU on domestic policies, politics, and polities across not only member states, but also candidate countries and more recently, beyond. This volume builds on a classic conceptualisation of Europeanisation by Radaelli (2003, p. 30), who sees it as 'processes of (a) construction (b) diffusion and (c) institutionalisation of formal and informal rules, procedures, policy paradigms, styles, "ways of doing things" and shared beliefs and norms which are first defined and consolidated in the making of EU decisions and then incorporated in the logic of domestic discourse, identities, political structures and public policies'. This conception of Europeanisation contains three key elements—*research design*, *theoretical core* and *operationalisation of domestic change*—which, when considered together, constitute the epistemological pillars of the Europeanisation research programme. It should be acknowledged that the domestic politics of member states, as different from candidate countries, shape the formation of EU level interactions, rules, policies or norms in the first place, as illustrated in the concepts of 'uploading' and 'downloading' to indicate the interrelated but analytically distinct processes of Europeanisation (Bulmer & Radaelli 2005; Börzel 2002). The focus of this volume is on the latter, i.e. on the ways in which and the extent to which downloading takes place.

In terms of *research design*, which is an integral component of the Europeanisation research programme, existing research can be categorised into three types with respect to their overall design. In a recent volume, Radaelli succinctly summarises (2012, p. 9) these design types with the help of the equation $Y = f(X)$ where X denotes the cause (i.e. the EU input), Y denotes the effect (i.e. domestic change) and f denotes the causal relationship between X and Y. The first type of Europeanisation research focuses on X (read, the EU input) as its point of departure and adopts a top-down research design whereby the degree of compatibility or distance between EU practices, inputs or frameworks on the one hand and domestic practices in policies, politics or polity on the other leads to 'adaptational pressure' (Heritier et al. 2001; Cowles, Caporaso & Risse 2001; Börzel 1999). In this type of research, analysis starts from the supposed cause (i.e. the EU input) and traces its impact all the way down at the domestic level, engaging in a search for 'effects of causes' (Exadaktylos & Radaelli 2009).

The second type of Europeanisation research focuses on *Y* (or domestic change) as its point of departure and adopts a bottom-up research design that aims to overcome the inbuilt bias of top-down research design, tending to find the EU input as *the* cause driving domestic change (Radaelli 2006; Quaglia & Radaelli 2007; Bulmer & Radaelli 2005; Radaelli & Franchino 2004; Bull & Baudner 2004). The criticism against top-down research design is that the incompatibility between the EU and domestic levels is taken as a structural variable, whereas 'the actualisation of this structural property (i.e. fit or misfit) requires agency. Agents give meaning to the objective structure and strategically choose an action to accomplish a project (not exogenously defined as material gains)' (Bache, Bulmer & Gunay 2012). In adopting a bottom-up approach to research design, this second type of Europeanisation studies starts its analyses at the domestic level where the impact takes place and trace the possible causes, be they at the national or international level, including the EU, thus engaging in a search for 'causes of effects' (Exadaktylos & Radaelli 2009).

The third type of Europeanisation research to which this volume aims to contribute is the one that treats *f* as its research focus. In order to do so, the contributions in this volume explore the relationship between the EU input and domestic change in their chosen public policy domains in terms of the constellation of ideas, interests and institutions characterising the political economies of their respective country case studies. In this genre, the contributions in volume identify both the relevant EU-level inputs, frameworks or agendas in the policy area they have chosen (*X*), on the one hand, and the magnitude and direction of domestic change (*Y*), on the other. They do so, however, only to lay the ground for the next analytical stage of unpacking the relationship between *X* and *Y* through analysing the interaction among ideas, interests and institutions (*f*), concepts deeply embedded in the new institutionalist literature as discussed below. In doing so, the contributions make a conscious effort to capture not only 'reactions' but also 'more complex and creative' uses of, and adaptation to, the EU (Radaelli & Pasquier 2007, p. 38). By focusing on *f*, the contributions in this volume aim to go beyond following the bottom-up research designs characterising the second type of Europeanisation research. Therefore, most of the contributions in this volume remain alert to possible causes (at the national or international level) other than the EU in their analyses of the relationship between the EU and domestic change.

In terms of *theoretical core*, the new institutionalisms that have dominated political science as well as sociology and economics during the past three decades or so constitute the theoretical underpinnings of the Europeanisation research programme (Bulmer 2007). As one recent survey of the literature observes, studies on Europeanisation 'have mobilised all strands of the "new institutionalist approaches"—historical, rational choice and sociological' (Graziano & Vink, forthcoming, p. 11). What unites institutionalists in general is the view that 'institutions matter' and institutionalists working within the Europeanisation research programme concur. They are, however, divided in emphasising different factors explaining dynamics of continuity and change at the domestic level and the role that the EU plays therein. Rational choice institutionalists identify veto points and facilitating institutions

(Börzel 2005; Börzel & Risse 2007), while historical institutionalists emphasise historical legacies and temporality (Brusis 2002; Bulmer 2009; Goetz 2009) and sociological institutionalists highlight the role of norm entrepreneurs (epistemic communities and advocacy coalitions) and resonance of ideas (Checkel 2001; Börzel 2005; Börzel & Risse 2007) as key intervening variables mediating the impact of the EU at the domestic level. The differentiated emphases by scholars subscribing to different variants within new institutionalisms on what may be summarised as ideas, interests and institutions are consistent with the comparative political economy literature that also uses this triptych in portraying dynamics in a given public policy domain, as we elaborate below.

In *operationalising domestic change*, which involves 'a change in the logic of political behaviour' (Radaelli 2003, p. 30), as implied in the definition of 'Europeanisation' quoted above, contributions to this volume follow a combination of the set of categories introduced by Radaelli (2003, p. 37) and Börzel and Risse (2003, pp. 69–70). Bache (2008, p. 12) elaborates on these categories of change as follows:

- 'Transformation' refers to a situation in which existing domestic practices, policies, rules or preferences are replaced 'with new ones' so that the degree of change is high.
- 'Accommodation' is observed if existing domestic practices, policies, rules or preferences 'adapt' to the EU without involving a change in 'their essential features'.
- 'Absorption' is a situation where EU practices, policies, rules or preferences are 'incorporated' 'without substantially modifying' existing domestic practices, policies, rules or preferences.
- 'Inertia' is a situation where there is no change which can be in the form of 'lags', 'delays' and 'sheer resistance' (Radaelli 2003, p. 37).
- Finally, 'retrenchment' occurs when the incompatibility between EU practices, policies, rules or preferences and existing domestic practices, policies, rules or preferences expands even further from before interaction with the EU begins.

These categories, which are the possible 'outcomes of Europeanisation', gauge the 'magnitude' and 'direction' of change (and, by implication, continuity) in public policy and governance (Radaelli 2003, p. 37).

Unpacking Continuity and Change through Ideas, Interests and Institutions

In addressing the dynamics of domestic change in Southern Europe during the 1990s, Featherstone and Kazamias (2000) focused on the interplay of structure and agency in painting broader substantive landscapes as their point of departure. Given the limited focus on comparative political economy in the present volume, however, we follow the research strategy of the 'new generation of political economists' as depicted in a recent survey of this literature (Blyth 2009, p. 196). Following this strategy, contributions in this volume survey the unfolding empirical terrain of South European political economies through the 'troika of concepts'—ideas, interests and institutions—that is now generally taken to define ontologically 'what political economy is' (Blyth 2009, p. 193).

In this literature, *ideas* are generally conceptualised as roadmaps, strategic 'weapons' in the battle for control, and narratives that shape understandings of events (as 'frames of reference'). Ideas that are exemplified in the literature are presented at three different levels ranging from the more specific (at the policy level) to the more general (at the philosophy level). At one extreme, scholars focus on specific, concrete 'policy ideas' (i.e. 'policy solutions') presented by policymakers at the policy level. At the other extreme, at the philosophical level, are the all-encompassing, general 'worldviews' comprising 'public philosophies', 'public sentiments' or 'deep core' which underlie the more specific policy and programmatic ideas. In between these two extremes at the programme level remain 'programmatic ideas' which take the form of 'policy paradigms', 'frames of reference', 'programmatic beliefs', 'policy cores' or 'problem definitions' (Schmidt 2008, pp. 306–307). Conceptualised at these three levels, ideas are of two types. Cognitive ideas (which may be referred to as 'causal ideas') define policy problems as well as methods with which to solve them. They 'provide the recipes, guidelines, and maps for political action and serve to justify policies and programmes by speaking to their interest-based logic and necessity' (Schmidt 2008, p. 306). Normative ideas speak to the appropriateness of policies and provide legitimacy by attaching values to political action. In this way, they address 'how ... programmes as well as ... policies resonate with a deeper core of ... principles and norms of public life, whether the newly emerging values of a society or the long-standing ones in the societal repertoire' (Schmidt 2008, pp. 306–307).

Interests are generally identified in the comparative political economy literature with the (generally fixed) preferences, material interests and dominant strategies of major actors (either individuals or groups) in domestic political economies. They are the main building blocks of the literature on distributive coalitions. The coalitions depicted in this literature include organised functional interests (employers and trade unions), class-based coalitions (upper classes, middle classes, working classes), factor-based coalitions (abundant-factor coalition vs. scarce-factor coalition), producers' groups or sectoral interests (including those engaged in industrial, financial, domestically oriented, export-oriented sectors), workers (high-skilled vs. low-skilled or white-collar vs. blue-collar), political parties (with given ideological positions for whatever reason), policymakers (bureaucrats vs. politicians) and diverse (and often competing) interests within bureaucracies (such as treasury officials vs. central bankers). In the comparative political economy literature, these actors' preferences and hence interests are generally shaped through their 'class positions, what assets they have, how fungible those assets are, how exposure to particular economic shocks impact agents' resource portfolios' (Blyth 2009, p. 197).

In the comparative political economy literature, *institutions* are generally defined as conventional systems of formal and informal rules constraining and enabling human behaviour and structuring social interactions by, for example, allocating power among actors, and structuring policymaking and procedures of how decisions are adopted (adapted from Bache [2008] and Hall [1997]). Given their primary interest in public policy, the types of institutions that comparative political economists focus on are those which are 'fundamentally shaped by and through processes at the level of the nation-state' (Morgan et al. 2010, p. 2). Such a conception of institutions in the literature builds on an influential definition whereby institutions represent 'the political dimensions of economic management': 'the formal rules, compliance procedures, and standard operating practices that structure the relationship between individuals in various units of the polity and the economy' (Hall 1986, p. 19). In a broader definition that transcends the limited contours of comparative political economy, institutions are conceived as 'the rules of the game in a society or, more formally,... the humanly devised constraints that shape human interaction' which 'structure incentives in human exchange, whether political, social, or economic' (North 1990, p. 3).

Let us now turn to how comparative political economists use these concepts. As Blyth (2009) shows, scholars of diverse traditions identify *one* of these three concepts as the explanatory principle having primary (if not exclusive) independent impact on their particular *explananda*. Different approaches, each emphasising one of these concepts, in time amounted almost to 'research programmes' in and of themselves as depicted by Hall (2005, p. 131): 'the field of comparative political economy has seen successive research programmes focused on the role of interests, institutions, and ideas in politics, each with important insights'. Hall continues, '[b]ecause these developed seriatim, however, they speak to each other only occasionally, and ... [a]ll too often, the literature counter-poses explanations based on interests, ideas, or institutions as if they were alternatives'. Among the explanatory alternatives in the comparative political economy literature, the point of departure for scholars who emphasise actors' interests underlying (or as prior to) any other variable is asking, 'in whose benefit would it be for outcome X to pertain over outcome Y?' (Blyth 2009, p. 196). These scholars typically take actors' preferences as exogenous and explain outcomes relying on deductive reasoning. Other scholars who see ideas as the explanatory principle start their analyses by identifying 'social constructions agents use to decode and navigate the political economy' (Blyth 2009, p. 197). These scholars reject the view that 'agents know their preferences and know the appropriate strategies for advancing them' (Eichengreen 1998, p. 999). Seeing actors' preferences as entirely endogenous, it is ideas that 'construct' actors' interests and thereby determine strategies and choice. Still another group of political economists focus on institutions as the chief explanatory principle. In these accounts, scholars suggest that institutions come prior to interests in that interests are 'refracted through institutions' (Blyth 2009, p. 197) and therefore it is the institutional contexts that actors find themselves that determine action. In all of these alternative narratives, ideas, interests and institutions are each conceptualised as what comes prior to the others; and in this respect they are presented as competing variables chasing after the outcome to be explained. In these narratives, 'one of the three I's pushes the process at the expense of the other two factors', aiming to establish a 'hierarchy of variables' (Palier & Surel 2005 cited in Jenson 2010, p. 8). Therefore, each of these three I's constitutes the dominant explanatory principle in alternative research programmes with their own ontological foci and epistemological foundations.

The present volume, however, aims to part ways with this literature by exploring ways of harnessing ideas, interests and institutions for reaping the benefits of combinative causality. In formulating our research questions, we follow Heclo (1993 cited in Jenson 2010, p. 8), who advises that, 'in trying to account for change and continuity, these are categories that need each other'. In exploring the 'co-dependency' among ideas, interests and institutions, therefore, this volume aims to 'follow the strands of ideas, interests and institutions as they intertwine and enfold in dynamic processes' (Heclo 1993 cited in Jenson 2010, p. 8). In this way, contributions in this volume strive to show how the relationship between ideas, interests and institutions is reflexive (i.e. how each is constitutive of the others) in dynamic political economic processes in different public policy domains.

The Structure of this Volume

The case studies that follow are theoretically informed empirical surveys, analysing processes of transformation in Southern European countries. They are designed to follow a common theoretical and methodological template in order to be able to reach a set of comparative conclusions. Each case study identifies EU input (key formal and informal rules, procedures, frames of reference, mechanisms and governance structures) and discusses the degrees and dimensions of (mis)fit between the EU and domestic levels. The case studies portray the interplay of the specific ideas, interests and institutions in explaining continuity and change at the domestic level during the 2000s. In doing so, each contribution aims to trace the extent to which the dynamic processes of continuity and change in domestic political economies are in fact shaped by the EU models, frameworks, structures, rules and policies.

The case study on Greece by Blavoukos, Caramanis and Dedoulis (2013) focuses on the foundation of the Accounting and Auditing Oversight Board (ELTE) in 2003. The authors see this institutional development as a turning point in formal accounting and auditing practices in Greece. Prompted by EU pressure, this development, as in other areas of public policy, exemplifies the introduction of formally independent bodies and agencies in policymaking in Greece. However, this institutional development maintained a highly politicised mode of governance in this policy area, in particular through the political appointment of experts. Such politicisation has effectively undermined the purpose of ELTE's raison d'être. The authors conclude, therefore, that although the nature of the EU input suggests that the degree of change should be policy transformation, empirical evidence points to mere absorption or accommodation at best. Although the EU may have promoted the independence of regulatory institutions, pressures stemming from the EU in that direction failed to bring about a transformation in terms of the role of the state in public policymaking in this policy domain. The authors also add that the establishment of ELTE owed as much to EU pressures as to the government's preferences towards polishing its tainted reputation following the Athens stock exchange crisis. In this domestic context, the authors concluded that the government instrumentally used the EU pressures in the area of accounting and auditing to legitimise policy preferences that were subsequently embodied in ELTE.

In the Italian case study, Quaglia (2013) asks to what extent, how and why two key domains of domestic political economy, namely, macroeconomic policies and financial services regulation, have been Europeanised in Italy over the course of the 2000s. The author assesses the impact of the European Monetary Union's (EMU's) macroeconomic framework and the EU's financial services regulation by tracing the changing interests, ideas and institutions in these policy areas in search of identifying the causal mechanisms through which change came about (or was resisted). The author concludes that over the last decade the changes in the Italian political economy that were reflected in these policy domains can be characterised by varying degrees of Europeanisation. The extent to which these domains were Europeanised depended on the level of institutionalisation in each of the policy domains at the EU level. The Europeanisation outcomes ranged from transformation to retrenchment. The unfolding domestic interest constellations in many cases reinforced the institutional change prescribed by the EU. These changes often went hand in hand with the emergence of policy entrepreneurs sponsoring domestic change who were keen to exploit at the national level the external constraints imposed by the EU. Quaglia underlines two main findings of the Italian case study that feed into the broader literature on the Europeanisation of domestic political economies, especially in the case of Southern Europe. First, the general trend is to foster the convergence of the Southern European model towards an EU model, largely informed by a German-inspired stability-oriented approach to macroeconomic policies and Anglo-Saxon-inspired market-friendly regulation in financial services. Second, despite such convergence across the EU towards these dominant models, some distinctive domestic features remain prevalent, as confirmed by the chronic problems marring Italian fiscal policy.

The Maltese case study by Azzopardi (2013) investigates the changes in the labour market within the context of Europeanisation processes. The author evaluates formal and informal structures of the economy by relying on the dynamic interaction of ideas, interests and institutions to analyse whether and how Europeanisation of the Maltese labour market has occurred. The findings indicate that changes have occurred in the legislative framework, language and values about work, but resistance and continuity were evident in other areas, such as practices of flexicurity, undeclared work and a low level of female labour force participation. The author indicates that in the Maltese case study there were different forms of limited change (inertia, retrenchment and absorption) with no incidence of transformation indicating wholesale change. She concludes that on the whole there appears to be a shift in ideas, interests and institutions in the Maltese political economy as a result of EU pressures. Europeanisation is more evident on the formal policy level, but was not so clear on the informal societal level in terms of, for example, how people structure their relationships with the labour market. The author concludes by presuming that this is mainly due to the persistence of the traditional family roles and the informal structures that tend to be stronger than formal ones in everyday societal relationships.

The case study on Portugal by Royo (2013) identifies the basic changes in the Portuguese economy that occurred as a result of European integration. It focuses, in particular, on the country's fiscal policies and performance during the period 1999–2008, the decade prior to the global financial crisis. While mapping the limits of convergence, the author focuses on institutions, ideas and interests to account for the difficulties that Portugal experienced in complying with the Stability and Growth and Pact. The author argues that one of the fundamental reasons for the under-performance of the Portuguese economy prior to the current crisis was the lack of fiscal discipline and the adoption of ad hoc measures for controlling the rampant budget deficit. The Portuguese case study demonstrates that the impending EU pressures themselves cannot produce change; the process of economic reform has to be owned by domestic actors who will be willing to carry them out. The Portuguese experience of Europeanisation, the author contends, shows that countries wishing to join the Eurozone need to have a sound budgetary position, which is supposed to provide some fiscal space for manoeuvring once the country is inside the Eurozone. The author concludes that otherwise, as in the case of Portugal, the opportunity for sustained structural reform and the improvement in fiscal discipline afforded by the introduction of the euro will effectively be lost.

In the case study on Spain, Moreno (2013) focuses on processes of Europeanisation of the Spanish welfare political economy, which experienced decades of international isolation and ideological and economic autarchy prior to EU membership. The Spanish case study constitutes an example of a country graduating from peripheral to core status within the EU as well as in the international economic order. During the period analysed (2000–10), the Spanish welfare political economy was reformed in line with the country's aspirations to develop a mature welfare state similar to those that exist in other EU members. To this end, policies were implemented in all pillars of the welfare edifice. The author discusses a series of significant policy changes including the adoption of the EU recommendations in labour activation policies, the increase in female participation in the formal labour market and the establishment of a national system for long-term care. The Spanish case study confirms the general claim that 'benchmarking' and 'best practices' can induce socio-economic convergence towards the EU average. The author questions the sustainability of the post-1945 European welfare state model, due to the ongoing realignments in the world economy and the shortcomings in EU governance mechanisms. The concluding remarks underline the fact that domestic actors in Spain will continue to closely watch the developments at the EU level as the main point of reference in reforming their welfare political economy.

In the case study on Turkey, Bolukbasi and Ertugal (2013) analyse the extent to which the accession process prompted a transformation in the area of employment policy, which, like many others, they perceive to be the most salient problem in the country and which at the same constitutes *the* policy area with the greatest misfit between the EU and Turkey, in terms of both policy performance and institutional structure. The authors' overall finding is that there were varying degrees of change across different components of employment policy in Turkey in response to the EU pressures with no incidence of inertia and retrenchment contrary to theoretical expectations. They also claim that domestic change is a result of policy learning, pointing to the significance of ideas. These changes take place, however, only when they are in accordance with the preferences of powerful domestic actors. In the domains characterised by a medium to higher degree of change (i.e. transformation in labour law and accommodation in Active Labour Market Policies (ALMPs), objectives and instruments), the framing effects of the European Employment Strategy (EES) policy paradigm and the selective usage of ideas by these dominant domestic interests become causally significant. In cases of lower degrees of change, however, it is the path-dependent institutional factors that account for the policy outcomes, as in the cases of lifelong learning and social security systems and procedures in governance.

These case studies are followed by a framing article. The article by Balkir, Bolukbasi and Ertugal (2013) summarises the comparative findings from the cases examined. It provides answers to the key questions that are raised in the first section of this introductory article. After reviewing the wide range of EU inputs (frames, models, policies, etc.) that the case studies focus on, the authors trace domestic continuity and change in South European political economies by use of the categories (i.e. transformation, accommodation, absorption, inertia and retrenchment) used for operationalising domestic change. They then summarise the significant ideas, interests and institutions that feature in the case studies to unpack the relationship between the EU and domestic political economies. The article concludes by specifying the conditions under which the EU has an impact on South European political economies.

Notes

[1] While the workshop that led to this volume also incorporated a case study on Cyprus, focusing on the differentiated impact of the EU on environmental policies in the divided island, the author in the end withdrew the article.

[2] We thank Susannah Verney, who invited us to explicitly emphasise the 'political' in political economy.

[3] The authors use the term 'periphery' in a descriptive sense where they identify Southern Europe with 'the economic inequality compared to northern EU states; the historically distinctive mode of the region's economic development and social stratification as a consequence of "late industrialisation" and the relatively greater importance of agriculture and services; the financial dependence on EU development aid; the structural power of Germany in shaping the EU's policy agenda in many areas; and the lesser bargaining strength of the "south" in EU treaty negotiations' (Featherstone & Kazamias 2000, p. 2).

References

Azzopardi, R.M. (2013) 'All hands on deck! How Europeanised is the Maltese labour market?', *South European Society and Politics*, vol. 18, no. 2, pp. 177–196.

Bache, I. (2008) *Europeanisation and Multilevel Governance*, Rowman & Littlefield, Lanham, MD.

Bache, I., Bulmer, S. & Gunay, D. (2012) 'Europeanisation: a critical realist perspective', in *Research Design in European Studies: Establishing Causality in Europeanisation*, eds T. Exadaktylos & C.M. Radaelli, Palgrave Macmillan, Basingstoke, pp. 64–84.

Balkir, C., Bolukbasi, H.T. & Ertugal, E. (2013) 'Europeanisation in the "Southern Periphery": comparative research findings on the EU's impact on domestic political economies', *South European Society and Politics*, vol. 18, no. 2, pp. 259–280.

Blavoukos, S., Caramanis, C. & Dedoulis, E. (2013) 'Europeanisation, independent bodies and the empowerment of technocracy: the case of the Greek auditing oversight body', *South European Society and Politics*, vol. 18, no. 2, pp. 139–157.

Blyth, M. (2009) 'An approach to comparative analysis or a sub-discipline within a sub-field? Political economy', in *Comparative Politics. Rationality, Culture and Structure*, eds M.I. Lichbach & A.S. Zuckerman,, 2nd edn, Cambridge University Press, Cambridge, pp. 193–219.

Bolukbasi, H.T. & Ertugal, E. (2013) 'Europeanisation of employment policy in Turkey: tracing domestic change through institutions, ideas and interests', *South European Society and Politics*, vol. 18, no. 2, pp. 237–257.

Bolukbasi, H.T., Ertugal, E. & Ozcurumez, S. (2010) 'The impact of the EU on Turkey: toward streamlining Europeanisation as a research program', *European Political Science*, vol. 9, no. 4, pp. 464–480.

Börzel, T. (1999) 'Towards convergence in Europe? Institutional adaptation to Europeanisation in Germany and Spain', *Journal of Common Market Studies*, vol. 37, no. 4, pp. 573–596.

Börzel, T. (2002) 'Member state responses to Europeanisation', *Journal of Common Market Studies*, vol. 40, no. 2, pp. 193–214.

Börzel, T. (2005) 'Europeanisation: how the European Union interacts with its member states', in *Member States and the European Union*, eds S. Bulmer & C. Lequesne, Oxford University Press, Oxford, pp. 45–69.

Börzel, T. & Risse, T. (2003) 'Conceptualising the domestic impact of Europe', in *The Politics of Europeanisation*, eds K. Featherstone & C.M. Radaelli, Oxford University Press, Oxford, pp. 57–80.

Börzel, T. & Risse, T. (2007) 'Europeanisation: the domestic impact of European Union politics', in *Handbook of European Union Politics*, eds K.E. Jorgensen, M.A. Pollack & B. Rosamond, Sage, London, pp. 483–525.

Brusis, M. (2002) 'Between EU requirements, competitive politics and national traditions: re-creating regions in the accession countries of Central and Eastern Europe', *Governance*, vol. 15, no. 4, pp. 531–559.

Bull, M. & Baudner, J. (2004) 'Europeanisation and Italian policy for the Mezzogiorno', *Journal of European Public Policy*, vol. 11, no. 6, pp. 1058–1076.

Bulmer, S. (2007) 'Theorising Europeanisation', in *Europeanisation. New Research Agendas*, eds P. Graziano & M.P. Vink, Palgrave Macmillan, Basingstoke, pp. 46–58.

Bulmer, S. (2009) '*Politics in Time* meets the politics of time: historical institutionalism and the EU timescape', *Journal of European Public Policy*, vol. 16, no. 2, pp. 307–324.

Bulmer, S. & Radaelli, C. M. (2005) 'The Europeanisation of national policy', in *The Member States of the European Union*, eds S. Bulmer & C. Lequesne, Oxford University Press, Oxford, pp. 338–359.

Campbell, J.L. (2010) 'Institutional reproduction and change', in *The Oxford Handbook of Comparative Institutional Analysis*, eds G. Morgan, J.L. Campbell, C. Crouch, O.K. Pedersen & R. Whitley, Oxford University Press, New York, pp. 87–115.

Checkel, J. (2001) 'The Europeanisation of citizenship?', in *Transforming Europe: Europeanisation and Domestic Change*, eds M.G. Cowles, J. Caporaso & T. Risse, Cornell University Press, Ithaca, NY, pp. 180–197.

Cowles, M. G., Caporaso, J. & Risse, T. (eds) (2001) *Transforming Europe: Europeanisation and Domestic Change*, Cornell University Press, Ithaca, NY.

Eichengreen, B. (1998) 'Dental hygiene and nuclear war: how international relations looks from economics', *International Organisation*, vol. 52, no. 4, pp. 993–1012.

Exadaktylos, T. & Radaelli, C.M. (2009) 'Research design in European studies: the case of Europeanisation', *Journal of Common Market Studies*, vol. 47, no. 3, pp. 507–530.

Featherstone, K. & Kazamias, G. (2000) 'Introduction: Southern Europe and the process of "Europeanisation"', *South European Society and Politics*, vol. 5, no. 2, pp. 1–24.

Goetz, K.H. (2009) 'How does the EU tick? Five propositions on political time', *Journal of European Public Policy*, vol. 16, no. 2, pp. 202–220.

Graziano, P. & Vink, M.P. (2013) 'Europeanisation: concept, theory and methods', in *The Member States of the European Union*, eds S. Bulmer & C. Lequesne, Oxford University Press, pp. 31–54.

Hall, P.A. (1986) *Governing the Economy: The Politics of State Intervention in Britain and France*, Oxford University Press, Oxford.

Hall, P.A. (1997) 'The role of interests, institutions and ideas in the comparative political economy of the industrialised nations', in *Comparative Politics. Rationality, Culture and Structure*, eds M. I. Lichbach & A. S. Zuckerman, Cambridge University Press, Cambridge, pp. 174–207.

Hall, P.A. (2005) 'Preference formation as a political process: the case of monetary union in Europe', in *Preferences and Situations: Points of Intersection between Historical and Rational Choice Institutionalism*, eds I. Katznelson & B. R. Weingast, Russell Sage Foundation, New York, pp. 129–160.

Hall, P.A. (2013) 'The political origins of our economic discontents: contemporary adjustment problems in historical perspective', in *Politics in the New Hard Times: The Great Recession in Comparative Perspective*, eds M. Kahler & D. Lake, Cornell University Press, Ithaca, NY, pp. 129–149.

Heclo, H. (1993) 'Ideas, interests and institutions', in *The Dynamics of American Politics: Approaches and Interpretations*, eds L.C. Dodd & C. Jillson, Westview Press, Boulder, CO, pp. 366–392.

Heritier, A., Kerwer, D., Knill, C., Lehmkuhl, D., Teutsch, M. & Douillet, A.-C. (2001) *Differential Europe. The European Union Impact on National Policymaking*, Rowman & Littlefield, Lanham, MD.

Jenson, J. (2010) 'Ideas and policy: the European Union considers social policy futures', American Consortium on European Union Studies, ECAS Cases, No. 2010/2, available online at: transatlantic.sais-jhu.edu/bin/y/d/2010.2_ACES_Cases_Jenson.pdf

Moreno, L. (2013) 'Spain's catching up with the EU core: the implausible quest of a "flying pig"?', *South European Society and Politics*, vol. 18, no. 2, pp. 217–236.

Morgan, G., Campbell, J.L., Crouch, C., Pedersen, O.K. & Whitley, R. (2010) 'Introduction', in *The Oxford Handbook of Comparative Institutional Analysis*, eds G. Morgan, J.L. Campbell, C. Crouch, O.K. Pedersen & R. Whitley, Oxford University Press, New York, pp. 1–11.

North, G. (1990) *Institutions, Institutional Change and Economic Performance*, Cambridge University Press, Cambridge.

Palier, B. & Surel, I. (2005) 'Les "trois I" et l'analyse de l'Etat en action', *Revue Française de Science Politique*, vol. 55, no. 1, pp. 7–32.

Pontusson, J. (1995) 'From comparative public policy to political economy: putting political institutions in their place and taking interests seriously', *Comparative Political Studies*, vol. 28, no. 1, pp. 117–147.

Quaglia, L. (2013) 'The Europeanisation of macroeconomic policies and financial regulation in Italy', *South European Society and Politics*, vol. 18, no. 2, pp. 159–176.

Quaglia, L. & Radaelli, C.M. (2007) 'Italian politics and the European Union: a tale of two research designs', *West European Politics*, vol. 30, no. 4, pp. 924–943.

Radaelli, C.M. (2003) 'The Europeanisation of public policy', in *The Politics of Europeanisation*, eds K. Featherstone & C.M. Radaelli, Oxford University Press, Oxford, pp. 27–56.

Radaelli, C.M. (2006) 'Europeanisation: solution or problem', in *Advances in European Union Studies*, eds M. Cini & A.K. Bourne, Palgrave Macmillan, New York, pp. 56–76.

Radaelli, C.M. (2012) 'Europeanisation: the challenge of establishing causality', in *Research Design in European Studies: Establishing Causality in Europeanisation*, eds T. Exadaktylos & C.M. Radaelli, Palgrave Macmillan, Basingstoke, pp. 1–16.

Radaelli, C.M. & Franchino, F. (2004) 'Analysing political change in Italy', *Journal of European Public Policy*, vol. 11, no. 6, pp. 941–953.

Radaelli, C.M. & Pasquier, R. (2007) 'Conceptual issues', in *Europeanisation. New Research Agendas*, eds P. Graziano & M.P. Vink, Palgrave Macmillan, Basingstoke, pp. 35–45.

Royo, S. (2013) 'Portugal in the European Union: the limits of convergence', *South European Society and Politics*, vol. 18, no. 2, pp. 197–216.

Schmidt, V. A. (2008) 'Discursive institutionalism: the explanatory power of ideas and discourse', *Annual Review of Political Science*, vol. 11, pp. 303–326.

Verney, S. (2009) 'Flaky fringe? Southern Europe facing the financial crisis', *South European Society and Politics*, vol. 14, no. 1, pp. 1–6.

Europeanisation, Independent Bodies and the Empowerment of Technocracy: The Case of the Greek Auditing Oversight Body

Spyros Blavoukos, Constantinos Caramanis and Emmanouil Dedoulis

The establishment of independent oversight bodies constitutes an important institutional reform in the European Union context. Based on technocratic expertise, they aim to curtail the state's policymaking and supervisory role. During the last decade, such bodies have been established in Greece, illustrating the ideational and institutional impact of the Europeanisation process. By examining the Greek independent oversight board for accounting and audit practices, we posit that its highly politicised mode of governance has undermined the purpose of its instigation and operation. Although such externally induced institutional reforms entail some ideational and institutional change, their full transformative potential has yet to be realised in Greece.

The ascendance of independent regulatory and oversight bodies in the Greek policymaking system has been associated with the country's European trajectory, illustrating the impact of Europeanisation in both ideational and institutional terms. In accordance with the focus of this volume our main research question is whether the European Union (EU) has been, and continues to be, the primary source of adjustment pressure vis-à-vis the establishment of these independent bodies. Within this context, we examine the establishment and operation of the independent oversight board for external audit practices, ELTE (Επιτροπή Λογιστικής Τυποποίησης και Ελέγχων – Accounting Standardisation and Auditing Committee), in the 2000s.[1]

The increased role of ideas and institutions in public policymaking is related to the ascendance of three relatively novel elements in contemporary policymaking: the rediscovery of efficiency as a primary policy goal; an awareness of the strategic importance of policy credibility; and, partly deriving from the former two, an increased willingness to delegate policymaking power to technocratic bodies enjoying considerable political independence (Majone 1996, p. 611). Whereas the United States (US) political system features a long tradition of delegation of regulatory authority to independent commissions and boards, this trend has appeared much more recently in European countries, especially in those that have traditionally placed a strong emphasis on parliamentary sovereignty (Majone 1994). However, because elected legislatures are incapable of committing subsequent legislatures, public policies are vulnerable to reneging. Thus, besides providing technical expertise, independent bodies and agencies come into play to ensure the continuity and credibility of a given public policy, largely insulated from the electoral cycle (Shepsle 1991).

However, the establishment of these independent authorities does not guarantee their independent institutional performance, with membership emerging as a critical condition in this respect. The public administration literature refers to the ascendance of a 'new patrimonialism', in which political leaders attempt to gain control over appointments to public offices and greater loyalty from civil servants (Peters & Wright 1996, pp. 628–629). This phenomenon is more frequent in continental European countries, which have traditionally adopted more positive attitudes vis-à-vis the intermingling of political and administrative elites, and even more so in the countries of Southern Europe and Greece, which have traditionally featured strong elements of clientelism and 'extended politicisation' at the top and at the bottom (Sotiropoulos 2004a; Spanou 1996). Thus, the staffing of an independent body may become an indirect form of continuing state control, negating the real transformative potential of these institutional efforts. This occurs in particular in cases of strong single-party majority governments, such as the Greek political setting, where the party in power faces few constraints on colonising the state apparatus with governing-party elites.

Our case study has been chosen thematically and country-wise on two grounds: First, auditing has been promoted as a fundamental mechanism in the context of the EU internal market, as it facilitates trust and credibility for investment activity and financial transactions. Thus, EU pressures in this field are quite concrete and prescriptive, especially during the last two decades, theoretically leaving little space for domestic political manoeuvrability and obfuscation. In this respect, conditions are very conducive for *transformation* to occur, as outlined in the introduction to this volume (Balkir, Bolukbasi & Ertugal 2013). If this is not the case, however, then we need to consider the implications for the Europeanisation effect and substantially lower the threshold of any expectations for policy and institutional convergence and isomorphism in other fields. Second, Greece is an interesting case, as 'extended politicisation' is a critical component of the domestic political and policymaking modus operandi. Thus, new ideas—especially externally induced ones—have to struggle with long-established, often institutionalised, policymaking practices and deeply entrenched interests.

We argue that, despite the governmental rhetoric of successful institutional reform in conformity with EU blueprints, ELTE became subject to the highly politicised domestic mode of governance and the all-pervasive role of political parties. Our research demonstrates that ELTE does not yet live up to the institutional expectations that accompanied its genesis. This raises questions about its contribution to the actual curtailment of the state's policymaking role and indicates the limitations of the external empowerment of domestic technocracy. Analytically, we posit that institutional reform and actual policy implementation should be distinguished, with the former not necessarily leading to the latter. The policy outcome of institutional reform is filtered through personnel selection, the pattern of which reproduces to some extent the pre-existing policymaking ethos and dependencies.

Our analysis is based on a combination of primary and secondary sources. The former consists of interviews with a former minister of economy and a secretary-general in the same ministry, as well as six members of the independent authority and an eminent professional, all personally involved in the preparatory and operational stages of ELTE. (See Appendix for the list of interviewees.) Although limited in number, the seven interviews comprise high-level state officials and the political leadership of the ministry in charge. All the individuals concerned were either directly involved in, or knowledgeable of, the process of ELTE's genesis, staffing and modus operandi.

In the next section, we provide an overview of the EU actions in this field and the insights of the most relevant, Greek-focused, Europeanisation literature, in order to identify the expected direction of change. Following that, we elaborate on the degree of incompatibility between EU and domestic policy before proceeding in the next two sections to discuss the effects of Europeanisation in terms of continuity and change, as well as to account for our findings. We conclude by summarising our main arguments and drawing together generalised insights regarding the internalisation of Europeanisation pressures in Greece.

EU Policymaking on Auditing: Expected Changes in the Greek Context

A significant body of literature has underlined that auditing has remained a central issue in public debates in the aftermath of corporate crises and collapses (Sikka 2009; Humphrey, Loft & Woods 2009; see also Cooper & Robson 2006). Its role in facilitating trust in investment activities has often been discussed and arguments have recently emerged in favour of instituting authorities independent of the profession and the state to effectively regulate auditing practices (Sikka & Willmott 1995a; 1995b). For instance, in the aftermath of the Enron episode, the US established an independent oversight body under the Sarbanes–Oxley Act (US Congress 2002).

During the last two decades, the EU has taken specific action to harmonise national systems of auditing oversight. Having identified considerable differences between national audit regimes, which made it difficult for international investors and other users to make meaningful comparisons of the financial statements audited, the European Commission outlined a programme to review important issues ranging from auditing standards to national systems of oversight (European Commission 1998). Fearing corporate collapses in Europe analogous to those in the US, the European Commission issued a Recommendation in 2001, calling for the establishment of national independent oversight bodies that would effectively facilitate the operation of the market. It set out, inter alia, the basic conditions for the national monitoring systems, defining proper public oversight procedures and requiring a majority of non-professionals (such as representatives of business, securities regulators and shareholders) to be on the bodies (European Commission 2001). The promulgations of the Recommendation constituted the basis of the new Eighth Directive 2006/43/EC, issued in 2006, which actually required member states to establish such bodies in order to ensure robust public oversight over the audit profession (European Commission 2006).

The analysis of the mechanisms of pressure internalisation and the individual member state's responses to it has illustrated that one important conditioning factor of the Europeanisation effect is the variation in the type of the EU mode of governance in each field and the nature of the consequent commitments. The more binding these commitments are, the less space they allow for flexibility in the domestic adjustment process (Bulmer & Radaelli 2005). In our case, adjustment pressures were of a legally binding nature and consisted of a concrete institutional model for domestic compliance (i.e. positive integration),[2] thus generating expectations of *transformation* in the relevant fields of domestic policymaking. The Recommendation and the Directive had a strong prescriptive institutional element in the format, composition and role of the independent body that would take up the monitoring position. At the same time, the emphasis placed on the independence of the body and its technocratic staffing exercised broader ideational pressures vis-à-vis the role and broader empowerment of technocracy and independent authorities in Greece more generally.

These high-level pressures were conditioned by the domestic political and institutional setting, which constitutes the 'intervening variable' in the adaptation process, shaping the scope and extent of national response to Europeanisation pressures (Radaelli 2003, pp. 46–50). Earlier research has illustrated that in the Greek case '[t]he Europeanisation of Greek politics essentially revolved around a single, overriding issue: the redefinition of the role, size, scope, functions and morphology of the state' (Ioakimidis 1996, p. 40). Participation in the European integration process held out the prospect of economic rationalisation and political reform, reinforcing a political culture of modernisation and extroversion. However, the specific domestic political contours of the 1980s and early 1990s severely affected Greek–European Community/EU relations and the impact of Europeanisation (Mitsos 2000).[3] Whereas some segments of the Greek polity and society rapidly and extensively internalised the influence of EU membership, other vital elements of government and administration failed to do so (Ioakimidis 2000). Furthermore, parts of the political system only adhered rhetorically to the induced modernisation following membership, in order to better serve and reproduce parochial clientelistic patterns and practices. This particular interaction resulted in a dualistic political system of organisational and behavioural adaptation to Europeanisation, which created pockets of adaptational inertia and resistance within the Greek administration and policymaking system more generally.

In practice constituting a synonym of modernisation, 'Europeanisation' has been instrumentally used to nurture a wider reform paradigm, especially from the second half of the 1990s onwards. As in other countries, the EU, and especially its European Monetary Union (EMU) component, has often been invoked domestically by the Greek government as an 'external constraint' to achieve otherwise elusive reform (Tinios 2006; Papadimitriou 2005; Featherstone 2003). Even in cases where the EU did not directly mandate a specific reform agenda and thus the 'commitment devices' were relatively weak, it nevertheless had an indirect impact, contributing to the legitimisation of a particular course of action in domestic political discourse, as for example within the broad agenda of privatisation (Pagoulatos 2006).

This reform process, however, has not always been smooth. Strong resistance and consequent electoral concerns have more than once negated the reform dynamics of Europeanisation. In many cases, formal and informal veto forces have clashed with, and prevailed over, the reform-prone upper strata of the political executive. This can be clearly illustrated by the attempted 2001 pension system reform, the problematic reform of the Greek labour market over the years, and the restructuring of Olympic Airways/Airlines (Featherstone & Papadimitriou 2008; Sotiropoulos 2004b; Featherstone, Kazamias & Papadimitriou 2001). These case studies of abandoned reform seemingly confirm the classification of Greece as a 'world of neglect' in terms of political culture, where EU compliance is not a goal per se, or, at best, as a 'world of domestic politics', in which compliance is only one goal among many and domestic concerns frequently prevail. However, this would most probably result in a simplified categorisation that failed to acknowledge significant progress over time in other sectors, such as public procurement (Dimitrakopoulos 2007). True, Greece has remained one of the least effective or responsive member states in implementing EU-initiated policies (Spanou 2008). Still, a more nuanced approach is required, capable of capturing the dualistic nature of Greek policymaking's adaptation to Europeanisation, with certain policy areas still far from internalising EU-induced change.

The problematic response to calls for reform associated with Europeanisation also illustrates the limits of technocratic empowerment, an issue of direct relevance to the role of independent bodies and authorities in the Greek policymaking system. The prevalence of political parties in the domestic political arena has nurtured a weak civil society and a lack of associational culture. However, this situation may be changing, not least because of the opening of the Greek polity and society since EU membership was obtained (Mouzelis & Pagoulatos 2003). As a result, only a relatively small elite of experts is actively engaged in the policymaking process. These individuals are frequently associated with more than one organisation, thus creating a membership overlap among think-tanks, government- or party-funded research institutes, and universities. The common element among these experts, and the critical criterion of their participation in the process, is their clear political affiliation with a particular party. This means that, in practice, most of the intellectual activity with a potential input into public policy takes place close to political parties, or is somehow affected by party competition more generally (Ladi 2006, pp. 62–63). The lack of an effective and independent community of policy expertise has played its role in previous rounds of pension (Featherstone 2005) and labour market reforms (Papadimitriou 2005). It creates a closed circuit that uses almost exclusively party-affiliated experts as personal advisors or indeed as decision-makers—for example in independent authorities—in an attempt to legitimise reforms (Monastiriotis & Antoniades 2009).

The implications of this highly politicised atmosphere for the operation of independent authorities, if and when they are created, are straightforward, revealing a very low 'goodness of fit' between EU policies and domestic practices in this field (cf. Knill 2002; Knill & Lenschow 1998). Party identification or at least association is a necessary condition for the appointment of most experts in such bodies in order to ensure compliance with government policy and avoid agency losses. In the words of a former minister:

> There are two kinds of risks associated with independent authorities. Either they will not do the job they are established for, or they will be overactive, causing problems for the operation of the market ... [in Greece] there are gross excesses with them ... we have granted them responsibilities they cannot handle effectively within the Greek context ... and they lack democratic legitimisation. On the other hand, they are in a position to hold the Minister to ransom ... and blackmail the government ... because they have all the information and the Minister is very vulnerable to adverse publicity. (Interview 1)

Within this context, '[m]inisters have always held the view that independent authorities should be held at arm's length ... to be independent but not so much so' (interview 2).[4]

The Development of Greek Auditing and the Establishment of ELTE

Corporate auditing in Greece began in the mid 1950s when the auditing profession, SOL,[5] was established through a state legislative initiative. Prioritising public purposes such as reducing errant corporate activities and limiting tax evasion, the state incorporated the auditing institution into its own centralised, hierarchical system of regulation. State officials supervised and monitored the activities of the auditing profession and governed issues such as audit fees, appointments of auditors, disciplinary processes and the formulation of by-laws (Dedoulis & Caramanis 2007). Furthermore, the auditing profession was subject to state control in relation to leadership selection, interest articulation and policy formulation. Until 1992, the quasi-state institute also constituted the only audit firm enjoying a legally sanctioned monopoly in the market for statutory audits.

In the early 1990s, the liberalisation of the local economy, a direct corollary of further European integration, brought about changes in the domestic political and economic context that necessitated the modernisation of the auditing profession. Demands for comparable and reliable financial information from international investors, shareholders and managers and the growth of local branches of multinational audit firms (which first set foot in the country in the 1960s) created significant pressures to reform the local profession. Responding to broader calls, the state abolished the state-regulated SOL and reorganised the auditing profession (Caramanis 2002; 2005). Under the new structure both local and multinational audit firms were incorporated into a new professional body, SOEL,[6] which was endowed with the privilege of self-governance. The institutions of the profession became the means with which to represent and advance the interests of its constituent members—issue standards, codes of ethics, by-laws and guidance—as well as exercising disciplinary action and quality control inspections.

However, the privilege of self-regulation of the profession was soon abolished. In 2003, Law 3148/2003 established ELTE, which would exercise control over SOEL, depriving it of almost all regulatory and oversight powers, including, inter alia, quality control inspections and disciplinary action. A necessary precondition for the effective operation of the new oversight board was its institutional independence. In a parliamentary debate, the Minister of Economy, N. Christodoulakis, underlined the importance of relying upon internationally accepted standards when structuring the proposed body in order to ensure the institute's independence from the state.[7] The organisation of the body was, in a number of respects, based on the 2001 EU Recommendation that called for the majority of members to be market representatives. ELTE was governed by a seven-member Administrative Council (AC), headed by the chairman and two vice-chairmen appointed by the Ministry of Economy. The four remaining members were nominated by the Bank of Greece, the Hellenic Capital Markets Commission, the Confederation of Greek Industries and SOEL. ELTE's chairman and the two vice-chairmen comprised a separate three-member organ, ELTE's Executive Committee (EC).

Within the hierarchical structure of ELTE, two committees were set up with distinctive responsibilities, in order to facilitate the advisory, oversight and regulatory operations. The Accounting Standardisation Committee (SLOT) would advise various constituencies on the application of the International Accounting Standards and the Greek Chart Accounts, while the Quality Inspections Committee (SPE) would perform quality controls on the work of professional auditors. The former was a five-member committee which was to be headed by one of the two vice-chairmen of ELTE and four other members. SLOT's members were to be appointed by ELTE's AC. The latter would be a seven-member committee headed by the second vice-chairman and would comprise a senior judge, one member of SLOT and four members nominated by the Bank of Greece, the Hellenic Capital Markets Commission, SOEL and the Ministry, respectively. The initial law was accompanied by high expectations cultivated by members of the government and the major opposition party (Greek Parliament 2003b). As evidenced by the minutes of the parliamentary debate, the support garnered in parliament for the establishment of ELTE primarily stemmed from the fact that the creation of an independent auditing oversight board was an EU Recommendation (Greek Parliament 2003b).

Besides the EU Recommendation, the formation of ELTE was also related to the 1999 Athens Stock Exchange crisis and its political repercussions. In the late 1990s, the Athens Stock Exchange exhibited unprecedented growth followed by an intensive downward spiral. This fluctuation, which turned stock market euphoria into a drama, gave rise to significant public concerns about the role of politicians and various institutions.[8] This growing public discontent was accompanied by explicit corruption allegations against senior members of PASOK (Pan-Hellenic Socialist Movement), the governing party at that time. In response, the government prioritised, inter alia, the establishment of the independent oversight board to strengthen audit function, thereby minimising the likelihood of a similar crisis reoccurring. Endorsing the EU rhetoric of the 2001 Recommendation, Minister Christodoulakis, in various comments and public statements, stressed the importance of this development.[9] Thus, three years before the issuance of the legally binding EU Directive, a domestic crisis accelerated the establishment of the independent body ELTE, contributing to the EU's/European ideational ascendance in the domestic policymaking system.

ELTE in Operation: The Institutionalisation of Local Constraints

Appointing the Protagonists

From its inception, ELTE was entrapped in the acknowledged weaknesses of the Greek political system. Two successive governments failed (or did not really intend) to take the necessary measures that would enable the newly established body to develop as an independent and effective institution.

The government filled the three leading posts of ELTE's EC in August 2003, appointing an active certified auditor and senior partner in a big-four audit firm as chairman. Two political affiliates of PASOK were appointed as the two vice-chairmen of ELTE, but their competencies and appropriateness for the specific posts were openly questioned (interview 3). Interestingly, the PASOK government neglected to fill the remaining posts of ELTE's AC and the positions in SLOT and SPE, as the country was heading for elections in March 2004. As ELTE's main organs remained understaffed, crucial operations, including quality inspections of audit work and disciplinary processes, could not be properly organised and conducted.

PASOK lost the 2004 elections. New Democracy (ND) came to power and the newly appointed minister of economy, G. Alogoskoufis—despite his parliamentary statements during the passing of the initial law (Greek Parliament 2003b)—appeared to place little emphasis on ELTE's function. 'Indeed, the Ministry's leadership merely marginalised if not ignored accountancy issues' (interview 1; this was also underscored by interviewee 2). Within this context, the oversight body remained inactive for eight months. The ND government's involvement in ELTE's affairs commenced in late December 2004, when article 18 of Law 3301/2004 was enacted. The importance of this legislative intervention lay in the fact that it changed ELTE's membership composition. The new law prescribed that the heads of SLOT and SPE (ELTE's two vice-chairmen), posts that should have been filled by SOEL according to the initial law, would be filled by the government and would be taken over by state officials. This reorganisation of the membership resulted in the state obtaining significant influence, if not control, over those committees' workings, substantially limiting ELTE's independence.

Two months later, in February 2005, the government changed ELTE's vice-chairmen. Two civil servants from the Ministry of Economy, widely regarded as political affiliates to the new minister and thereby inextricably related to ND, became vice-chairmen (interview 1). The two officials had played an influential role in determining the selection criteria prescribed in article 18 of the Law 3301/2004 (interview 2). However, the Chairman who had been appointed by the PASOK government remained in position. Interestingly, the Minister of Economy maintained that, although ELTE's Chairman had not been a 'political' friend, since he had been appointed by the previous government, he had to remain in position in order to project the idea of cohesion and continuity (interview 1). The Minister explicitly admitted that the two vice-chairmen were ND party devotees, 'but it is important that the Chairman was not ... ideally no one should be ... but, you know, a vicious circle has long been set in public administration' (interview 1). Thus, retaining the Chairman of ELTE appointed by the previous government appears primarily to have served a legitimising purpose. The government then appointed the four members of SLOT, selecting a practitioner and three accounting academics (*Government Gazette* 2009). However, it was a year later before it filled SPE's posts. Understandably, the criteria adopted for selecting part of the membership and the various delays in staffing the remaining posts substantially impeded the oversight board's operations.

The Oversight Body's Workings in Question

For the first five years since its inception, the body remained essentially idle, very much due to the state's inaction with regard to staffing. At the same time, the prevailing political indifference towards accountancy matters had affected the attitudes of ELTE's members, which prolonged the oversight body's inertia. In various cases, the Minister had communicated to several parties, including the Secretary-General of the Ministry of Economy and ELTE's EC, that ELTE and, more generally, accounting and auditing regulation were not his priority, despite occasional public statements to the contrary (interviews 1 and 2). Within this context, ELTE showed no sign of seeking to undertake an essentially active role.

A member of SLOT met with the Secretary-General of the Ministry of Economy in July 2006 to expose the difficulties that ELTE encountered. A report was requested which would then be forwarded to the Minister. The report was submitted in October 2006 and, inter alia, stressed ELTE's weakness in facilitating the advancement of Greek accountancy. Attention was also drawn to the criteria applied regarding the selection of ELTE's membership and to the significance of its independence from the Ministry, two necessary preconditions for the effectiveness of the oversight body (Member of ELTE 2006a). According to the testimony of this individual, the Secretary-General admitted that the situation was much worse than revealed in the report and seemed to disagree with certain decisions[10] that had been taken by the Minister and ELTE's leadership (interview 3). The problems raised in the report were also conveyed to ELTE's leadership in writing (Member of ELTE 2006b; 2006c; 2006d).

Several members of the oversight body also reported those issues to the Secretary-General, whilst three senior state officials informed the Minister himself (interview 4). In a similar vein, a new five-page report was submitted by the SLOT member, who underscored the challenges and pointed out that the credibility of pivotal institutions remained in question, a situation that constituted a real threat to the operation of the market (Member of ELTE 2007). Shortly after, the member of SLOT was unexpectedly replaced.

In January and November 2008, two more letters were sent by the same former member of SLOT, exposing a conflict-of-interest situation in which two senior members of ELTE had been involved (Member of ELTE 2008a; 2008b). Specifically, addressed to the Minister of Economy, the first letter argued that the Chairman of ELTE had been appointed as a non-executive director of a large listed Greek bank and later as head of the General Directorate of the Bank's Internal Control (from July 2008), while the Vice-Chairman of ELTE had become chairman and chief executive officer of a large pension fund. The second letter had a similar content and was addressed to the membership of ELTE's AC. Three members of the AC agreed with the issues underscored; however, they did not want to get involved and consequently they took no action (interviews 5, 6, 7).

The Member of SLOT also met with the Secretary-General of the Ministry of Economy to explain the situation. According to his own account,

> I met with the Secretary in his office in the presence of the Director General of the Ministry ... I was in a mood to test their attitude and I explained to them that I would communicate the details of the ELTE case to members of the Economics Committee of Parliament and, if that had no effect, I would write to the EU Competition Commissioner, Charlie McCreevy. I think they were both deeply shocked. I remember the Secretary saying '... you are right but ... you know ... this is not compatible with our political culture'. (Interview 3)

The attitudes of ELTE's members sealed the oversight board's institutionalised links with the political leadership and attested to the lack of 'true independent, qualified, committed and tough-minded individuals among their members' (interview 3). Interesting insights into ELTE's workings were given by a reputable professional with considerable experience of the mechanisms and mentalities of the various accountancy committees. He argued that, in most cases, political affiliation and loyalty to the political leadership constituted the main criteria for ministers in selecting the oversight authorities' membership (interview 8). He openly questioned the competence of ELTE's membership and described their prevailing attitude as primarily characterised by reluctance to challenge established relationships and connections with political leadership, as this would jeopardise the remuneration they received from being a member of ELTE (interview 8).

In 2006, as previously mentioned, the EU issued the Eighth Directive 2006/43/EC, which required the establishment of a system of public oversight over audit practice, including the performance of audit quality inspections. Although the transposition of the Directive entailed reforms to the existing system, the basic organisation and structure of ELTE remained in place whilst it met, at least on paper, the EU prescriptions.

However, ELTE's role was soon called into question publicly. The debate was instigated by an academic survey of the state of accounting and auditing which received wide coverage by the financial press and major professional journals and focused on the role of the oversight authorities.[11] The survey revealed that these authorities were in need of significant improvements on a number of issues, including reliability, transparency, staffing and independence from political and economic centres of power (Caramanis & Papadakis 2008). Cabinet reshuffling in early 2009 resulted in the replacement of Minister Alogoskoufis by J. Papathanasiou but did not bring about the removal of the Secretary-General who supervised ELTE. The change of minister raised expectations for a change in ELTE's administrative council, given the main features of the Greek clientelistic political system and especially following the adverse publicity surrounding ELTE mentioned above (interview 4). Change in personnel did occur in April 2009. The Minister appointed as chairman of ELTE an individual with significant international academic and consulting experience in the United Kingdom (UK), and as vice-chairman a retired big-four partner who was working in a freelance consulting capacity at the time of his appointment (*Government Gazette* 2009).

The new chairman expressed his views on ELTE's contribution from 2003 to 2009 in the influential professional journal *Accountancy Greece*. He acknowledged that, 'although there was a clear legislative requirement for ELTE to perform quality control inspections since its establishment in 2003, the institution remained dormant and totally inactive until April 2009' (*Refenes*, 2011, p. 29). He also mentioned that ELTE's main priority since he had taken over was to instigate quality controls. Indeed, the 2009 change in ELTE's membership appears to have initiated some modest action. The first quality inspections of audit firms took place in autumn 2009, after ELTE was given permission by the Ministry of Economy to appoint suitably qualified staff on a fixed-term one-year contract. On 14 April 2010, ELTE organised a one-day conference where a summary of the quality control results was presented to interested parties (professionals, state officials, academics and so on). However, the actual report has not been made available and it therefore remains unknown whether ELTE took any disciplinary action or imposed any fines on deviant practices. Since then, however, ELTE has been left without staff to conduct quality inspections. The one-year contracts of its staff expired in summer 2010 and the government has apparently failed to renew them or to give permission for new appointments.

Ideas, Interests and Institutions: Insights from the Case of ELTE

The case of ELTE illustrates the ascendance of independent bodies and agencies in the Greek public policymaking setting, internalising EU pressure. Given the overwhelming presence of the Greek state in the domestic public policymaking process, one would expect that the emergence of independent, regulatory and oversight actors would substantially alter the terms of policymaking. In this respect, the EU influences and constraints, in the form of Recommendations and Directives, generate expectations of policy *transformation*. However, our empirical evidence suggests a mere *absorption* of the EU pressures, at best their *accommodation*. True, both policy and institutional adaptation has occurred. However, it seems that only a superficial adjustment has transpired, despite the legally binding and highly prescriptive nature of EU pressures.

In terms of ideas, we can distinguish between the impact of EU pressures at different levels. At the micro-ideational level of specific policies and the meso-ideational level of policy programmes, adaptation owed much to the cognitive realisation of the regulatory benefits associated with ELTE and independent agencies more generally. However, at the macro-level of the policymaking role of the state, the predominant character of the state has not been challenged. As a result, the omnipresent and all-encompassing state has retained its control over domestic policymaking process, limiting in practice the independent function of oversight institutions. Thus, although Europeanisation may have nurtured a greater domestic ideational adherence to independent regulatory actors, it has not yet brought about a curtailment of and a paradigmatic shift vis-à-vis the role of the state in public policymaking.

In terms of interests, caution is required before establishing direct causality between Europeanisation and induced reform. Our case clearly suggests that Europeanisation may not be the sole or even the prime agent of change. Converging domestic elements, such as the 1999 Athens Stock Exchange crisis, emerged as catalysts of change, creating an environment conducive to reform, opening 'opportunity windows' for institutional adaptation to EU prescriptions and conditioning the Europeanisation effect. The establishment of ELTE owed much to the government's intention to polish its tarnished image and restore public confidence in the stock exchange after the crisis. In this respect, pressures emanating from the EU public policy domain were internalised successfully, in the form of ELTE, and used instrumentally for domestic political motives to legitimise government action. This allowed the government to adopt EU-enthused reform rhetoric as a response to the crisis without actually losing control of the policymaking process. Furthermore, in the case of Greece, our findings call into question the 'external constraints' argument, according to which EU pressures bring about the empowerment of domestic technocracy at the expense of political party opportunism. Although ELTE constitutes a primary example of an institution with a high technocratic capture potential, the inappropriate selection of the appointed experts has hindered its operation. This is the case because most experts were party-affiliated and selected largely based on their political identification, which rendered them extremely sensitive about upsetting the governmental agenda. As a matter of fact, there is a tight policymaking nexus comprising politicians and members of epistemic communities, wherein academics, for example, often move into the central political arena.

Finally, in terms of institutions, the creation of ELTE per se constitutes an important institutional development. Independent agencies have traditionally featured very low in the Greek policymaking system, clearly indicating a problematic relationship with governmental authorities. This relationship owes much to the pervasive policymaking role of the state as mentioned above, which is in itself a by-product of the historical development of the Greek state and the political culture it has nurtured. ELTE's gestation created the façade of a far-reaching institutional reform, especially given the lip service paid to it by the highest echelons of the domestic political executive. The result has been a new institution characterised by a traditional—in political terms—modus operandi. The body's inaction throughout its existence due to problematic staffing means that almost no quality inspection has been conducted and no disciplinary action has been taken in a conscious attempt to avoid thorny issues and the subsequent political cost.

Conclusions

The foundation of ELTE in 2003 was heralded as a turning point in accounting and auditing practice in Greece. The creation of the body owed much to the 1999 Athens Stock Exchange crisis and its broader political repercussions, facilitating a swift adjustment to the EU agenda on this issue. Thus, Europeanisation should not be misunderstood as the sole agent of change. The functioning of this EU-inspired, independent oversight board faltered when it came up against some problematic features of the domestic policymaking system, losing a large part of its transformative potential. Even highly prescriptive EU-originated reforms are filtered through the domestic political system, often leading to gaps between the intended purpose and actual policy outcome. In our case, of particular interest is the state's delay in making the body fully operational by postponing its staffing and, more importantly, by the appointment to key positions of policy experts with a clear party affiliation. These features undermined not only ELTE's effectiveness but also its independence, making it, in essence, another state-controlled agency.

The ELTE case provides many insights into public policymaking in Greece as well as the impact of Europeanisation on that. It reiterates earlier findings regarding the superficial nature of Greek public policy adaptation in certain policy fields. Institutional reform does occur as a response to EU developments but is often shallow and a mere façade, pointing to *absorption* or *accommodation* of EU pressures rather than *transformation* of the domestic policymaking system. Europeanisation has not yet triggered any policy paradigm shift vis-à-vis the role of independent bodies in the Greek policymaking system. In practice these bodies have functioned as vehicles for pushing forward governmental agenda priorities. The state proceeds to create such allegedly independent authorities but maintains control indirectly through the appointment of party-associated experts who influence the operation of these bodies in accordance with the governmental agenda. This is also telling with regard to the status of the expert/state relationship, professionals often relinquishing their independence and the administration then utilising them for legitimising purposes. The repercussions of these findings are significant, especially as their potential for generalisation is high because they pertain to many forms of oversight bodies and independent authorities in Greece across different fields. At the same time, the findings provide a research agenda for other South European countries to explore similar constraints within their own Europeanisation processes.

Notes

[1] Besides ELTE, other independent authorities were also established around this period, such as the Hellenic Competition Commission (in 1995), the Greek Ombudsman (in 1997), the Hellenic Data Protection Authority (in 1997) and the Regulatory Authority for Energy (in 2000).

[2] Alternatively, they may only change domestic opportunity structures, dismantling the national regulatory and policymaking system without entailing concrete and specific modality blueprints (i.e. negative integration). In their weakest form, they may have no institutional impact at all but bring about changes in domestic beliefs and expectations (i.e. the domestic policy-framing dimension), not only vis-à-vis the policy content but also with regard to policy agency (Knill 2002).

[3] Until 1985, adjustment pressures were successfully blocked, to a large extent on ideological and economic grounds, the first PASOK government centrally orchestrating resistance. In the post-1985 period, the reinforced involvement of European structures in the management of the Greek economy (through the Integrated Mediterranean Programmes and most significantly the Structural and Cohesion Funds) and the invigoration of the integration process (Single European Act, Maastricht Treaty) increased EC/EU appeal and strengthened Europeanisation pressures (Kazakos 1994).

[4] Similar attitudes towards the role of independent authorities are not uncommon in the Greek policymaking system. For instance, the Ministry of Economy has often taken measures to limit the role of independent authorities over the past few years. To give two examples: Law 3691/2008 turned the pre-existing independent authority for money-laundering into a committee under the direct supervision of the Ministry of Economy, while Law 3756/2009 brought the Greek Capital Markets Commission under even closer control of the Ministry of Economy.

[5] SOL = the Body of Sworn-in Accountants (Σώμα Ορκωτών Λογιστών – ΣΟΛ).

[6] SOEL = the Body of Sworn-in Auditors Accountants (Σώμα Ορκωτών Ελεγκτών Λογιστών – ΣΟΕΛ).

[7] '[O]ur purpose is only one ... (to) bring it away from the operation of the state, so that it will be able to adapt to international developments and will be capable of overseeing companies and inspecting auditors ... we use the recipes that are available internationally to improve the context in which the markets operate and investors make decisions' (Greek Parliament 2003b, p. 4269, authors' translation).

[8] A political debate on this issue took place in parliament. Leading figures from the centre-right party, ND, and other opposition parties accused the governing PASOK of playing a key role in the overvaluation of stocks with a view to winning the 2000 elections (Greek Parliament 2003b, pp. 5351–5352; see also 2003a).

[9] Indicatively, see the Minister's public speeches to key business organisations, such as the Hellenic Bank Association (19 March 2002), the Federation of Greek Industries (14 May 2003) and the Athens Stock Exchange Conference (8 March 2002). Furthermore, he stated that '[i]n order to increase transparency in the operation of companies, the Ministry ... establishes a committee of accounting standardisation and supervision, which will secure the transparency and quality of the statutory audits ... In this way, it is expected that investors' faith in listed companies will be restored' (*Ministry of National Economy Bulletin*, 9 July 2002; see also 23 July 2002; 9 February 2002; 22 August 2003: available online at: www3.mnec.gr).

[10] On one occasion for instance, the Secretary-General was required to give his consent to a ministerial decision that appointed a member of the disciplinary council who did not hold the qualifications prescribed by the law (interview 3).

[11] See *Epsilon7*, 17 October 2008, pp. 4–7; *Naftemporiki*, 17 October 2008; *Kerdos*, 19 October 2008, *Vima*, 6 January 2009.

References

Balkir, C., Bolukbasi, H. T. & Ertugal, E. (2013) 'Europeanisation and dynamics of continuity and change in domestic political economies in the "Southern Periphery"', *South European Society and Politics*, vol. 18, no. 2, pp. 121–137.

Bulmer, S. & Radaelli, C. M. (2005) 'The Europeanisation of national policy', in *The Member States of the European Union*, eds S. Bulmer & C. Lequesne, Oxford University Press, Oxford, pp. 338–359.

Caramanis, C. (2002) 'The interplay between professional groups, the state and supranational agents: Pax Americana in the age of "globalisation"', *Accounting, Organizations and Society*, vol. 27, pp. 379–408.

Caramanis, C. (2005) 'Rationalisation, charisma & accounting professionalisation: perspectives on the intra-professional conflict in Greece, 1993–2001', *Accounting, Organizations and Society*, vol. 30, pp. 195–221.

Caramanis, C. & Papadakis, V. (2008) *Η εφαρμογή των Διεθνών Λογιστικών Προτύπων στην Ελλάδα* [The Application of the International Accounting Standards in Greece], Athens University of Economics & Business.

Cooper, D. & Robson, K. (2006) 'Accounting, professions & regulation: locating the sites of professionalisation', *Accounting, Organizations and Society*, vol. 31, pp. 415–444.

Dedoulis, E. & Caramanis, C. (2007) 'Imperialism of influence and the state–profession relationship: the formation of the Greek auditing profession in the post WWII era', *Critical Perspectives on Accounting*, vol. 18, pp. 393–412.

Dimitrakopoulos, D. (2007) 'Institutions and the implementation of EU public policy in Greece: the case of public procurement', *Hellenic Observatory Papers on Greece & Southeast Europe*, no. 2.

European Commission. (1998) 'Communication from the Commission on the statutory audit in the European Union: the way forward', *Official Journal of the European Union*, C 143, 8 May, p. 12–16.

European Commission. (2001) 'Commission Recommendation of 15 November 2000 on quality assurance for the statutory audit in the European Union: minimum requirements', *Official Journal of the European Union*, L 091, 31 March, pp. 91–97.

European Commission. (2006) 'Directive 2006/43/EC of the European Parliament & of the Council of 17 May 2006 on statutory audits of annual accounts & consolidated accounts, amending Council Directives 78/660/EEC & 83/349/EEC & repealing Council Directive 84/253/EEC', *Official Journal of the European Union*, L 157, 9 June, pp. 24–86.

Featherstone, K. (2003) 'Greece and EMU', *Journal of Common Market Studies*, vol. 41, no. 5, pp. 923–940.

Featherstone, K. (2005) '"Soft" co-ordination meets "hard" politics: the European Union & pension reform in Greece', *Journal of European Public Policy*, vol. 12, no. 4, pp. 733–750.

Featherstone, K. & Papadimitriou, D. (2008) *The Limits of Europeanisation. Reform Capacity and Policy Conflict in Greece*, Palgrave Macmillan, Basingstoke.

Featherstone, K., Kazamias, G. & Papadimitriou, D. (2001) 'The limits of external empowerment: EMU, technocracy and reform of the Greek pension system', *Political Studies*, vol. 49, no. 3, pp. 462–480.

Government Gazette (2009) *'Υπ' αριθμ. 17779/524/3.4.2009 απόφαση αντικατάστασης Προέδρου και Ά Αντιπροέδρου του Διοικητικού Συμβουλίου της Επιτροπής Λογιστικής Τυποποίησης και Ελέγχων (ΕΛΤΕ)*, (Decision 17779/524 Re: Changes in the Composition of ELTE's Administrative Committee), National Printing Office, Athens.

Greek Parliament. (2003a) *Διαρκής Επιτροπή Οικονομικών Υποθέσεων συζήτηση για το νομοσχέδιο 3148/2003* [The Official Proceedings of the Discussion of Law 3148/2003 Before the Standing Committee of Economic Affairs], 17 April 2003, Athens.

Greek Parliament. (2003b) *Επίσημα Πρακτικά Βουλής, Συνεδρίαση ΡΆ Προκαταρκτική εξέταση περί ευθύνης Υπουργών* [The Official Proceedings of the ΡΆ Parliamentary Meeting on Investigation of the Ministers' Responsibility], 17 June.

Humphrey, C., Loft, A. & Woods, M. (2009) 'The global audit profession and the international financial architecture: understanding regulatory relationships at the time of financial crisis', *Accounting, Organizations and Society*, vol. 34, pp. 810–825.

Ioakimidis, P. C. (1996) 'Contradictions in the Europeanisation process', in *Greece in a Changing Europe: Between European integration & Balkan Disintegration?* eds K. Featherstone & K. Ifantis, Manchester University Press, Manchester.

Ioakimidis, P. C. (2000) 'The Europeanisation of Greece: an overall assessment', *South European Society & Politics*, vol. 5, no. 2, pp. 73–94.

Kazakos, P. (1994) 'Greece and the EC: historical review', in *Greece and EC Membership Evaluated*, eds P. Kazakos & P. C. Ioakimidis, Pinter, London, St Martin's Press, New York.

Knill, C. (2002) 'The national impact of European Union regulatory policy: three Europeanisation mechanisms', *European Journal of Political Research*, vol. 41, no. 2, pp. 255–280.

Knill, C. & Lenschow, A. (1998) 'Coping with Europe: the impact of British and German administrations on the implementation of EU environmental policy', *Journal of European Public Policy*, vol. 5, no. 4, pp. 595–614.

Ladi, S. (2006) 'The role of experts in the reform process in Greece', in *Politics and Policy in Greece*, ed. K. Featherstone, Routledge, London, pp. 57–74.

Majone, G. (1994) 'The rise of the regulatory state in Europe', *West European Politics*, vol. 17, pp. 77–101.

Majone, G. (1996) 'Public policy and administration: ideas, interests and institutions', in *A New Handbook of Political Science*, eds R. E. Goodin & H. -D. Klingemann, Oxford University Press, Oxford, pp. 610–627.

Member of ELTE. (2006a) *Αναφορά σχετικά με την εσωτερική κατάσταση λειτουργίας της ΕΛΤΕ, υπόψη του Γενικού Γραμματέα στο Υπουργείο Οικονομικών* [Report to the Secretary-General of the Ministry of Finance Regarding the State of Affairs in ELTE], 2 October.

Member of ELTE. (2006b) *Επιστολή προς τον Πρόεδρο και μέλη του διοικητικού Συμβουλίου της ΕΛΤΕ* [Letter to the President and to the Members of ELTE's Administrative Council], 1 November.

Member of ELTE. (2006c) *Επιστολή προς τα μέλη του Διοικητικού Συμβουλίου της ΕΛΤΕ σχετικά με τη συμμετοχή στο συμβούλιο του EGAOB για τα Διεθνή Ελεγκτικά*

Πρότυπα της 16ης Νοεμβρίου 2006 και Ποιοτικού Ελέγχου της 20ης Νοεμβρίου 2006 [Letter to Members of ELTE's Administrative Council on Greece's Participation in EGAOB ISA Meetings of 16 November 2006 and EGAOB Quality Assurance Meetings of 20 November 2006], 28 November.

Member of ELTE. (2006d) *Επιστολή προς τον Πρόεδρο της ΕΛΤΕ και του ΣΛΟΤ με την οποία ζητείται να ακολουθηθεί η ορθή διαδικασία έγκρισης και υπογραφής των αποφάσεων του ΣΛΟΤ* [Letter to the Chairman of ELTE and to the Chairman of SLOT Asking for the Proper Signing of all Pronouncements of SLOT by Its Members], 19 December.

Member of ELTE. (2007) *Αναφορά στον Υπουργό των Οικονομικών σχετικά με την κατάσταση στην ΕΛΤΕ* [Report to the Minister of Economy about ELTE's Situation. Ministry of Economy], Register number 427, 24 January.

Member of ELTE. (2008a) *Επιστολή στον Υπουργό των Οικονομικών σχετικά με την κατάσταση στην ΕΛΤΕ* [Letter to the Minister of Economy about the Situation of ELTE's. Ministry of Economy], Register number 192, 22 January 2008.

Member of ELTE. (2008b) *Επιστολή στον Υπουργό των Οικονομικών, συνοδεύουσα την υποβλειθείσα έκθεση για τις επιπτώσεις από την εφαρμογή των ΔΛΠ στην Ελλάδα* [Letter to the Minister of Economy, Accompanying a Report Submitted on the Results of a Survey about the Impact of the Application of IFRS in Greece], Register number 8698, 18 November.

Mitsos, A. (2000) 'Maximising contribution to the European integration process as a prerequisite for the maximisation of gains', in *Contemporary Greece and Europe*, eds A. Mitsos & E. Mossialos, Ashgate, Aldershot.

Monastiriotis, V. & Antoniades, A. (2009) 'Reform that! Greece's failing reform technology: beyond "vested interests" & "political exchange"', *Hellenic Observatory Papers on Greece & Southeast Europe*, no. 28.

Mouzelis, N. & Pagoulatos, G. (2003) 'Κοινωνία πολιτών και ιδιότητα του πολίτη στη μεταπολιτευτική Ελλάδα', [Civil society and citizen's capacity in post-war Greece] *Greek Political Science Review*, vol. 22, pp. 5–29.

Pagoulatos, G. (2006) 'The politics of privatisation: redrawing the public–private boundary', in *Politics and Policy in Greece*, ed. K. Featherstone, Routledge, London, pp. 136–158.

Papadimitriou, D. (2005) 'The limits of engineering collective escape: the 2000 reform of the Greek labour market', *West European Politics*, vol. 28, no. 2, pp. 381–401.

Peters, B. G. & Wright, V. (1996) 'Public policy and administration, old and new', in *A New Handbook of Political Science*, eds R. E. Goodin & H. -D. Klingemann, Oxford University Press, Oxford, pp. 628–641.

Radaelli, C. M. (2003) 'The Europeanisation of public policy', in *The Politics of Europeanisation*, eds K. Featherstone & C. M. Radaelli, Oxford University Press, Oxford, pp. 27–56.

Refenes, A. (2011) '*Στις «δύσκολες χρονιές» αυξάνουν τα κρούσματα «ωραιοποίησης» των οικονομικών καταστάσεων* [During 'difficult years', 'creative reporting' increases]', *Accountancy Greece*, vol. 2, pp. 26–31.

Shepsle, K. A. (1991) 'Discretion, institutions and the problem of government commitment', in *Social Theory for a Changing Society*, eds P. Bourdieu & J. S. Coleman, Westview Press, Boulder, CO, pp. 245–263.

Sikka, P. (2009) 'Financial crisis and the silence of the auditors', *Accounting, Organizations and Society*, vol. 34, pp. 868–873.

Sikka, P. & Willmott, H. (1995a) 'Illuminating the state–profession relationship: accountants acting as Department of Trade and Industry investigators', *Critical Perspectives on Accounting*, vol. 6, no. 4, pp. 341–369.

Sikka, P. & Willmott, H. (1995b) 'The power of independence: defending & extending the jurisdiction of accounting in the United Kingdom', *Accounting Organisation and Society*, vol. 20, no. 6, pp. 547–581.

Sotiropoulos, D. (2004a) 'Southern European public bureaucracies in comparative perspective', *West European Politics*, vol. 27, no. 3, pp. 405–422.

Sotiropoulos, D. (2004b) 'The EU's impact on the Greek welfare state: Europeanisation on paper?', *Journal of European Social Policy*, vol. 14, no. 3, pp. 267–284.

Spanou, C. (1996) 'Penelope's suitors: administrative modernisation and party competition in Greece', *West European Politics*, vol. 19, no. 1, pp. 97–124.

Spanou, C. (2008) 'State reform in Greece: responding to old and new challenges', *International Journal of Public Sector Management*, vol. 21, no. 2, pp. 150–173.

Tinios, P. (2006) 'Pension reform in Greece: "reform by instalments" – a blocked process?', in *Politics and Policy in Greece*, ed. K. Featherstone, Routledge, London, pp. 180–197.

US Congress. (2002) 'Public Law 107 – 204 – Sarbanes–Oxley Act of 2002', available online at: http://www.gpo.gov/fdsys/pkg/PLAW-107publ204/content-detail.html

Apendix. List of Interviews

1. (Former) Minister of National Economy, 14 July 2010
2. (Former) Secretary-General of Ministry of National Economy, 14 July 2010
3. (Former) Member of ELTE, 10 March 2009
4. (Former) Member of ELTE, 10 January 2009
5. (Former) Member of ELTE, 24 November 2006
6. (Former) Member of ELTE (Vice-Chairman of Capital Market), 21 November 2008
7. (Former) Member of ELTE (Vice-Chairman of Capital Market), 21 November 2008
8. (Former) Member of ELTE (senior manager in the Bank of Greece), 22 November 2008
9. Professional auditor, 23 November 2008

The Europeanisation of Macroeconomic Policies and Financial Regulation in Italy

Lucia Quaglia

This research asks to what extent, how and why two key domains of domestic political economy, namely, macroeconomic policies and financial services regulation, have been Europeanised in Italy over the last decade. The impacts of Economic and Monetary Union and European Union financial services regulation are assessed by tracing the change in interests, ideas and institutions in these policy areas and identifying the causal mechanisms through which change came about (or was resisted). It is concluded that the degree of Europeanisation and its effects have been uneven across different elements of the political economy and some distinctive national features have remained.

The Italian political economy underwent significant changes in the third stage of Economic and Monetary Union (EMU), which gave new impetus to financial integration in Europe and is generally the end point of most research on Europeanisation in Southern Europe (see, for example, Featherstone & Kazamias 2001). Whereas the adaptation of Italy to EMU has been examined in the academic literature, especially approaching the final stage (Della Sala 1997; Ferrera & Gualmini 1999; Radaelli 2002; Sbragia 2001; for a later period see Quaglia & Furlong 2008), financial services governance in Italy has attracted limited academic attention.[1]

Following the framework set out in the introductory article of this volume (Balkir, Bolukbasi & Ertugal 2013), this research asks to what extent, how and why two key domains of domestic political economy, namely, macroeconomic policies and financial services regulation, have been Europeanised in Italy. It considers the extent to which the European Union (EU) is contributing to domestic change in these policy areas, which constitute ideal test cases for the Europeanisation literature. Indeed, they represent, respectively, an example of 'strong' Europeanisation, whereby the domestic effects of the EU are pronounced in the macroeconomic field, especially monetary policy; and 'weak' Europeanisation, whereby the domestic effects of the EU are less visible in the financial domain.

These policy areas, which were substantially affected by the establishment of EMU, are interlinked in that EMU gave a major impetus to financial market integration and regulation in the EU. Subsequently, the global financial crisis severely affected the conduct of macroeconomic policies in the EU and the very survival of EMU. For this reason, the time frame for this research spans from the establishment of EMU to the present, although a reference to earlier periods is necessary in order to trace change and investigate causality.

The paper proceeds as follows. The second section outlines the research design and concisely reviews the literature on the Italian variety of capitalism, paying special attention to its variety of financial capitalism. The third section traces the evolution of macroeconomic policies in Italy over the last decade or so. The fourth section discusses the evolution of financial regulation in Italy, focusing on banking and securities markets. Whereas the third and fourth sections primarily explain the influence of the EU on interests, ideas and institutions, the fifth section teases out the influence of ideas, interest and institutions on the various domains of political economy in Italy. The concluding section summarises the main findings that can travel beyond the country study examined in the paper and feed into the broader literature on Europeanisation.

The Research Design

Following the template outlined in the introduction to the volume (Balkir, Bolukbasi & Ertugal 2013), this research investigates the effects of certain EU policies, namely EMU and financial services regulation (the independent variables), on the respective domestic political economy domains of a member state (the dependent variables). Hence, causation moves from the EU level to the domestic level. However, Europeanisation is a two-way process, where downloading influence from the EU to the national level is paralleled by and/or interacts with uploading trends whereby national actors try to shape EU policies. Interests, ideas and institutions are the intervening variables through which the EU affects the domestic environment of the member states. Although these variables can be applied to any policy domains, they assume specific configurations with reference to macroeconomic policies and financial services regulation.

To begin with, the EU could trigger a change of domestic institutions. For example, the provisions concerning EMU contained in the Maastricht Treaty (to be precise, the Treaty on European Union [TEU]), and in subsequent EU legislation, prescribed a high degree of independence for the central banks of the member states of the euro area (see Dyson & Marcussen 2009). Hence, the statutes of many central banks, including the Italian central bank, the Banca d'Italia, had to be amended for them to become members of the Eurosystem.

Second, the EU could alter the configuration of interests in the member states. For example, certain private-sector actors, first and foremost large financial companies, supported the removal of national barriers to financial integration throughout the EU (Mügge 2010). This meant that the most competitive part of the Italian financial industry had potentially something to gain from further market integration and the opening up of national financial systems.

Finally, the EU could foster a change in the policy paradigm (or causal ideas) held by domestic elites, such as the diffusion of the stability-oriented paradigm in the making of EMU from Germany to other member states (Dyson 1994; McNamara 1998; Marcussen 2000; Quaglia 2004a). Besides cognitive (causal) ideas that provide mental road maps for policy-makers, the ideational literature also considers normative ideas. For example, Risse et al. (1999) argued that elites' perception of their material interests with regard to the euro was deeply influenced by their visions of European political order, to be understood in the framework of identity politics.

EU influence can be either direct or indirect. It is direct when changes in the domestic political economy are prescribed by the EU. This happens often, but not always, in the institutional domain, where domestic institutions may be changed to comply with EU rules (e.g. central bank independence in the Eurosystem). However, domestic institutions could change as a result of isomorphism, whereby a given institutional configuration is considered as functional to deal with domestic issues and is imported into the national environment. In this case, EU influence is indirect. This was the case for the social pacts adopted in Italy in the run-up to EMU, which drew on the German concertation in labour policy and were widely praised by the EU. The influence of the EU is generally indirect whenever it affects the ideas (or policy paradigms) of domestic elites or the configuration of interest groups involved in a policy domain, which then affect the policy outcome.

Of course, domestic change may be the result of the interaction of all the three intervening variables mentioned above, not least because it is difficult to neatly distinguish between interests, ideas and institutions. For example, changes concerning the monetary policy paradigm have often gone hand in hand with the institutional reforms towards central bank independence. Alternatively, domestic change can be purely endogenous, a fact often overlooked by the somewhat predetermined literature on Europeanisation (Radelli 2003). For example, some authors stress the domestic sources of fiscal adjustment (Stolfi 2008) or of financial reforms (Perez & Westrup 2010). In other cases, the encounter with Europe is a marginal episode that does not alter what is at stake in domestic political economy or can lead to inertia or open resistance, as in labour market reform (Quaglia & Radaelli 2007). Finally, in other cases, domestic change is the result of international as opposed to purely European factors. For example, capital requirements for banks in the EU (and hence in its member states) are set on the basis of global standards agreed by the Basel Committee on Banking Supervision (BCBS) and then incorporated into EU directives (Christopoulos & Quaglia 2009).

Before proceeding with the analysis, it is useful to outline the Italian model of capitalism, which encapsulates the foundations of the domestic political economy.[2] It is difficult to pigeonhole the Italian model of capitalism, for Italy is neither a liberal market economy (like the UK) nor a coordinated market economy (like Germany). Some authors argue that, to some extent, the Italian variety of capitalism resembles the 'statist' French model, the main difference being that the public authorities are less efficient in Italy than in France (Schmidt 2002). Indeed, Della Sala (2004, p. 1045) labels it as 'dysfunctional state capitalism'. In the macroeconomic realm, the Italian model, as in several other Southern European states, has been characterised by a vast public debt, which persisted to the 2000s; a large public deficit, which, however, turned into a primary surplus (i.e. net of interest payment) in the 1990s; and higher than EU average inflation, which, however, substantially decreased in the 1990s.

Until the 1990s, state intervention in the Italian economy was extensive and inefficient, as was the welfare state. Protective labour market legislation benefited those who were already employed, reducing flexibility in the labour market. The state took part in labour negotiations, although tripartite agreements in income policy were successfully managed only in the run-up to the final stage of EMU (the so-called *concertazione*) (Molina & Rhodes 2007). In the 2000s, there was an attempt to make the labour market less rigid by introducing more flexible wage structures and contracts.

In terms of corporate governance, before the 1990s many companies, even large ones, tended to be family owned and family managed, often through interlocking ownership managed by the powerful merchant bank Mediobanca (Della Sala 2004).[3] This was a family type of capitalism created by an underdeveloped capital market and outdated legislation that discouraged shareholder involvement. In contrast to Germany, before the revision of Italy's banking legislation in 1993 there was a complete separation between banks and industry in terms of ownership and shareholding (Deeg 2005).

Until the 1990s the Italian financial system was mainly 'bank oriented', in that it was characterised by extensive activity of financial intermediation performed by banks (Ciocca 2005, p. 4). Thus it resembled the situation in Germany, rather than the British 'market-oriented' system, where securities markets were already well developed in the 1980s. Before the reform of the 1990s the Italian banking sector was largely state-owned and characterised by two anomalies. The first of these was the division between public long-term credit institutions (*istituti di credito speciale*) and short-term credit institutions (*istituti di credito ordinario)*, with few private banks and many public savings banks and cooperative banks. Each of these categories was, in turn, divided into several different segments, on top of which there were geographical boundaries that restricted their activity. The second anomaly of the Italian banking system was the low degree of competition as a result of internal and external protectionism (Monti 1998).

EMU and Macroeconomic Governance in Italy

Against the odds, Italy managed to join the third and final stage of EMU from its inception (Ferrera & Gualmini 1999; Radaelli 2002; Sbragia 2001). Joining EMU brought about several changes in Italy: some of them were direct and explicitly prescribed by EMU membership, as in the case of monetary policy, whereas others were indirect, as in the case of structural reforms. Finally, there were instances of limited or no change.

The main change brought about by EMU in Italy concerned *monetary policy*. In approaching the final stage of EMU, monetary policy in Italy remained relatively tight, with a clear anti-inflationary priority. When the third stage of EMU began in 1999, the conduct of this policy was transferred to the European Central Bank (ECB). This can be seen as the most extreme case of transformation because a policy that was previously (at least formally) decided at the domestic level was transferred to the EU level, to be precise the euro-area level. It should, however, be noted that even prior to the establishment of EMU the monetary policy conducted by the Italian monetary authorities to a large extent deliberately followed the monetary policy of the leading central bank in Europe, the Bundesbank (Giavazzi & Pagano 1988).

It is also noteworthy that, except for the direct legal changes prescribed by EMU/ECB legislation, and the operational changes needed to take part in the Eurosystem, the Italian central bank exhibited limited adaptation to the EMU framework prior to 2005. According to newspaper accounts, the Governor of the Bank of Italy (and the governors of other large central banks in the Eurosystem) opposed the centralisation of some tasks, for example payment systems, at the ECB. Indeed, the Bank of Italy opened a state-of-the-art facility outside Rome for processing payments in the late 1990s. Central banking governance in Italy was reformed in 2005, when the new savings law (*legge sul risparmio*) was passed, after having been (at times heatedly) discussed since 2002, and after contributing to the resignations of two successive Treasury ministers. Overall, the change introduced in December 2005 was relatively small, but it was significant precisely because in the past it had been successfully opposed, principally by the Bank of Italy and by some political forces, which therefore acted as veto points. This topic is elaborated in the following section on financial services regulation in Italy.

The conduct of *exchange-rate policy* underwent a major transformation as a result of EMU. In the 1980s and early 1990s, the Italian monetary authorities had used exchange-rate policy, especially membership of the Exchange Rate Mechanism (ERM) as an external constraint (Dyson & Featherstone 1996; 1999), to bring about domestic changes, in particular to conduct an anti-inflationary monetary policy (Giavazzi & Pagano 1988; Frieden 1994). After the withdrawal of the Italian lira from the ERM in 1992 and until 1996, when the lira re-entered the ERM, this policy was characterised by a depreciating lira, which improved the competitiveness of Italian exports, fostering an export-led boom that sustained Italian economic growth in a phase of fiscal retrenchment (Spaventa & Chiorazzo 2000). In 1999, the conduct of exchange-rate policy was transferred to the authorities of the euro area (the ECB and Council of Economic and Finance Ministers (ECOFIN)).

Overall, in these two policy areas, namely monetary and exchange rate policies—which are strictly interconnected, in that exchange rate policy largely depends on the conduct of monetary policy—the main changes concerned the institutional aspect. Indeed, domestic institutions, first and foremost the central bank, lost competences that were transferred to the supranational (euro area) level, whereby the primary objective assigned to the ECB by the TEU was price stability. Moreover, in preparation for EMU membership, the Banca d'Italia completed its path towards full independence from the political authorities, as prescribed by the relevant central banking provisions of EMU.

This formal institutional change completed a process of ideational shift that had already begun in the 1980s, when the stability-oriented paradigm advocated by the Bundesbank spread across Europe. The new policy paradigm, which centred on the concept of central bank independence and the benefits of low inflation, had gained ground in academic as well as policy-making circles from the 1980s onwards (Dyson 1994; McNamara 1998; Marcussen 2000). In Italy, an anti-inflationary monetary policy was implemented, not without difficulties, by the Italian central bank, which was therefore the main agent of change in the 1980s and 1990s. In this case, the process of learning seems to have been somewhat deeper than in the case of fiscal policy examined below, partly because there is an established literature in economics on this subject (Alesina & Summers 1993; Cukierman 1992).

Partly this learning was because the monetary policy elite (i.e. central bankers) rather than the fiscal authorities (i.e. politicians) were primarily involved in the policy change, and the new paradigm of central bank independence and the benefits of low inflation served well the interests of central bankers. As well as the central bank, the financial sector is traditionally inflation averse, and so are the economic forces that are most exposed to external competition (Frieden 1994; Walsh 1999). Thus, the process of European monetary integration that culminated in EMU modified the constellation of domestic interests, providing a window of opportunity for those supporting macroeconomic policy changes at the domestic level.

Fiscal policy had undergone a major adjustment in the 1990s in order for Italy to join the final stage of EMU. Although there were some remarkable changes in revenues and primary expenditures, what made it possible for the fiscal adjustment to meet the fiscal convergence criteria (in particular the criterion of the deficit-to-GDP [gross domestic product] ratio) was the reduction in interest payments on the Italian public debt as a result of lower nominal interest rates, which in turn were linked to the prospect of joining EMU (Spaventa & Chiorazzo 2000).

Once the third stage of EMU began, the fiscal convergence criteria of the TEU were substituted by the rules of the Stability and Growth Pact, which, however, proved to be rather flexible in practice (Heipertz & Verdun 2010). When the Stability and Growth Pact came under strain because even its main supporter, Germany, had problems in compliance, the Berlusconi government strongly supported the suspension and the reform of the Pact. Indeed, the Italian presidency in the second half of 2003 was perceived by many small member states and EU institutions as sympathetic to the suspension of the Pact for France and Germany (Quaglia 2004a). Hence, domestic actors, first and foremost the Italian government, tried to ease the external constraint on fiscal policy imposed by the Pact by changing the rules of the game at the EU level. In 2005, after further deterioration of the budgetary situation in Italy, there was a formal warning to Italy from the European Commission.

Despite the fact that the bonus of the lower interest payments on the staggering Italian public debt continued after Italy joined the euro area, this bonus was not used to pay back the outstanding debt, as was wisely done, for example, in Belgium. In contrast, in Italy, especially during the Berlusconi governments, there was a reduction of the primary budget surplus, which produced an upward trend in the public-sector borrowing requirement. The European Commission also criticised Italian fiscal policy for several one-off or temporary measures. Overall, the adaptation of Italian fiscal policy to the requirements imposed by the EU and by EMU remained problematic; hence, it has been an instance of accommodation rather than transformation (Radaelli 2002).[4] Furthermore, the pressure exerted by the EU on the conduct of Italian fiscal policy was stronger in approaching the final stage of EMU because there was a concrete penalty (i.e. exclusion from EMU) attached to the failure to meet the convergence criteria. Afterwards, EU pressure diminished because the 'hard' rules of the Stability and Growth Pact were not hard enough.

There seems to have been some (thin) learning through the assimilation of the German-inspired stability-oriented culture, but the paradigm change was not as deep as in the case of monetary policy, for two main reasons. To begin with, there is no consensus in the academic literature about the optimal conduct of fiscal policy, nor is there a consensual view amongst fiscal policy-makers, unlike in the central banking community.

In addition, there are clear-cut winners and losers in the implementation of fiscal policy, so the latter tends to be more politicised than monetary policy. As in the case of monetary policy, there was also a realignment of domestic interests, leading to the formation of a weak constituency that had a stake in budgetary rectitude (Walsh 1999). This constituency was led by the Bank of Italy and the employers' organisation Confidustria was part of it. The former regarded sound fiscal policy as part of the stability-oriented culture, flanking the conduct of an anti-inflationary monetary policy, whereas for the employers' organisation (and its members) it was instrumental to reduce the fiscal pressure (i.e. tax burden).

Besides direct EMU pressure on the monetary, exchange-rate and fiscal policies of the member states, there was also indirect pressure on other economic policies. Within the euro area, the national authorities could no longer use the exchange rate as an instrument of macroeconomic adjustment and they could no longer set the level of interest rates. Thus, the EMU policy framework triggered a process of competition between national economic systems, requiring domestic adjustments in order to restore and maintain competitiveness (Quaglia & Radaelli 2007). In Italy, such indirect

EMU pressure highlighted the need for structural reforms, especially in the sclerotic labour market, which are, however, outside the scope of this paper.

Here it is important to note that the locking in of the exchange rate, together with a rigorous monetary policy and the lack of substantive structural reforms, endangered the competitiveness of the Italian economic system, with negative repercussions on the balance of payments. The current account, which had been in surplus for most of the 1990s, turned negative from 1999 onwards. Rates of growth and measures of competitiveness have been among the lowest in the eurozone and in Europe. All these suggest that Italy has been subject to limited and delayed adaptation to EMU. Since joining the eurozone, Italy has lost considerable economic competitiveness because it has failed to undertake the substantial structural reforms necessary to adapt to life with the single currency.

The EU and Financial Services Regulation in Italy

The Italian banking system and its regulation underwent significant changes in the 1990s, which continued well into the 2000s. This was accompanied by the (somewhat delayed) reform of securities markets regulation. In both sectors, direct and indirect EU pressure (such as EU directives, competition policy, financial integration, fiscal constraints) as well as domestic sources of change (such as 'reform-minded' policy-makers at the Bank of Italy and the Treasury) played a crucial role in the evolution of the financial system in Italy. Then the global financial crisis brought into the spotlight other aspects of the Europeanisation of financial regulation in the member states.

The traditional segmentation in the *banking sector* came to an end with the transposition in 1992 of the Second Banking Directive issued in 1988, which introduced the all-purpose universal bank in Italy as well as in other EU member states (Story & Walters 1997). Italian banks therefore became 'universal' banks, which are banks potentially able to perform a variety of financial activities, whereas in the past there had been different types of banks able to perform only specific activities (such as the *istituti di credito speciale* for long-term loans, etc.). Hence, the implementation of the second banking directive was a watershed event for Italy, leading to institutional change.

Over the 1990s, the banking system was privatised, modernised and consolidated (see Deeg 2005; Panetta 2004). The big and powerful public banks were privatised and nowadays there are no big public banks in Italy. This was partly the result of indirect EU influence because the privatisation process in the banking sector as elsewhere in the economy was triggered by fiscal adjustment and the need to raise public revenues by selling off public banks and other state enterprises. EU competition policy also played a role in encouraging privatisation (Monti 1998). In the reform process, policy entrepreneurs at the Bank of Italy and the Treasury[5] were often able and willing to use creatively the external constraints posed by the EU to bring about domestic changes. Some of them (e.g. Treasury Minister Giuliano Amato) repeatedly pointed out the need to embrace a different (more modern) approach to banking in Italy, based on the concept of efficiency, not on rent-seeking and the protection of the status quo.

In the 2000s, EMU and the completion of the single financial market, a project sponsored by the Commission and the ECB and supported by some member states and the most competitive parts of the financial industry (Mügge 2010), unleashed a process of regulatory competition in the EU. This spearheaded the modernisation and consolidation of national banking systems, as witnessed in Italy. Between 1995 and 2005 the number of banks in the country dropped from 970 to 785 (Barber 2005). The two largest Italian banks, Unicredit and Intesa San Paolo, have become among the largest in Europe (Bank of Italy 2008b).

Until the early 2000s, there was a relatively limited penetration of foreign banks and financial institutions, for a variety of reasons. These included: the complex national regulatory environment; the preferences of Italian consumers for national brand names, i.e. Italian and often local banks; the role of Mediobanca; and the lukewarm (if not overtly hostile) attitudes of the public authorities, first and foremost the Bank of Italy during the governorship of Antonio Fazio (1993–2005). After the establishment of EMU, and the endorsement of the Financial Services Action Plan (FSAP) by the EU, foreign banks tried to penetrate the Italian market. The Bank of Italy, under Fazio's governorship, reacted by endeavouring to protect the *italianitá delle banche* (basically, Italian ownership of the banks operating in Italy). As part of the Bank's 'grand design' for reshaping the Italian banking system, Governor Fazio consistently opposed foreign shareholdings and never authorised a foreign takeover, in an attempt to prevent, or at least to slow down, foreign penetration of the Italian market (*Financial Times*, 11 February 2005).

In 2005, two cases made the headlines across Europe because they involved foreign banks and related to two proposed takeovers of Italian banks in 2004–05: one of Banca Nationale del Lavoro by a Spanish group, Banca Bilbao Vizcaya Argentaria; and the other of Banca Antoniana Popolare Veneta (Antonveneta) by ABN Amro. In both cases, Governor Fazio intervened to block the foreign takeover bid, while endorsing counterbids launched by two Italian financial institutions, Banca Popolare di Lodi and Unipol, respectively. (Unipol is an example of bank-assurance, that is a financial group that combines banking and insurance.) Both foreign banks involved in the attempted takeovers complained to the European Commission, which had given its authorisation on the grounds that the bids did not jeopardise competition in the banking sector. An antitrust enquiry launched by European Competition Commissioner Neelie Kroes was dropped on the grounds of lack of conclusive evidence. The European Internal Market Commissioner, Charlie McCreevy, also expressed his concern in a letter to Governor Fazio in 2005 (Buck 2005). This was a case of temporary domestic retrenchment to EU pressure, which, however, could not be resisted in the end.

Pressure from other EU member states, EU bodies and financial markets, coupled with the support of domestic forces keen to open up the Italian banking system, led to the resignation of Fazio in autumn 2005, followed by a change of competition policy in the banking sector in Italy (Quaglia 2008). The Law on Savings, which had been initiated by the centre-right government following some major domestic policy failures (the bankruptcy of Parmalat and the Ciro junk bonds), was revised and passed in haste in the wake of a scandal that involved the Governor of the Bank of Italy, Antonio Fazio, who had repeatedly opposed foreign takeovers of Italian banks.

During the drafting of the Law on Savings, which amended central banking legislation, the Italian government requested the ECB's legal opinion three times (May 2004, October 2005 and December 2005) and some of the suggestions put forward by the ECB were eventually included in the final draft. Interestingly, in September 2005, Prime Minister Berlusconi tried to enlist the support of the ECB not only for the national legislation in the making, as prescribed in the TEU, but also in order to topple the Governor of the Bank of Italy by soliciting the direct intervention of the ECB on this matter. The ECB, however, refrained from intervening, on the grounds that this was not part of its remit. This was a failed attempt by the Italian government to deploy EU pressure to unblock a domestic political impasse on the reform of the Bank of Italy.

The law introduced three important amendments to the legislation concerning the central bank: the ownership of the central bank was changed, so that only the state and public bodies were allowed to hold shares of the bank's capital; the governance structure of the bank was rendered more pluralistic and transparent;[6] and the bank's powers concerning banking competition policy were transferred to the Competition Authority. In the past, the central bank was entirely responsible for competition policy in the banking sector as well as having extensive and discretionary supervisory powers.

Financial integration triggered by EMU, the Commission-led project concerning the completion of the single financial market and the application of EU competition policy have modified the constellation of interests in Italy, so that the most outward-oriented part of the financial system has become keen to exploit the opportunities provided by financial integration in Europe. Nowadays, the Italian banking system is as open to foreign operators as that in other EU countries[7] and in some cases higher, and foreign banks have acquired major Italian banks (e.g. the Banca Nazionale del Lavoro was acquired by BNP Paribas). Moreover, Italian banks have increasingly been active abroad (Bank of Italy 2008b), mainly through subsidiaries, which was one channel of exposure of Italian banks to the global financial crisis. Such exposure topped €148 billion in December 2008.

As far as *securities markets* legislation is concerned, the vast majority of the 42 measures envisaged in the FSAP (2001) for the completion of financial market integration in the EU mainly concerned securities markets and post trading (notably, securities clearing and settlement). They subsequently found their way into four so-called 'Lamfalussy directives', named after the process through which they were negotiated and implemented. These directives were: the Prospectus directive (2003), the Market Abuse directive (2003), the Transparency directive (2004) and the Market in Financial Instruments directive (MiFID) (2004).

Compared with banking and insurance, securities was the sector of most intense activity in the EU in the 2000s, partly because market integration had lagged behind in this field (Story & Walter 1997) and a period of catch-up was therefore overdue, and partly because technical innovations increased the potential for cross-border securities trading. Moreover, unlike the banking sector, where international rules, such as the

Basel II Accord, are well developed due to the activity of the BCBS, securities markets were subject to limited international regulation. Hence, EU regulatory activity in the securities sector was all the more necessary.

The Lamfalussy directives were based on a regulatory approach that prioritised financial market integration; thus they were designed primarily to open up national markets. Notable examples were the MiFID and the Prospectus directive. The MiFID, which updated the existing Investment Services directive (ISD) issued in 1993, set common rules for securities and derivatives markets and permitted investment firms to operate throughout the EU by using a 'single passport', which allowed financial firms to conduct business across Europe with the approval of their home authorities. The Prospectus directive allowed capital to be raised throughout the EU on the basis of one set of documents—the prospectus—and gave bond issuers a choice of regulator.

The EU rules issued in the early 2000s were also intended to foster competition and market efficiency, as in the case of the Market Abuse directive and the Transparency directive. The directive on insider dealing and market manipulation (also known as the 'Market Abuse directive') was designed to promote market integrity in the field of financial instruments, harmonising the provisions concerning market abuse in the EU. The directive on transparency requirements with regard to information on issuers whose securities are admitted to trading on a regulated market (the so-called 'Transparency directive') upgraded the information to be made available to investors.

These pieces of legislation were informed by a market-making approach, which prioritised efficiency and competition, rather than a market-shaping approach, privileging financial stability, consumer protection and in some cases the protection of national operators (Quaglia 2010). Part of the content of the new EU rules was a far cry from the securities market legislation in place in Italy, where competition was not regarded as a major concern and in some cases market-opening had been resisted by the public authorities and parts of the financial sector. This meant that with the domestic transposition of the relevant directives a different set of priorities were introduced into Italian financial legislation. The implementation of these rules in Italy was an example of institutional adaptation to an alien regulatory approach.

Moreover, the implementation of these directives in Italy also modified the configuration of domestic interests, providing new opportunities to the most competitive parts of the industry. For example, the big Italian banks are potential winners from the elimination of the so-called concentration rules in the MiFID directive (interviews, Brussels 2007). The merger of the Borsa Italiana (Italian stock exchange) and London Stock Exchange was another tangible effect of the internationalisation of securities trading in Italy, which had winners and losers. In both instances, there was a recasting of domestic interests. In the first case, the most competitive Italian banks were able to undertake financial transactions that prior to the introduction of the MiFID directive were the prerogative of the Stock Exchange. Hence these banks won out at the expenses on the Italian Stock Exchange. In the second case, the (less competitive and less internationalised) Borsa Italiana, was acquired by a global player, the London Stock Exchange.

Interests, Ideas, Institutions and Domestic Political Economy in Italy

So far the analysis has primarily focused on the effects of the independent variable (the EU) on the intervening variables (interests, ideas and institutions). This section links these intervening variables to the dependent variable, that is, to change in domestic political economy. It also evaluates the importance of these changes for the Italian variety of capitalism.

Across the policy areas examined, namely macroeconomic policies and financial regulation, the *institutional* change triggered by the EU (together with the ideational factor mentioned below) has to some extent moved the Italian political economy towards the German model in macroeconomic policies and towards the British model in financial services regulation. It is widely acknowledged that Germany had a predominant influence in the establishment of EMU, from which the UK opted out. The German macroeconomic model is based on the concept of central-bank independence, 'sound money' and 'sound public finance' (Dyson 1994). The institutional changes prescribed by EMU had a direct (transformative) impact on three components of domestic political economy: central banking, monetary policy and exchange-rate policy. There are no hard EU rules on fiscal policy, hence this domain was less subject to change than monetary policy was.

By contrast, the UK has been very influential in shaping EU financial services regulation over the last decade (Posner & Veron 2010; Quaglia 2010). The British model of financial regulation is based on market-making measures and a light-touch regulatory philosophy, which were questioned after the global financial crisis that severely hit the UK (though some large continental countries, first and foremost Germany, were also badly affected by the crisis). Many of the institutional changes introduced in Italy in the 2000s as a consequence of EU financial regulation were initially resisted by some domestic forces. Subsequently, these changes contributed to the modernisation of the Italian variety of financial capitalism.

In macroeconomic policies and financial regulation, the EU fostered domestic *ideational* change, although to different extents across policy areas, being more pronounced in the case of the stability-oriented monetary policy and less so in fiscal policy and financial regulation. The EU and some (large) member states acted as 'exporters of ideas' towards the Italian economic and political elites (Quaglia 2004b). The German-inspired stability-oriented economic paradigm was embraced by policy-makers at the Bank of Italy and Treasury. The same policy-makers were also exposed to Anglo-Saxon ideas about financial regulation, on which, however, there was not a consensus within the EU, in contrast to the realm of monetary policy. Prior to the global financial crisis, the market-making approach promoted in the EU by the UK at times clashed with the market-shaping approach that prevailed in Italy and other continental countries. After the crisis, the market-shaping approach regained ground in the EU (Quaglia 2010), as suggested by the raft of EU legislation passed on rating agencies, hedge fund managers, over-the-counter derivatives, etc.

In both policy domains, EU pressure triggered a reconfiguration of domestic interests. In the case of EMU, a macroeconomic adjustment coalition supported Italy's membership of EMU (Walsh 1999), although once membership was secured the coalition partly disbanded and was less able to push through the domestic structural reforms that were needed. In the case of financial market integration, an outward-oriented coalition emerged in the most competitive part of the financial sector in Italy. By contrast, the more inward-oriented (and generally less competitive) part of the financial sector, with the support of friendly politicians and the Bank of Italy during the Fazio governorship, initially acted as a veto point towards financial market integration.

The reshaping of domestic interests triggered by the EU generated policy entrepreneurs who acted as agents of change in the policy domains examined. It also created domestic veto players that sometimes opposed the process of change; the most notable case was the slowing down of financial opening in Italy in the early 2000s. Unlike in EMU, where winners and losers from the policy change were somewhat diffused, in financial regulation there are clear-cut winners and losers, hence it is more likely that the latter will act as veto points. Moreover, the 'permissive consensus' supporting Italy's membership of EMU (Sbragia 2001), which was seen as a deepening of European integration, was not present in the financial regulation.

The main domestic agents facilitating the Europeanisation of the Italian political economy were mostly those at the interface between Italy and the EU, as in the case of the Bank of Italy (an exception was the last period of the Fazio governorship), or those having something to gain from deepening economic and financial integration, such as large financial groups keen to exploit the opportunities posed by a single financial market in Europe. These agents of change sometimes resorted to a two-level game (Putnam 1988), played at the domestic and EU levels. They were motivated by common interests, as in the case of competitive financial institutions keen to open up the Italian market in the 2000s. However, the glue of these coalitions was sometimes ideational, as in the case of the macroeconomic policy elite that had embraced the stability-oriented paradigm and was keen to undertake a major fiscal adjustment in Italy in the 1990s.

In terms of outcomes, domestic change was more pronounced—that is to say, it amounted to a real transformation—when there were 'hard' EU rules (for example, treaty provisions) prescribing domestic institutional change, as in the case of monetary policy and exchange rate policy in EMU. The fiscal convergence criteria of the TEU also triggered a major fiscal adjustment in the run-up to EMU. Domestic change was quite significant—that is, it fell in between transformation and accommodation—when EU hard rules (first and foremost, EU legislation) prescribed certain institutional changes, such as in the case of financial regulation. When EU rules were less hard, as proved to be the case with the Stability and Growth Pact, domestic change, which had been significant at first, was partly reversed afterwards, especially once the Stability and Growth Pact was weakened. When only soft EU rules were present (i.e. they were the main source of EU pressure) or EU pressure was indirect, the domestic outcome was often inertia, as in the case of the insubstantial structural reforms (for a summary, see Table 1).

Table 1 A summary of the main findings

Policy domain	Independent variable: EU	Intervening variable 1: Institutions	Intervening variable 2: Interests	Intervening variable 3: Ideas	Dependent variable: Domestic Outcome
Monetary policy	EMU project (1990 onwards), building on the EMS (1979):	Domestic institutional change (1990s):	Change of domestic constellation of interests (1980s–1990s):	Change of domestic monetary policy paradigm (1980s–1990s):	Transformation:
	TEU, related legislation	Legal changes prescribed by TEU and EU legislation, e.g. organisation of the central bank, its policy competence	Empowerment of actors supporting price stability and central bank independence, i.e. Bank of Italy	Spread of the stability-oriented paradigm, especially amongst monetary elite	Policy shifted to supranational level in 1999, priority of price stability for ECB
Exchange rate policy	EMU project (1990 onwards), building on the EMS (1979):	Domestic institutional change (1990s):	Change of domestic constellation of interests (1980s–1990s):	No shared exchange-rate policy paradigm in the EU:	Transformation:
	TEU, related legislation	Legal changes prescribed by TEU and EU legislation, e.g. organisation of the central bank, its policy competence	Empowerment of actors supporting the exchange rate as external constraint, i.e. Bank of Italy, part of the Treasury	No domestic learning	Policy shifted to supranational level in 1999, priority of price stability for ECB
Fiscal policy	Some EU 'hard' and 'not so hard' rules:	Limited domestic institutional change (1990s onwards):	Limited change in domestic constellation of interests (1990s onwards):	Limited change in fiscal policy paradigm domestically (1990s onwards):	Accommodation:
	Fiscal convergence criteria (prior to 1999), Stability and Growth Pact (1999 onwards)	Difficult compliance with the Stability and Growth pact, attempt to reform it at the EU level	Limited empowerment of sound fiscal policy supporters, e.g. Bank of Italy, Confindustria	Spread of the sound public finance paradigm, but fiscal policy elite (politicians) less susceptible to learning	Fiscal adjustment in the run-up to 1999, somewhat looser policy afterwards
Financial regulation	EU hard rules:	Change in domestic institutions:	Change in domestic constellation of interests (2000s):	No clear evidence of ideational change:	Initial retrenchment/ transformation:
	FSAP, banking and securities markets legislation, competition policy	Domestic implementation of EU legislation, reform of the Bank of Italy	Set of actors (competitive Italian banks) supporting market integration	Market-shaping paradigm still strong in Italy	Fazio affair, opening up of the Italian financial sector

Conclusion

Over the last decade the Italian political economy has been Europeanised to a large extent through a variety of mechanisms, first and foremost institutional pressure, and a vast array of outcomes, which range from transformation to retrenchment. The stronger causal mechanism operated through institutional pressure. The change of domestic constellations of interests in many cases reinforced the institutional change prescribed by EU rules, as in the case of the formation of the domestic stability-oriented coalition. Moreover, the change of domestic constellations of interests often went hand in hand with the emergence of policy entrepreneurs sponsoring domestic changes and keen to exploit at the national level the external constraints posed by the EU. Ideational change seems to have had the weakest effect at the domestic level and it is difficult to tease out some genuine instances of learning, except for the stability-oriented paradigm, which gained good currency amongst the macroeconomic policy elites that coalesced around the Bank of Italy.

There are two main findings that can travel beyond the Italian case study, feeding into the broader literature on the Europeanisation of national political economies, especially in Southern Europe.

First, the degree of Europeanisation and its effects have been uneven across different elements of the political economy, but the general trend has been to foster the convergence of the Southern European model towards an EU model largely informed by a (German inspired) stability-oriented approach to macroeconomic policies, and (Anglo-Saxon-inspired) market-friendly regulation in financial services, prior to the crisis. Second, despite the fact that the Europeanisation of domestic political economies has encouraged convergence across the EU, some distinctive (Southern European?) features have remained. This is demonstrated by the chronic problems with unsustainable fiscal policy (in particular, in the Italian case, a very high level of public debt) and by the relative resilience of Southern European financial systems to the global banking crisis per se (Quaglia 2009), due to the traditional business model of their banks and the national regulatory framework in place.

Acknowledgements

I wish to thank the European Research Council (Grant 204398 FINGOVEU) for financial support for this research, and the reviewers and the editors for their perceptive comments on an earlier draft of this paper. The paper was written while I was a visiting fellow at the Max Planck Institute in Cologne.

Notes

[1] In political science, there is also a vast literature on the Europeanisation of Italy (Fabbrini 2003; Cotta, Isernia & Verzichelli 2005) and on Italy and the EU more generally (Di Palma, Fabbrini & Freddi 2000; Giuliani 2001; 2006; della Cananea 2000; Hine 2001).

[2] The literature on varieties of capitalism is vast. For some comprehensive analyses, see Amable 2003, Hancké, Rhodes & Thatcher 2007; Hall & Soskice 2001; Schmidt 2002.

[3] Mediobanca was an Italian investment bank active in managing corporate affairs in the postwar period. Despite the changes experienced by the Italian financial system in the 1990s and the death of the founding father of Mediobanca, Enrico Cuccia, the role of the bank remains important in the new century (*Financial Times*, 4 March 2005).

[4] Another institutional change took place in 2001 when the Ministry of Finance, in charge of the revenue side of the budget, was merged with the reformed Treasury, creating the 'super-ministry' for the economy. The newly created Ministry for the Economy was thus responsible for the revenue and expenditure side of the state budget.

[5] Like the Treasury Ministers Giuliano Amato and Guido Carli (also a former governor of the Bank of Italy) and the Director General of the Treasury Mario Draghi.

[6] A term mandate for the Executive Board, including the governor, was introduced, whereas previously their mandate was unlimited. Second, collegial decision-making and greater transparency within the Executive Board were established.

[7] In 2007, the market share of foreign banks in Italy approached 19 per cent. In Germany, France and Spain in 2006 the market share of foreign banks averaged 10.5 per cent (Saccomanni 2008).

References

Alesina, A. & Summers, L. (1993) 'Central bank independence and macroeconomic performances', *Journal of Money, Credit and Banking*, vol. 25, no. 2, pp. 151–163.

Allen, F. & Gale, D. (2000) *Comparing Financial Systems*, MIT Press, Cambridge, MA.

Amable, B. (2003) *The Diversity of Modern Capitalism*, Oxford University Press, Oxford.

Balkir, C., Bolukbasi, H. T. & Ertugal, E. (2013) 'Europeanisation and dynamics of continuity and change in domestic political economies in the "Southern Periphery"', *South European Society and Politics*, vol. 18, no. 2, pp. 121–137.

Bank of Italy (2008a) *Annual Report*, Rome.

Bank of Italy (2008b) *Bollettino Economico*, October.

Barber, T. (2005) 'Institution's defences under siege from all sides', *Financial Times*, 17 February.

Buck, T. (2005) 'Italian bank governor denies protectionism', *Financial Times*, 18 February.

Ciocca, P. (2005) *The Italian Financial System Remodelled*, Palgrave Macmillan, Basingstoke.

Cotta, M., Isernia, P. & Verzichelli, L. (eds) (2005) *L' Europa in Italia*, Il Mulino, Bologna.

Christopoulos, D. & Quaglia, L. (2009) 'Network constraints in EU banking regulation: the case of the capital requirements directive', *Journal of Public Policy*, vol. 29, no. 2, pp. 1–22.

Cukierman, A. (1992) *Central Bank Strategy, Credibility, and Independence: Theory and Evidence*, MIT Press, Cambridge, MA.

Deeg, R. (2005) 'Change from within: German and Italian finance in the 1990s', in *Beyond Continuity: Institutional Change in Advanced Political Economies*, eds W. Streeck & K. Thelen, Oxford University Press, Oxford, pp. 169–202.

Della Cannanea, G. (2000a) 'Italy', in *The National Coordination of EU Policy: The European Level*, eds. H. Kassim, B. Peters and V. Wright, Oxford University Press: Oxford, pp. 129–46.

Della Cannanea, G. (2000b) 'Italy', in *The National Coordination of EU Policy: The European Level*, eds. H. Kassim, B. Peters and V. Wright, Oxford University Press: Oxford, pp. 99–113.

Della Sala, V. (2004) 'The Italian model of capitalism: on the road between globalisation and Europeanisation?', *Journal of European Public Policy*, vol. 11, no. 6, pp. 1041–1058.

Della Sala, V. (1997) 'Hollowing out and hardening the state: European integration and the Italian economy', *West European Politics*, vol. 20, no. 1, pp. 14–33.

Di Palma, G., Fabbrini, S. & Freddi, G. (2000) *Condannata al Successo? L'Italia nell'Europa Integrata*, Il Mulino, Bologna.

Dyson, K. (1994) *Elusive Union*, Longman, London.
Dyson, K. & Featherstone, K. (1996) 'Italy and EMU as "Vincolo Esterno": empowering the technocrats, transforming the state', *South European Politics and Society*, vol. 1, no. 2, pp. 272–299.
Dyson, K. & Featherstone, K. (1999) *The Road to Maastricht*, Oxford University Press, Oxford.
Dyson, K. & Marcussen, M. (eds) (2009) *The Changing World of Central Banking*, Oxford University Press, Oxford.
Fabbrini, S. (ed.) (2003) *L'Europeizzazione dell'Italia: l'Impatto dell'Unione Europea sulle Istituzioni e le Politiche Italiane*, Laterza, Rome.
Featherstone, K. & Kazamias, G. (eds) (2001) *Europeanisation and the Southern Periphery*, Frank Cass, London.
Ferrera, M. & Gualmini, E. (1999) *Salvati dall'Europa?*, Il Mulino, Bologna.
Frieden, J. A. (1994) 'Making commitments: France and Italy in the European monetary system, 1979–1985', in *The Political Economy of European Monetary Integration*, eds B. Eichengreen & J. Frieden, Westview Press, Boulder, CO, pp. 25–46.
Giavazzi, F. & Pagano, M. (1988) 'The advantage of tying one's hands', *European Economic Review*, vol. 24, pp. 1055–1082.
Giuliani, M. (2001) 'Europeanisation and Italy: a bottom up process?', in *Europeanisation and Southern Periphery*, eds K. Featherstone & G. Kazamias, Frank Cass, London, pp. 47–72.
Giuliani, M. (2006) *La Politica Europea*, Il Mulino, Bologna.
Hall, P. A. & Soskice, D. (eds) (2001) *Varieties of Capitalism: The Institutional Foundations of Comparative Advantage*, Oxford University Press, Oxford.
Hancké, B., Rhodes, M. & Thatcher, M. (eds) (2007) *Beyond Varieties of Capitalism: Conflict, Contradictions, and Complementarities in the European Economy*, Oxford University Press, Oxford.
Heipertz, M. & Verdun, A. (2010) *Ruling Europe: The Politics of the Stability and Growth Pact*, Cambridge University Press, Cambridge.
Hine, D. (2001) 'European Policy-making and the Machinery of Italian Government', in *Europeanization and Southern Periphery*, ed. K. Featherstone and G. Kazamias, Frank Cass: London, pp. 25–46.
Hine, D. (2002) 'European policy-making and the machinery of Italian government', in *Europeanisation and Southern Periphery*, eds K. Featherstone & G. Kazamias, Frank Cass, London, pp. 25–46.
McNamara, K. (1998) *The Currency of Ideas: Monetary Politics in the European Union*, Cornell University Press, Ithaca, NY.
Marcussen, M. (2000) *Ideas and Elites*, Aalborg University, Aalborg.
Molina, O. & Rhodes, M. (2007) 'Industrial relations and the welfare state in Italy: assessing the potential of negotiated change', *West European Politics*, vol. 30, no. 4, pp. 803–829.
Monti, M. (1998) *Intervista sull'Italia in Europa*, Laterza, Rome.
Mügge, D. (2010) *Widen the Market, Narrow the Competition*, ECPR, Colchester.
Panetta, F. (ed.) (2004) *Il Sistema Bancario Italiano negli Anni Novanta. Gli Effetti di una Trasformazione*, Il Mulino, Bologna.
Perez, S. A. & Westrup, J. (2010) 'Finance and the macroeconomy: the politics of regulatory reform in Europe', *Journal of European Public Policy*, vol. 17, no. 8, pp. 1171–1192.
Posner, E. & Véron, N. (2010) 'The EU and financial regulation: power without purpose?', *Journal of European Public Policy*, vol. 17, no. 3, pp. 400–415.
Putnam, R. (1988) 'Diplomacy and domestic politics: the logic of two-level games', *International Organization*, vol. 42, no. 3, pp. 427–460.
Quaglia, L. (2004a) 'The Italian presidency of the European Union in 2003', *Journal of Common Market Studies Annual Review*, vol. 42, no. 4, pp. 53–56.

Quaglia, L. (2004b) 'Italy's policy towards European monetary integration: bringing ideas back in?', *Journal of European Public Policy*, vol. 11, no. 6, pp. 1096–1111.

Quaglia, L. (2008) *Central Banking Governance in the European Union: A Comparative Analysis*, Routledge, London.

Quaglia, L. (2009) 'The response to the global financial turmoil in Italy', *South European Society and Politics*, vol. 14, no. 3, pp. 7–18.

Quaglia, L. (2010) 'Completing the single market in financial services: the politics of competing advocacy coalitions', *Journal of European Public Policy*, vol. 17, no. 7, pp. 1007–1022.

Quaglia, L. & Furlong, P. (2008) 'Italy in the eurozone: surviving the first decade', in *European States and the Euro*, ed. K. Dyson, Oxford University Press, Oxford, pp. 204–221.

Quaglia, L. & Radaelli, C. M. (2007) 'Italian politics and the European Union', *West European Politics*, vol. 30, no. 4, pp. 924–943.

Radaelli, C. M. (2002) 'The Italian state and the euro: institutions, discourse and policy-regime', in *European States and the Euro – Europeanisation, Variation, and Convergence*, ed. K. Dyson, Oxford University Press, Oxford, pp. 212–237.

Radaelli, C. (2003) 'The Europeanization of Public Policy', in *The Politics of Europeanization*, ed. K. Featherstone and C. Radaelli, Oxford University Press, Oxford, pp. 27–56.

Risse, T., Engelmann-Martin, D., Knop, H. J. & Roscher, K. (1999) 'To euro or not to euro? The EMU and identity politics in the European Union', *European Journal of International Relations*, vol. 5, no. 2, pp. 147–187.

Saccomanni, F. (2008) 'Il processo di internazionalizzazione del sistema bancario: la presenza delle banche estere in Italia', available online at: http://www.bancaditalia.it/interventi/intaltri_mdir/saccomanni190208/Saccomanni_190208.pdf

Sbragia, A. (2001) 'Italy pays for Europe: political leadership, political choice and institutional adaptation', in *Transforming Europe: Europeanisation and Domestic Change*, eds J. Caporaso, M. Green Cowles & T. Risse, Cornell University Press, Ithaca, NY, pp. 79–96.

Schmidt, V. A. (2002) *The Futures of European Capitalism*, Oxford University Press, Oxford.

Spaventa, L. & Chiorazzo, V. (2000) *Astuzia o Virtu'? Come Accadde che l'Italia fu Ammessa all'Unione Monetaria*, Doninzelli, Rome.

Stolfi, F. (2008) 'The Europeanisation of Italy's budget institutions in the 1990s', *Journal of European Public Policy*, vol. 15, no. 4, pp. 550–566.

Story, J. & Walter, I. (1997) *Political Economy of Financial Integration in Europe: The Battle of the System*, Manchester University Press, Manchester.

Walsh, J. I. (1999) 'Political bases of macroeconomic adjustment: evidence from the Italian experience', *Journal of European Public Policy*, vol. 6, no. 1, pp. 66–84.

All Hands on Deck! How Europeanised Is the Maltese Labour Market?

Rose Marie Azzopardi

This paper investigates the Maltese labour market within the context of the Europeanisation process. It explains the EU's labour market policies and presents studies in the field. The main focus is the case study of Malta, which evaluates formal and informal structures of the economy and uses the dynamics of the interaction of ideas, interests and institutions to analyse whether and how Europeanisation of the Maltese labour market has occurred. The findings indicate that different changes have occurred in the legislative framework, language and values about work, but resistance and continuity are evident in other areas such as flexicurity, undeclared work and a high level of female labour market inactivity.

'Europeanisation' is a term that has been 'stretched' (Radaelli 2000) and has 'many faces' (Olsen 2001). It can incorporate diverse processes, impacts and changes in the political economy of a country. The effect influences institutional moulds that have developed historically and become embedded in a particular society through political transformations. Europeanisation of public policies looks at how national policies are shaped and changed because of the integrative forces of the European Union (EU) (see for example Radaelli 2003; Haverland 2006). Following Balkir, Bolukbasi and Ertugal (2013), Europeanisation is considered in this paper as the impact of European integration on the domestic political economy (see also Vink 2003). More specifically it reflects changes in ideas, interests and institutions, or the 'trois I' (three I's) referred to by Palier and Surel (2005), concepts introduced into the literature by Heclo (1994) and Hall (1997).

One of the areas where Europeanisation has been evaluated is the labour market, and this is the main focus of this paper. It evaluates the impact of the European employment policies on the labour market in Malta. This is particularly important because Malta stands out as the EU member state with the lowest rates of employment (56.8 per cent), activity (61 per cent) and female employment (40.7 per cent) (2010 third quarter data), when compared with the other 27 member states (Massarelli, Giovannola & Wozowczyk 2010). Have the aims and goals of the European employment strategy had any impact on the Maltese labour market? What are the reasons for a high level of inactivity? What policies can be adopted to get every able body on board the employment ship? These are some of the questions this research seeks to answer.

The research methodology draws on official statistics, documents and ten interviews conducted with experts in the field. These included academics and representatives of both employers and unions (a list is shown in the Appendix). The semi-structured interviews were based on eight questions dealing with inactivity, governmental policies, the driving factor behind change in employment policy, familiarity with the European Employment Strategy (EES), social dialogue fora, the move from passive to active labour market policies (ALMPs), private sector practices and public sector efficiency. Primary data were generated and analysed using the software package HyperResearch™ Version 2.0.

Following this introduction, the remainder of the paper is divided into four sections. The first section explains the EU's labour market policies within the framework of the Lisbon Agenda and the Europe 2020 strategy. The second section provides a review of various studies on the impact of Europeanisation on the labour markets. The third section describes the Maltese labour market and examines the dynamics of the interaction of ideas, interests and institutions in order to analyse whether and how Europeanisation of the Maltese labour market has occurred. The last section concludes by using Radaelli's classification of the Europeanisation process to assess the Maltese labour market.

The EU's Employment Policies

The main European policy for the labour market is embodied in the Lisbon Strategy, launched during the European Council of March 2000 in response to two challenges: one external (globalisation) and one internal (ageing). The strategy is based on three pillars: the economic (turning the EU into a 'competitive, dynamic, knowledge-based economy'); the social (creating an active labour market policy with investment in human resources, education and training, and combating social exclusion); and the environmental (added in Goteborg June 2001, to sustain growth without damaging the environment). The strategy's relaunch in 2005 emphasised jobs and growth. A key component of the Lisbon Strategy is the EES, or Luxembourg Process, initially introduced in November 1997 and making the coordination of member states' labour market policies a priority for the EU, but harmonisation was not on the agenda (Fleckenstein 2006). The Europe 2020 strategy for smart, inclusive and sustainable growth further emphasised the need to increase labour market flexibility and participation.

The EES is a means whereby member states encourage the sharing of information and best practices in order to create more and better jobs There are four main aspects to the EES: 24 integrated guidelines (drawn up by the European Commission) that tackle 'the issues of improving employability, developing entrepreneurship, encouraging adaptability and equal opportunities' (Fleckenstein 2006, p. 285); the national reform programmes, drawn up by each member state for a three-year period, and annual implementation reports; the Commission's annual report (which analyses reform and implementation programmes submitted by the member states); and recommendations adopted by the Council for each member state. (See Goetschy [1999] for a detailed discussion.)

The EES 'has been a catalyst to develop and deepen employment analysis at EU level (and although it) remains fragile, it can now be seen as a credible vehicle for dealing with employment at EU level' (Fischer & Tholoniat 2006, p. 16). The Open Method of Coordination (OMC), which originated with the EES, 'provided a new framework for cooperation between Member States by directing national policies towards common objectives in areas which fall within the competence of the Member States, such as employment, social protection, social inclusion, education, youth and training' (Commission of the European Communities 2010, p. 22). To achieve the targets set by the Lisbon Strategy, financial support is offered through Progress 2007–2013 and the European Social Fund (ESF).

More important are the reforms and labour market policies (LMPs) adopted by each member state, to tackle labour markets' problems such as segmentation and skills shortages, by encouraging more training, offering more educational opportunities, instilling a more positive approach to prolonging the working life of individuals, and creating more inclusive labour markets.

LMPs differ across countries but essentially they all cover three types of interventions: *services* (all publicly funded activities for jobseekers including those of the public employment service); *measures* (including training, job rotation and job sharing, employment incentives, supported employment and rehabilitation, direct job creation and start-up incentives); and *supports* (out-of-work income maintenance and support, and early retirement schemes). The first two are ALMPs while the latter are passive policies (Van Berkel & Hornemann Moller 2002). Moving from passive to active policies means that the unemployed are not merely provided with income but are enticed to participate in the labour market, leading to wider inclusion. The EES 'diffuses a paradigm of activation through the member states, aimed at influencing the domestic policy-making arena's [sic] and tries to encourage active rather than passive policies' (Van Vliet & Koster, 2008 p. 6).

Some examples of ALMPs include measures pertaining to flexicurity, skills and lifelong learning. Flexicurity includes reforms to the taxation and social security benefits regimes, in order to encourage more people to work, thus lowering both the unemployment and inactivity rates. The acquisition of skills means providing people with the right capabilities to meet the eventuality of becoming redundant and to equip workers with the abilities needed for today's markets. It is futile for governments to try to retain jobs destined to migrate to more cost-effective and competitive countries. Also important is the reduction of the number of early school leavers, who normally lack exploitable skills or qualifications for a modern market economy. This is a new measure in the Europe 2020 strategy, ensuring that early school leavers are less than ten per cent and that at least 40 per cent of youths have a degree or tertiary-level diploma (the goals for Malta are less ambitious at 29 per cent for early school leavers and 33 per cent for tertiary level achievement). Skills and lifelong learning provide for the upgrading of knowledge and the acquisition of new competences.

Europeanisation of the Maltese labour market would entail increasing the participation rate, particularly of females and older workers. It would also provide for more youths to continue with their studies, thus reducing the high level of early school leavers and increasing the proportion of youths with tertiary-level qualifications. It would also lead to a higher proportion of workers engaging in lifelong learning programmes in order to keep abreast with innovative technology and new economic demands. From a purely policy perspective, the concept of flexicurity would require a reorganisation of taxation schemes in order to entice more people to participate in the labour market but also to act as a disincentive against the black economy. Changes would also need to be made to the social security system to make dependence on allowances less favourable and thus encourage labour market involvement, especially by healthy individuals and people with exploitable skills. Perhaps a reform to the minimum wage legislation, guaranteeing an adequate standard of living, would also work towards making a job worth engaging in, since the difference between the minimum wage and social security benefits may not be sufficient incentive to push individuals towards an employed status. An important point to keep in mind is that Malta joined the EU in 2004 and therefore the Europeanisation process is a relatively young one.

Europeanisation of Labour Markets in Europe

'Europeanisation' often implies that a 'misfit' has to exist between EU requirements and domestic circumstances for it to occur (Borzel & Risse 2000). Europeanisation can occur by *adaptation* (implementation of EU policy, the EES) and by *learning* (through the OMC and best practices of other member states). Causality is less possible to establish in the second type of Europeanisation but, as stressed by some authors (Majone 1989; Sabatier 1999), the roles of OMC and best practices are important to shape the 'dynamics of policy processes and in the shaping of their results' (Toller 2004, p. 7). A third mode is persuasion via *financial incentives* (Heidenreich & Bischoff 2008).

Drawing on the work of several authors (Hall 1993; Olsen 1996; Heritier 1998; Heritier & Knill 2001), Radaelli (2000) describes the outcomes of Europeanisation as taking four possible forms: *inertia* (when Europeanisation occurs involuntarily, if at all); *retrenchment* (where EU pressures continue to be resisted); *absorption* in the form of adaptation or accommodation (when some changes are taken up but these do not affect the fundamentals of the country); and *transformation* (which is deeper, as the very foundations need to change and lead to paradigm shifts). These processes imply changes in ideas, interests and institutions (for an extensive explanation, see Balkir, Bolukbasi and Ertugal 2013.

An analysis of literature on the Europeanisation of labour markets enables one to draw several conclusions. One is that there is huge variation in the ALMPs adopted by member states (see for example Zeitlin, Pochet & Magnussen 2005; Kvist & Saari 2007). The differences can be due to the diverse starting points of the member states, to variations in institutions, internal governance, social pacts, political structures and cultural attitudes. Furthermore, 'the reality is that the policy environment is neither static nor uniform' (Mendez, Wishlade & Yuill 2007, p. 17). Another conclusion is that both the EU and national political structures change each other; thus Europeanisation is a two-way process. 'A long-term challenge is to provide a better understanding of how different processes of change interact and make institutions co-evolve through mutual adaptation' (Olsen 2001, unpaged). However, studies do not always reach similar conclusions.

In a study of the EU15, Van Vliet and Koster (2008) maintain that 'the EES is associated with relative shifts from passive to active labour market policies across the member states' (p. 17). Furthermore, when social partners are involved (in the form of tripartite councils), there is a positive outcome in relation to expenditure on ALMPs. Another significant conclusion was that the 'peer review programme seems to have a stronger influence than the council recommendations' (ibid., p. 19), meaning that mutual learning and peer pressure, via the OMC, can have an impact.

Fleckenstein (2006) agrees that the EES can be considered an institutionalised learning mechanism, but due to 'the lack of strong supranational competencies and the insignificance of peer pressure ... the success of the strategy depends on the political will and voluntary action of member states' (p. 289). In the case of Germany, the researcher contends that the EES had 'limited' effect; rather, the reforms adopted by different governments were based on national driving factors.

In the Czech Republic, the EES 'did not create major adaptional [sic] pressure in the institutional sense that accession countries had to comply with EU employment norms ... [but] it triggered Europeanisation via cognitive and structural mechanisms' (Schuttpelz 2006, p. 166). This aided the reform process 'by altering the expectations and beliefs of domestic actors' (ibid., p. 155). Therefore, the EES was used as a 'blueprint' to formulate the local strategy. This assertion is made for all Central and Eastern European countries by Cerami (2007), who maintains that the EU had a critical part in the 'systemic transformation' of these ex-communist countries by introducing new ideas, interests and institutions in the realm of social and employment policies. In contrast, in a comparative analysis of Germany and the UK, Ardy and Umbach (2004) maintain that the EES appears to have had 'small visible impact on employment policy making, policy and performance' (p. v).

Afonso and Papadopoulos (2009) conducted a comparative analysis of labour market reforms in three small European states (Belgium, Austria and Switzerland), looking at two particular sectors: the opening up of labour markets and reforms in unemployment benefits. In the former, the EU 'factor' is strong, while in the latter it is weaker. Results indicate that Europeanisation does not undermine policy concertation, as had been anticipated, but in some cases it actually encourages more cooperation among the stakeholders in the policy elaboration process.

A study by Theophanous and colleagues (2007) looked at the evolution of labour law and the adoption of EU employment legislation in two small new member states, Cyprus and Malta, between 1995 and 2005. The adoption of the relevant acquis was in general successfully accomplished; however, this also resulted in changes in the way industrial relations were conducted, moving from soft to hard law in the case of Cyprus, but offering more legal protection to workers on both islands. In a sense it affected ideas, interests and institutions.

> The shift from job security to employability entails a cultural shift for both countries, mainly due to the idea that a lifelong job has not traditionally been associated with lifelong learning. However, the changes in the economies and labour markets of the two countries have forced them both to focus on the need to formulate training and employment policies and establish appropriate institutions to deal with these new demands. (Ibid., p. 68)

Sotiropoulos (2004) also analysed Greece, and concludes that the 'interplay of domestic interests and EU pressures led to important changes in this area. In a different vein, but also surveying Greece, Zartaloudis (2010) maintains that Europeanisation of the labour market occurred not because of legal implications via EES guidelines and recommendations (sticks) or through socialisation via the OMC (persuasion) but due to the financial incentives presented by the ESF (carrots).

This section has shown there are no guarantees that Europeanisation affects countries in the same manner. The following section presents the Maltese case study.

The Maltese Case Study

Malta is the smallest EU member state with a population of just over 0.4 million. Its economy is mainly service oriented, services accounting for 82 per cent of gross domestic product (GDP), with agriculture and fisheries producing only 1.8 per cent and the rest accounted for by manufacturing. Services include tourism, health and education, the arts, real estate, retailing, communication and financial services. The manufacturing base has in recent years diminished its role in the economy and has moved towards higher value-added products such as pharmaceuticals. Women account for 50.3 per cent of the population and perform better than men at all levels of education. However, their presence in the economy and in political life remains very low compared with males and also their European peers.

The evaluation of the Maltese labour market is divided into three parts: the first part presents descriptive statistics of the labour market; the second evaluates the outcomes of initiatives taken by the government in relation to the EES; and the last part appraises changes (if any) in ideas, interests and institutions to assess the Europeanisation impact. The analysis is based on official documents, data and interviews.

The Labour Market

During 2010, there were about 240,000 people in the 15–64 age group, considered the age range of potential workers. Data show that the labour supply of Malta (the employed and the unemployed) was only 177,206 or 50.7 per cent of the 15 + population. Those in employment were 165,152 or 47.2 per cent of the 15 + population. Of these, 144,131 were in full-time employment, the remaining 21,021 being part-time workers or on reduced hours. Over 60 per cent of part-timers (17,554) were women (National Statistics Office [NSO] Malta 2011).

Between 2000 and 2009, Malta had the lowest employment rate in the EU, the figure only improving marginally from 54.2 to 55 per cent compared with a move from 62.2 to 64.5 per cent in the EU's average rate. Malta also had the lowest female employment rate (37.6 per cent) compared with a rate of 58.4 per cent for the EU in 2009, Malta, however, registered an increase from 33.1 per cent in 2000. The male employment rate has witnessed an important decrease from 76.2 per cent in 2001 to 71.6 per cent in 2009, yet remains slightly higher than the EU average of 70.7 per cent.

Baldacchino (2003) maintains that the participation rate is effectively higher than the official figure but that women work either in the informal economy or perform unpaid work in family businesses. The restructuring of the Maltese economy, before and after accession to the EU, led to some job losses, particularly for women in low-paid sectors such as textiles and manufacturing.

The Beveridge curve shown in Figure 1 indicates that during the period 2002–05 the unemployment rate was higher than the availability of jobs on the market. This could be explained by the adaptation process entailed by EU membership in 2004, which led to the restructuring of the economy with several redundancies ensuing. The situation turned positive during 2006–08, when the economy created more jobs than the number of unemployed people. However, the international crisis had a negative effect on job creation and the situation returned to a higher level of unemployment by 2009, for which there was not a corresponding number of job vacancies. The problem may be due to low levels of job creation, skills mismatch, generous unemployment benefits or high income tax rates on low income. Data from the European Monitoring Centre on Change (EMCC) (2010) of Eurofound—European Foundation for the Improvement of Living and Working Conditions—indicate that in 2005–10 there were 4,517 redundancies, linked to restructuring, but 10,085 jobs had been expected to be created, mostly through expansions of existing companies. The redundancies occurred mostly in the textiles, manufacturing and shipyard areas, while new jobs were created in the health, electronics, banking, engineering and information and computing technology (ICT) sectors. This indicates a shift from low-level skill-based employment to more sophisticated and knowledge-based activity.

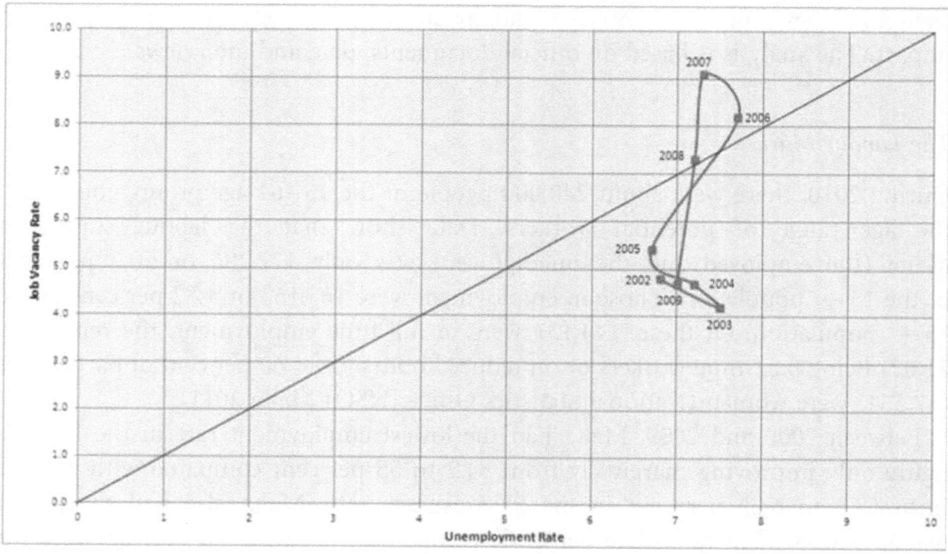

Figure 1 Beveridge curve* for Malta, 2002–09.
Sources: ETC annual reports for job vacancies and NSO Malta for labour force and unemployment rate. Job vacancy rate: author's calculations.
* The Beveridge curve shows the relationship between the availability of jobs on the market and the number of unemployed.

The EES

The following section compares Malta against the EES targets for 2000 and 2009 (see Table 1). The first two targets have already been covered in the section above. The employment of older workers (55–64 age category) is very low compared with EU27; it actually decreased in the ten-year period. This can be partially explained by the

Table 1 EES targets

Objective	Target	EU27 average 2000	EU27 average2009	Malta 2000	Malta 2009
Overall employment rate	70 (57)*	62.2	64.6	54.2	54.9
Female employment rate	60 (41)*	53.7	58.6	33.1	37.7
Employment rate of older workers	50 (35)*	36.9	46.0	28.5	28.1
Youth unemployment rate	5.73–9.00†	17.3	19.6	13.7	14.3
Long-term unemployment rate	0.73 – 0.63†	4.0	3.0	4.5	3.0
Labour market matching‡	Improvement	7.1	9.3	4.5	5.8
Gender pay gap	Reduction	n/a	17.6	n/a	9.2

Lifelong learning taken as a proxy indicating an improved skills base.
*Figures in brackets are the targets set by Malta in its National Reform Programme for 2005–08.
†Average of the three best member states in 2000 and 2009.
‡*Sources*: Eurostat and ETC Report 2009.

retirement age, which has only recently increased to 65 (it was 60 for women and 61 for men), but this increase has been staggered and people retiring now can still retain the old thresholds. The compulsory 65 retirement age is for those people born after 1962. The figure for youth unemployment is lower than the EU27 average. This could be linked to early school leavers (discussed below) and the lack of employability of such youths. The long-term unemployment rate is similar to the EU27 average and has improved over the ten-year period. No specific data were found for labour market matching, but the Employment and Training Corporation (ETC) Report provides a placement to vacancy ratio of 52 per cent for the year 2009. In the table a proxy was used (lifelong learning improving the skills base) and this crude indicator shows that there has been improvement, although the uptake remains relatively lower than the EU27 average. Although a gender pay gap continues to exist (mainly in the private sector), the situation in Malta is better than the EU27 average.

In general there has been marginal improvement in Malta in relation to several targets, although none of the targets set by the Maltese government (lower than the Lisbon targets and shown in brackets in Table 1) in its 2005–08 National Reform Programme (Ministry of Finance, the Economy and Investment 2010) has been achieved. The Joint Assessment of the Employment Policy Priorities for Malta (2001) summed up the problems facing the labour market at the turn of the century as follows:

> the challenges facing employment policy today relate to participation rates and skill levels ... particularly important in the context of an ageing population and a decline in birth rates ... As a result, concern arises over the relatively large number of people who are inactive. Low participation rates, particularly for women and, to a lesser degree, older workers, are to be addressed. The youth unemployment rate also needs close monitoring. The rise in educational attainment in Malta must be sustained and improved upon to address emerging skill shortages, which are particularly evident in the IT and construction sectors, in certain professions and in middle management. (p. 7)

This statement points to another aspect of the labour market: educational attainment affecting future workers. Access to all levels of education (including tertiary education) is free in Malta and has been since the 1970s, with non-compulsory education (over 16) actually providing for a monthly stipend to guarantee access to education, irrespective of family income. However, this has not helped to reduce the number of early school leavers or to encourage more youths to continue with higher education.

> The backbone of Malta's economic development is its human resources, where major improvements, in particular in reducing early school leaving, are needed. (Commission of the European Communities 2009, p. 38)

Malta had a lower school expectancy figure of 15.2 per cent in 2009, compared with 17.2 per cent for EU27, where 'school expectancy corresponds to the expected years of education over a lifetime' (Eurostat definition). This reflects the high level of early school leavers with the consequence that the level of 18-year-olds still in education was only 42.8 per cent compared with an EU average of 77.5 per cent in 2006, although the figure increased to 71.1 per cent by 2009. Compared with the EU27 (27.3 per cent), Malta had the highest (71) percentage of people aged 25–64 with the lowest educational attainment. However, people who did not consider tertiary education when leaving compulsory school are now returning to university. The proportion of students in vocational post-secondary schools is higher for males at 61.1 per cent than the EU average of 55.7 per cent, but lower for females at 37 per cent compared with 44.7 per cent. However, there are more women than men in tertiary education. In fact, 57.9 per cent of university students are women (compared with 55.3 per cent for the EU27) and this phenomenon has recurred every year since 1997. Unfortunately, there is a relatively low percentage of young people (20–29 years) on science and technology courses, which are considered essential, given the significance of innovation and scientific expertise in the EU's goal of knowledge-based economic growth. The figure was only six per 1,000 persons in the age group, compared with 13.9 for the EU (Eurostat).

Table 2 presents a summary of four objectives, action taken and the outcome (if data exist). Figures show an increase in female part-time work, an option that may be more amenable to juggling the work–life balance. The time is ripe for a national childcare policy, considering that more women are achieving tertiary education. Encouraging older people to contribute to the economy because of their experience has had some success. However, in most cases the beneficiaries are mainly engaged as consultants/experts on a part-time basis with government entities or have a family business. Less successful have been actions to tackle undeclared work, which continues in many areas of the economy and the level of such work 'is not necessarily low' (Camilleri-Cassar 2010), although no official data exist. Making work pay means the gap between social benefits and the minimum wage has to be significant enough to incentivise people to find employment. Malta was urged to step up

> efforts to attract more people, particularly women and older workers, into the labour market by, inter-alia, facilitating childcare; intensifying efforts to tackle undeclared work and encouraging participation in the labour market, including by tightening access conditions to the benefit system. (Commission of the European Communities 2009, p. 39)

Europeanisation would imply that government is replacing passive labour market policies with active ones. Yet the opposite occurred in 2009 when compared with 2008, funds moving from active to passive policies. The EU27 average spending on labour market policies for 2009 was 2.17 per cent of GDP, much higher than Malta's 0.51 per cent (the figure stood at 0.48 per cent in 1992). Most of the expenditure was on unemployment benefits, with 11,261 direct beneficiaries in 2009, an increase over 2008, possibly reflecting the repercussions of the international crisis. Labour market supports amounted to €21.88 million compared to only €1.73 million for labour market measures.

Table 2 Actions taken in Malta to meet labour market objectives

Objective	Year	Action	Outcome*
Promoting increased employment among women	2005	Tax credit for women returning to work after an absence of five years (with the amount increased again in 2009)	n/a
	2007	Deduction of childcare facilities fees for tax purposes	n/a
	2008	Paid maternity leave extended by one week to 14 weeks (as per EU directive); extra week initially paid out of public funding	2,396
	Various years	EU-funded projects, specifically targeting women, led by the ETC	n/a
Promoting increased employment among older workers	2008	Older workers campaign to promote the concept of lifelong learning	n/a
	2008	New legislation so that pensioners over 65 can still work without losing their pensions, regardless of amount earned from paid work	2,192
Making the benefit system more conducive to labour market participation	2008	People over 45 (unemployed for at least 5 years) encouraged to find self-employment with government paying social security contributions for the first year	n/a
	2008	Registered unemployed taking up short-term employment (not more than 13 weeks) will also have contributions credited to them from public funds	311
	2008	Child allowances payable to all children, irrespective of family income	38,000
	2008	Survivor's pension could be retained even if in employment and children still under 21 years of age	54
Intensifying efforts to tackle undeclared work	2008	Infringements mostly in the hospitality, cleaning and retailing sectors	2,175
	2008	Struck off unemployment register as they could not offer a valid reason for not accepting employment or training offered	2,032
	2008	Undeclared work will not lead to additional tax if declared within one year	n/a

n/a = not available
All figures refer to individuals, except for the Figure 38,000, which refers to families.
Source: Malta Progress Report 2009.

The number of people benefiting from labour market measures was only 759 (yet marginally up from 519 a year earlier), most of whom have undergone training while the rest enjoyed employment incentives or were involved in direct job creation schemes. No funds were made available for schemes focusing on job rotation/job sharing or supported employment and rehabilitation. There were 7,335 people registered with public employment services.

Some changes have also occurred in the educational field. The number of students attending full-time courses at university has not increased substantially but the number has increased for part-time ones. An important measure is the number of youths being encouraged to continue with their studies beyond the compulsory age of 16. The Malta College for Arts, Sciences and Technology (established in 2001) brought together in one institution pre-existing vocational and trade schools and also started offering new areas of study. In the first year it attracted 1,539 students. By 2009, there were 5,500 attending the nine institutes housed under the college. Furthermore, there were about 4,000 more attending part-time courses. The College offers over 120 courses from certificate courses to first degrees. However, children appear to be discouraged at a young age. The entrance exam from primary to secondary school normally sheds about half the pupils, those passing going to junior lyceum schools (having a higher status), while those failing go to general secondary schools and are labelled as non-achievers from the young age of ten. Recent changes to this system are expected to lead to a higher retention rate in the coming years.

Ideas, Interests and Institutions

'Ideas' include shared beliefs, values, conceptual language and legitimate justifications. To understand how the Maltese value work, the European Values Surveys (EVS) (ZACAT 2011) have been used. The late Maltese sociologist Anthony Abela (2000), who worked on the EVS project, described Maltese men as maintaining a traditional view of what the role of women in society should be, meaning women should primarily stay at home and take care of the family. Young people and highly educated women did not share this perspective, believing in equal opportunities to participate in the labour market and share household duties, including child-rearing. In principle, the experts interviewed agree with the validity of this analysis for today's society, where it has become more acceptable for women to pursue a career, yet the top echelons remain male dominated. Proposals (as suggested by women themselves during a research project) to enable women to participate more fully in the labour market include: more affordable childcare centres in all localities; flexible hours and teleworking; and more job opportunities (National Commission for the Promotion of Equality [NCPE] 2012). In fact only 22.4 per cent of women continued with a full-time job after motherhood while 17 per cent returned on a part-time/reduced/flexitime basis, and 71 per cent of these utilised grandparents as child-minders (ibid., pp. 248–249).

In recent years, the government has introduced several tax schemes for women to return to work after their family-related career break. Furthermore, the Foundation for Educational Services (a government entity) manages nine centres and operates three more as a public–private partnership. Prices range from a minimum €8 per month for a one-day-per-week use for low-wage families, to a maximum of €150 per month for a full week and a family earning more than €19,501 annually. Families with an annual income of less than €10,000 do not pay (for comparison the minimum wage for 2010 stood at just under €8,000). The total number of children in the nine centres, however, is only 347. The government aims to open other centres in the future. There are other private centres but data are not available.

An NSO study conducted in 2005 to understand the reasons for inactivity brought to light that people were in general happy with the status quo. In fact, 92.6 per cent of inactive/unemployed women did not want to change anything in the working-life pattern (NSO Malta 2006). Changes in flexible work conditions are more likely to encourage increased employment. As work conditions stood then, 53.9 per cent of respondents said they would like to work extra hours or have more flexible hours in order to be able to juggle life at home, by making use of time-off should the need arise. The situation differs between public and private sectors, with the former more likely to have such opportunities. Most interviewees agree that reduced hours, flexitime and teleworking have increased in the public sector in recent years, but the same cannot be said to be the case in the private sector. Private employers maintain that this is due to the small size of most private sector companies. Government policies in this regard are therefore facing issues that may be difficult to resolve. Private employers are not in a position to change working conditions and allow, for example, flexitime or teleworking. As one employer said, if there is a bookshop or café with established opening hours, how can the employee expect to start work at nine and not seven in the morning in order to take her/his child to school.

Another aspect of ideas is conceptual language. Terminology such as 'activation', 'making work pay', 'adequate and sustainable pensions' and 'lifelong learning' has spread through local political discourse and pervaded ministerial speeches and official reports. 'Of course, official statements are not automatically translated into real policies but the role that ideas developed at EU level have had on national policy outcomes should not be underestimated' (Cerami 2007, p. 7). Language is a medium to deliver ideas or to plant new priorities in people's minds and thus fertilise the ground for difficult but essential reforms. It is through language as a cognitive mechanism that new vocabulary and EU-related expressions have come to permeate articles in local newspapers, mirroring official verbal and written communications. Swiftly, EU policy priorities have become Maltese priorities and terms such as 'childcare centres', 'flexicurity', 'flexi-hours', 'reduced hours', 'family-friendly measures' and 'work–family balance' have gained currency in everyday speech. However, according to several interviewees, there is more talk than action on these matters. Furthermore, whilst action is possible in the public sector, it is more difficult to obtain in the private sector with its small-sized entities.

Any changes occurring that may require hardships or need sacrifices are generally presented as needed within the EU membership context and thus legitimately justified by the authorities. Examples mentioned by the interviewees included the changes in work conditions legislation, the one-week increase in maternity leave, the pressure on women to enter the labour market, the reduction in holidays, and awareness of the need for a social pact.

'Interests' refers to preferences and material interests of both individuals and groups. More explicitly, it can refer to vested interests in the realm of decision-making. Some reforms were resisted in Malta due to the lobbying power of certain interest groups. In other cases, compromises had to be found.

In 1981 the Maltese government introduced the initiative of 13 weeks' paid maternity leave. No further changes occurred until 2008, when an EU law decreed the minimum length of maternity leave as 14 weeks. This was fiercely opposed by private employers, who maintained they could not afford to pay for an extra week. Therefore, a compromise was reached in order to comply with EU legislation. The extra week was introduced, initially unpaid, but later fully paid through public funds even in the private sector. In this way, Europeanisation was in a sense accomplished, but interests maintained an upper hand in the ensuing negotiations. The Estrella Report suggesting that the increase from 14 weeks to 20 was heavily contested by employers in Malta, who maintained it would be too costly to put into practice. In the November 2011 budget speech, the government increased maternity leave by two weeks for 2012 and then again by two more in 2013, meaning that from 2013 onwards women can avail themselves of 18 weeks. A report commissioned by the employers' association, showing only the cost associated with this proposed measure, did not consider the benefits of having an increased female labour force. Due to vested interests, a realistic cost–benefit analysis was not undertaken. According to one interviewee, employers always oppose change unless it is an EU regulation.

Other changes were also initially opposed but in the end could not be blocked. Examples include the raising of the retirement age, the closing down of companies (sustained mostly through public funding) and the privatisation of public entities. Yet other changes continue to find opposition. One example is the reduction in access to social benefits. Resistance comes not from the social partners but from the beneficiaries themselves, and in this respect it is political interests in votes which are impeding reforms in the social security sector, and also in the health and education fields. Private pension funds have not caught on, signifying that private pension providers' interests have not yet made an impact on government policy. According to a human resource specialist, local people have developed the mindset that their social security contribution (amounting to one tenth of the salary) already guarantees them an adequate pension. Other interviewees maintained that pension funds are still considered risky ventures, while an economist suggested that some people may be saving for the future via safer means such as banks.

Europeanisation has undeniably infiltrated material interests in the case of EU funding possibilities. Whilst Malta was the most sceptical of the 2004 entrants, all social and economic actors (employers, unions, local councils, women's organisations, the self-employed, consultancies) have been influenced by the potential offered by EU funds, resulting in participation in the organisation of training courses, research and EU projects related to the labour market. Moreover, EU-related experts and consultants have mushroomed overnight, creating a class of people with new vested interests in the financial incentives aspect of the Europeanisation movement.

'Institutions' encompass all forms of formal and informal procedures that in various ways influence decision-making and policy-making. It refers to political, economic and social processes embodying forms of power in a country. Formally it relates to the legal aspect and informally it covers relationships in the socio-economic sphere. In essence, institutions incorporate legal and social norms.

Until 2002, the Maltese labour market was regulated by the Conditions of Employment Regulation Act (CERA) of 1952 and the Industrial Relations Act (IRA) of 1976. Although over the years these were updated to reflect changes in the work environment, it was only the need to align to EU labour law which made it imperative to overhaul the legislative framework. The Employment and Industrial Relations Act (EIRA) of 2002 'consolidated CERA and IRA, whilst ensuring increased protection for new types of working relationships based on the relevant EU Labour Directives' (Theophanous et al. 2007, p. 37). Reforms were introduced too slowly, even after EU accession, and in some cases only the minimum requirements of legislation were finally transposed into national law (ibid.). It is safe to say that, overall, the pressure of EU legislation was relatively strong. However, loopholes continue to be found, for example employers who engage people as self-employed rather than directly employed by the company. This means that those so employed will not have any rights to holidays, sick leave and other benefits deriving directly from the company.

According to an industrial relations expert, in new areas of expansion such as financial services there is more room for flexible working conditions. Furthermore, small and medium enterprises (SMEs), the majority of companies, tend to adopt a more informal atmosphere at work, working more like family holdings rather than bureaucratically structured and inflexible entities. The ETC, the main governmental institution offering labour market services provides a significant number of good schemes (mainly ESF funded), although these are generally limited in duration.

Europeanisation has not been as successful in the informal structures of the economy. Although the government has introduced several schemes to discourage undeclared work (such as a 15 per cent income tax flat rate on part-time work, and amnesties), such work remains diffused in the economy and appears to be governed by social norms that impede whistle-blowing, even though a special telephone number exists for anonymous reporting of abusers of the tax system. Work of this type is generally believed to be concentrated in the lower echelons of society, such as cleaning activities and maintenance work in private homes. However, according to several interviewees, it also permeates the professional sector such as in private teaching, the construction industry and the paramedic professions. There was general agreement among the interviewees that issues such as flexicurity and making work pay still had a long track to cover.

The Malta Council for Economic and Social Development (MCESD) is the organisation within which social dialogue is institutionalised. It was established in 2001 and replaced the original Council for Economic Development with the introduction of the social dimension. It is a tripartite organisation creating a dialogue between government, employers and workers' unions and acts as a consultative and advisory body to government. However, an institutionalised social pact is still elusive and not likely to happen in the near future, according to several interviewees. Although the real value of the MCESD is sometimes questioned, the fact that there are other organisations struggling to find representation on this body indicates that it is considered to have an important role in the power structure of society.

According to an industrial relations expert, social dialogue is very effective in the private sector, but more difficult to achieve in the public sector. The strength of trade unions may have diminished over time. Yet Malta has a relatively calm industrial relations environment, and this is due more to informal rather than formal processes. Dialogue is easier to obtain at the company level. Sectoral-level dialogue is not very evident and, though it is needed, no effort has been made to increase the partial coverage it now enjoys. The expert did not believe that social dialogue is in reality effective at the national level, as the main forum acts more as a sounding board than a real decision-making mechanism.

Malta has over the years borrowed the 'UK-bred practice of labour management relations', and has been recently influenced by European laws, but the Maltese have 'added our own special "new" ingredients into the industrial relations cauldron: local features include the paternalism and strong loyalty basis of employee relations in small, mainly family owned and family run businesses' (Baldacchino, Rizzo & Zammit 2003, pp. 5–6).

Conclusion

The European Commission's recommendations have over the past ten years resonated with the same message and spirit of encouraging a focus on 'retraining human resources' (Commission of the European Communities 1999, p. 22), 'reorienting labour market policies [by] increasing the overall employment rate ... in particular for women and long-term unemployed' (Commission of the European Communities 2003, p. 32) and stepping up 'efforts to attract more people, particularly women and older workers, into the labour market' (Commission of the European Communities 2009, p. 39). Yet, changes have certainly occurred during this decade. The formal structures, the language, certain ideas and preferences have become Europeanised; unfortunately not all hands are on deck. The problem lies in the difficulty of changing attitudes concerning employment, particularly within certain groups in society: the home-carers, low-skilled women, older workers, the inactive indolent and the perennial social security system parasites. Tackling undeclared work has had some effect but more progress is needed. Changes in the tax system have been haphazard and lacked significant impact. The dire situation of public finances has not been conducive to drastic changes in this revenue-generating mechanism. Meritocracy and equal opportunities need to be more evident. In this respect Europeanisation has not been influential, and this is creating serious inefficiencies in the labour force, particularly in the public sector, which has become top-heavy.

But there is also a new trend of less conservative behaviour, especially among the young and more educated. The new demands of modern life indicate that households need the comfort of more than one bread-winner in the family. The increased opportunities offering higher returns in other EU member states are taking their toll on the local labour market, with increasing numbers seeking employment abroad. It is urgent for labour market policies to rein in this resource haemorrhage and to cultivate and retain the skills needed for a changing economy.

Following the classification set out in Radaelli (2000), which types of Europeanisation have taken place in Malta? Some element of *inertia* has certainly been present: most Eurosceptics had to reluctantly convert to the EU reality. There has also been *retrenchment* where resistance to change continues and this is seen in high inactivity rates, untaxed work and resistance by employers to offering workers increased protection and benefits. In most cases *absorption* occurred, particularly in the legislative framework, where only the minimum requirements were generally transposed, thus without impacting on the fundamentals. *Transformation*, meaning significant paradigm shifts, has not occurred. Overall, there appears to be a shift in ideas, interests and institutions. Although not as dynamic or open as one might expect, changes are happening, even though certain interest groups such as employers would prefer to delay their entry and sustain more for continuity rather than transformative change. Unions are cautious in their approach too, as more regulation lessens their power in the negotiations arena. Government in turn is caught in the middle ground between the pressures from Europe and the demands of a small economy heavily reliant on its people for economic growth and on businesses for its economic activity. Therefore, whilst Europeanisation is more evident on the formal policy level, it is less clear on the informal societal level dealing with people and their relationships with the labour market and their work. This is mainly due to the traditional family roles (which are fortunately changing, since females are surpassing males in the educational field, but such changes remain limited to a small portion of society), and also to informal structures that tend to be stronger than formal ones in everyday social relationships.

Time will increase Europeanisation in the years to come; after all, changes in attitudes need time. As always Malta remains a colourful kaleidoscope with an adaptive disposition when circumstances, especially externally induced ones, require it. It is possible, through a concerted tripartite effort, for this small island economy to get more hands on deck and become more actively productive.

References

Abela, A. (2000) *Values of Women and Men in the Maltese Islands: A Comparative European Perspective*, Ministry for Social Policy, Commission for the Advancement of Women, Malta.

Afonso, A. & Papadopoulos, Y. (2009) 'Europeanisation, policy concertation and labour market reforms in small European states: a comparative analysis', National Centre of Competence in Research – Challenges to Democracy in the 21st Century, Working Paper No. 34.

Ardy, B. & Umbach, G. (2004) *Employment Policies in Germany and the United Kingdom: The Impact of Europeanisation*, Anglo-German Foundation for the Study of Industrial Society, London.

Baldacchino, G. (2003) *Factors Affecting Women's Formal Participation in the Malta Labour Market: Results of a Research Project*, Government Printing Press, Malta.

Baldacchino, G., Rizzo, S. & Zammit, E. (2003) *Evolving Industrial Relations in Malta*, Agenda, Malta.

Balkir, C., Bolukbasi, H. T. & Ertugal, E. (2013) 'Europeanisation and dynamics of continuity and change in domestic political economies in the "Southern Periphery"', *South European Society and Politics*, vol. 18, no. 2, pp. 121–137.

Borzel, T. & Risse, T. (2000) 'When Europe hits home: Europeanisation and domestic change', *European Integration online Papers*, vol. 4, no. 15, available online at: http://papers.ssrn.com/sol3/papers.cfm?abstract_id=302768

Camilleri-Cassar, F. (2010) 'Undeclared work in Malta', *Sunday Times of Malta*, 8 August.

Cerami, A. (2007) 'Europeanisation, enlargement and social policy in Central and Eastern Europe', Centre d'Etudes Europeennes, Cashiers Europeens No. 1/2007.

Commission of the European Communities (1999) 'Regular report from the commission on Malta's progress towards accession', available online at: http://ec.europa.eu/enlargement/archives/pdf/key_documents/1999/malta_en.pdf

Commission of the European Communities (2003) 'Comprehensive monitoring report on Malta's preparations for membership', available online at: http://ec.europa.eu/enlargement/archives/pdf/key_documents/1999/malta_en.pdf

Commission of the European Communities (2009) 'Implementation of the Lisbon Strategy structural reforms in the context of the European Economic Recovery Plan - annual country assessments', Brussels, COM(2009) 34/2 Volume 1, available online at: http://ec.europa.eu/archives/growthandjobs_2009/pdf/european-dimension-200812-annual-progress-report/annualass_en.pdf

Commission of the European Communities (2010) 'Lisbon Strategy evaluation document', Commission Staff Working Document, Brussels, 2 February, SEC (2010) 144.

ETC (2009) 'Annual report', available online at: www.etc.gov.mt

European Monitoring Centre on Change (2010) 'Latest restructuring cases for Malta', available online at: http://www.eurofound.europa.eu/emcc/erm/index.php?template=searchfactsheets&kSel = 1&page = 1&sel = 3&date = &totalRecords = 30&issearch = &nav = &order = date&type = DESC

Fischer, G. & Tholoniat, L. (2006) 'The European employment strategy in an enlarged EU', *Journal for Labour Market Research*, vol. 39, no. 1, pp. 123–142, available online at: http://econpapers.repec.org/article/iabiabzaf/

Fleckenstein, T. (2006) 'Europeanisation of German labour market policy?: the European employment strategy scrutinised', *German Politics*, vol. 15, no. 3, pp. 284–301.

Goetschy, J. (1999) 'The European employment strategy: genesis and development', *European Journal of Industrial Relations*, vol. 5, no. 2, pp. 117–137.

Hall, P. A. (1993) 'Policy paradigms, social learning and the state: the case of economic policy-making in Britain', *Comparative Politics*, vol. 25, no. 3, pp. 275–296.

Hall, P. A. (1997) 'The role of interests, institutions and ideas in the comparative political economy of the industrialized nations', in *Comparative Politics: Rationality, Culture, and Structure*, eds M. I. Lichbach & A. S. Zuckerman, Cambridge, Cambridge University Press, pp. 174–207.

Haverland, M. (2006) 'Does the EU cause domestic developments? Improving case selection in europeanization research', *West European Politics*, vol. 29, issue 1, pp. 134–146.

Heclo, H. (1994) 'Ideas, interests and institutions', in *The Dynamics of American Politics: Approaches and Interpretations*, eds L. Dodd & C. Jillson, Westview Press, Boulder, CO, pp. 366–392.

Heidenreich, M. & Bischoff, G. (2008) 'The open method of co-ordination: a way to the europeanization of social and employment policies?', *Journal of Common Market Studies*, vol. 46, no. 3, pp. 497–532.

Heritier, A. (1998) 'Differential Europe: administrative responses to community policy', paper presented at the Europeanisation and Domestic Change Conference, Florence, 19–20 June.

Heritier, A. & Knill, C. (2001) 'Differential responses to European policies: a comparison', available online at: http://papers.ssrn.com/sol3/papers.cfm?abstract_id=280910

Kvist, J. & Saari, J. (2007) *The Europeanisation of Social Protection*, Policy Press, Bristol.

Majone, G. D. (1989) *Evidence, Argument and Persuasion in the Policy Process*, Yale University Press, New Haven.

Massarelli, N., Giovannola, D. & Wozowczyk, M. (2010) 'EU-27 downward employment trend flattening out – latest labour market trends – 2010Q1 data', *Eurostat Statistics in Focus*, 46/2010.

Mendez, C., Wishlade, F. & Yuill, D. (2007) 'Made to measure? Europeanisation, "goodness of fit" and adaptation pressures in the EU Competition Policy and Regional Aid', European Policy Research Paper No. 61, European Policies Research Centre, Glasgow.

Ministry of Finance, the Economy and Investment (2010) 'National Reform Programme 2008–2010: annual progress report 2009', available online at: http://ec.europa.eu/archives/growthandjobs_2009/pdf/nrp2009/mt_nrp_en.pdf

NCPE (2012) 'Unlocking the female potential research report', ESF3-47, Outlook Coop, Malta.

NSO Malta (2006) 'Labour market: reconciliation between work and family life'. Press Release 24/2006.

NSO Malta (2011) 'Labour force survey Q3/2010', Press Release 003/2011, 6 January.

Olsen, J. P. (1996) 'Europeanisation and nation-state dynamics', in *The Future of the Nation-State*, eds S. Gustavsson & L. Lewin, vol. 1, part 3 Routledge, New York, pp. 245–286.

Olsen, J. P. (2001) 'The many faces of Europeanisation', ARENA Working Papers 01/2.

Palier, B. & Surel, Y. (2005) 'Les "trois I" et l'analyse de l'Etat en action', *Revue Francaise de Science Politique*, vol. 55, no. 1, pp. 7–32.

Radaelli, C. M. (2000) 'Whither Europeanisation? Concept stretching and substantive change', *European Integration Online Papers*, vol. 4, no. 8, available online at: http://eiop.or.at/eiop/texte/2000-008a.htm

Radaelli, C. (2003) 'The europeanization of public policy', in *The Politics of Europeanization*, eds K. Featherstone & C. Radaelli. Oxford, Oxford University Press, pp. 27–56.

Sabatier, P. (ed.) (1999) *Theories of the Policy Process*, Westview Press, Boulder, CO.

Schuttpelz, A. (2006) 'The Europeanisation of employment policy in the Czech Republic', *Croatian Journal of Social Policy*, vol. 13, no. 2, pp. 151–171, available online at: http://hrcak.srce.hr/index.php?show=clanak&id_clanak_jezik = 47829&lang = en

Sotiropoulos, D. A. (2004) 'The EU's impact on the Greek welfare state: Europeanisation on paper?' *Journal of European Social Policy*, vol. 14, no. 3, pp. 267–284.

Theophanous, A., Antoniou, M., Tirkides, Y., Ioannou, C., Azzopardi, R. M. & Georgiou, K. E. (2007) 'The evolution of labour law in the new member states of the European Union: 1995–2005 – country studies on Cyprus and Malta', study undertaken for the Employment, Social Affairs and Equal Opportunities Directorate-General of the European Commission.

Toller, A. E. (2004) 'The Europeanisation of public policies – understanding idiosyncratic mechanisms and contingent results', *European Integration Online Papers*, vol. 8, no. 9, available online at: http://eiop.or.at/eiop/texte/2004-009a.htm

Van Berkel, R. & Hornemann Moller, I. (2002) *Active Social Policies in the EU – Inclusion through Participation?* Policy Press, Bristol.

Van Vliet, O. & Koster, F. (2008) 'Europeanisation and the political economy of active labour market policies', paper presented for the NIG Annual Work Conference, Enschede, 20–21 November, available online at: http://docs.google.com/viewer?a=v&q = cache:UIG2xggZYDEJ:media.leidenuniv.nl/legacy/06-01-09-paper-olafvanvliet-europanisation.pdf

Vink, M. P. (2003) 'What is Europeanisation? and other questions on a new research agenda', *European Political Science*, vol. 3, no. 1, pp. 63–74.

ZACAT (2011) 'European values surveys', available online at: http://zacat.gesis.org/webview/index.jsp?object=http://zacat.gesis.org/obj/fCatalog/Catalog5

Zeitlin, J., Pochet, P. & Magnussen, L. (eds) (2005) *The Open Method of Co-ordination in Action: The European Employment Strategy and Social Inclusion Strategies*, PIE Peter Lang, Brussels.

Zartaloudis, S. (2010) 'Follow the money: tracing the Europeanisation of Greek employment policy with regard to public employment service's reform', paper presented at ECPR's Fifth Pan-European Conference on EU Politics, Porto, 23–26 June 2010.

Appendix. List of Interviewees

1. Dr Joe Azzopardi, human resources specialist, 5 December 2010.
2. Ms Anna Borg, lecturer at the Centre for Labour Studies, 9 December 2010.
3. Professor Lino Briguglio, economist, 24 November 2010.
4. Mr Michael Briguglio, sociologist, 29 November 2010.
5. Dr Manwel Debono, Director, Centre for Labour Studies, 29 November 2010.
6. Mr Joe Grech, employers' representative, 20 November 2010.
7. Mr Joe Muscat, employers' representative, 20 November 2010.
8. Professor Edward Zammit, industrial relations expert, 1 December 2010.
9. Union representative, 30 November 2010
10. Union representative, 7 December 2010.

Portugal in the European Union: The Limits of Convergence

Sebastián Royo

This article examines the integration experience of Portugal in the European Union in order to study how it has affected the country's fiscal policies in the decade prior to the global financial crisis, from 1999 to 2008. It focuses on three main variables to account for the difficulties that Portugal experienced in complying with the Stability and Growth Pact: institutions, ideas, and interests. The paper closes with some lessons from the Portuguese experience. The examination of this case will show that, to be successful, economic reform has to be a domestic process led by domestic actors willing to carry it out.

The date of 1 January 2011 marked the twenty-fifth anniversary of Portugal's accession to the European Community (EC). European integration followed the establishment of democracy in Portugal in the 1970s, a precondition for EC membership. By the 1970s, the country, in its relative isolation from Europe, had sharpened its desire to become part of the EC and most Portuguese supported the integration process. Indeed, in the second half of the past century, the EC epitomised in the eyes of Portuguese citizens the values of liberty, democracy, and progress absent in their country. In addition, although some economists expressed reservations about the impact of EC membership, most Portuguese entrepreneurs knew that their only future lay in Europe and that the modernisation of their country was contingent on European integration. Hence, belonging to the European club was a mission to be pursued. The treaties of accession were signed in 1985 and Portugal (and Spain) joined the EC on 1 January 1986. This long-awaited development had profound consequences for the EC and for Portugal (Royo 2003; Royo & Manuel 2003).

This article examines the effect of European Union (EU) membership on Portugal in accordance with the template provided by Balkir, Bolukbasi, and Ertugal (this volume). It identifies the basic changes in the Portuguese economy that occurred as a result of European integration and focuses, in particular, on the country's fiscal performance during the 1999–2008 period. The examination of this case sheds new light on the challenges (and opportunities) that countries face when trying to integrate regionally. It shows that countries do respond differently to similar challenges and pressures, and that there is still room for policy choices within a monetary union. These policy choices in turn affect economic performance.

The paper proceeds in five steps. Providing historical background information, the first section analyses briefly the overall economic consequences of EU integration for Portugal. The second section examines the fiscal rules associated with the European Monetary Union (EMU) membership. The third analyses the Europeanisation of Portugal's fiscal policies. Section four describes how institutions, ideas, and interests have hindered the compliance with EMU fiscal rules. The paper closes with an analysis of the lessons from the Portuguese experience.

EU Membership and the Portuguese Economy

From an economic standpoint, entry to European integration has contributed to the modernisation of the Portuguese economy (Lobo & Lains 2007; Royo 2004; Royo 2011). Although EC/EU membership has not been the only reason for this development (the economic liberalisation and modernisation processes started in the 1950s and 1960s), European integration has played a critical role. Indeed, it was the perspective of EC integration that gave a final push to the modernisation and liberalisation of the Portuguese economy. The 1972 Preferential Trade Agreement (PTA) between the EC and Portugal resulted in the further opening of European markets to the country. Additionally, the perspective of EU membership acted as an essential motivational factor that influenced the actions of policymakers and economic actors, thus acting as a catalyst for change as Portugal took unilateral measures in preparation for EC accession, including increasing economic flexibility, industrial restructuring, the adoption of value added tax (VAT), and trade liberalisation.

At the same time, the fact that most citizens supported integration facilitated the implementation of (in many cases, quite painful) micro- and macroeconomic reforms, which allowed the political and economic actors to adopt economic policies and business strategies consistent with membership and the *acquis communautaire*. (At the time of accession, the latter included the custom union, VAT, the Common Agricultural and Fisheries Policies, and the external trade agreements; and in subsequent years following the country's accession to the EU it also included the Single Market, Exchange Rate Mechanism [ERM], and EMU.)

Overall, EC/EU membership has had a very significant impact on economic policies and economic performance (Lains 2003). It has significantly constrained the economic strategies of successive Portuguese governments. In Portugal, with a strong history of state intervention in the economy, single market, EMU, and EU competition policies have diminished the state's role in the economy and constrained policy options. They have forced successive governments to deregulate the country's economy, privatise public companies, and eliminate subsidies that had been used to sustain noncompetitive industries. This process, however, was sometimes contentious. In Portugal, the privatisation of public companies required a constitutional change (finally approved in 1989) and governments often fought the European Commission over government aid to state companies.

As a result of EU accession, trade barriers to the EU have been eliminated; markets and prices have been deregulated and liberalised; the labour market has been the subject of limited deregulatory reforms; and a privatisation programme was started in the early 1980s to roll back the presence of the government in the economy and to increase the overall efficiency of the system (Royo 2003, pp. 291–292). In the 1990s, the country's desire to participate in the EMU led to the implementation of policies that resulted in fiscal consolidation and the independence of the central bank.

One of the main consequences of these developments has been a reduction in the economic differences that separated the country from the European average (Lobo & Lains 2007; Loureiro 1995). Pedro Pita Barros and Nuno Garoupa (1996) confirm that Portuguese income has shown a pattern of convergence to average EU income levels over time and that it grew after 1986. Indeed, average per capita income, which is the indicator of real convergence, improved from 55 per cent of the EC average in 1980 to 78 per cent of the EU average in 2008. This convergence of national income to 'European' levels has been one of the most important consequences of membership.

An additional outcome of EU membership has been to give Portugal additional macroeconomic credibility (Macedo 2003a). Portugal joined the European Exchange Mechanism in 1992. Hence, Portuguese governments were forced to tighten fiscal policy, use privatisation revenues to pay down debt (particularly in the 1980s), and further liberalise the economy. The culmination of this process was the largely unexpected participation of Portugal in the EMU. Indeed, contrary to initial expectations, Portugal fulfilled the conditions established by the Maastricht Treaty and on 1 January 1999 became a founding member of the EMU (see Table 1). This development confirmed the nominal convergence of the country with the rest of the EU.

Table 1 Compliance with the EMU convergence criteria, 1996–2009

	1996	1998	2008	2009
Inflation	3.1	2.3	2.6	−0.9
General government deficit (per cent of GDP)	4.5	2.8	−3.8	−9.0
General government debt (per cent of GDP)	58.3	62.9	71.5	83.0
Long-term interest rates (%)	8.6	6.8	3.64	4.0

Source: Eurostat and IMF.

Fiscal Policies in the EMU

The Treaty on European Union (TEU) stated that countries wishing to participate in the EMU would have to meet a number of criteria to ensure 'a high degree of sustainable [economic] convergence'. The so-called convergence criteria included budgetary discipline aimed at avoiding a government financial position that would include an excessive deficit. A protocol attached to the TEU included two possible variables: a public debt ratio that would not exceed 60 per cent of gross domestic product (GDP) or a budget deficit of less than three per cent of GDP.

In order to ensure the continuation of budgetary discipline after the launch of the euro, and at Germany's insistence, the European Council in December 1996 adopted the Stability and Growth Pact (SGP). Under the provisions of this pact, countries agree to respect two criteria: a deficit-to-GDP ratio of three per cent and a debt-to-GDP ratio of 60 per cent (Article 104). However, in response to political pressures from other member states concerned about the negative impact of austerity policies, Germany agreed to water down the original proposed terms and make fines for violations not automatic, but subject to approval by governments. Furthermore, according to the SGP, countries could invoke the exceptional nature of a deficit linked to an annual fall in GDP of more than two per cent in the case of a severe recession (annual fall in real GDP of at least 0.75 per cent).

The SGP also established a system of multilateral surveillance of national budgetary policies in which the European Commission, the Ecofin Council, and the European Central Bank (ECB) would play a role, as well as an Excessive Deficit Procedure (EDP) to deal with countries that violate the pact. The Council in 1997 approved the guidelines for the implementation of the pact. In 2005, the Council approved a new regulation on speeding and clarifying the implementation of the Excessive Deficit Procedure. The new regulation extended the procedural deadlines for Council decisions in the excessive deficit procedure, and expanded the relevant factors that the Commission has to take into account, when preparing a report under Article 104(3) of the treaty.

In March 2000 the European Council also approved the Lisbon Strategy, which aimed at making the EU 'the most competitive and dynamic knowledge-based economy in the world capable of sustainable economic growth with more and better jobs and greater social cohesion' by 2010. This initiative was motivated by the relatively low economic and productivity growth in the EU, and it led to the formulation of various policy initiatives to be taken by all EU member states, including economic, social, and environmental renewal and sustainability, among other areas. Unfortunately, a 2004 review of the Lisbon Strategy concluded that even if some progress had been made, most of the goals were not achieved, and in 2009 it was declared a failure. The non-binding character of the Lisbon Strategy contributed to this failure.

Both fiscal rules, which were binding, and broader EU governance initiatives, such as the Lisbon Strategy, which were not legally binding, were expected to have an impact on the domestic economic policies of the member states and on their economic performance in general (and fiscal policy, in particular). The rest of the paper shows, however, the limits of convergence in the light of any pressure in the sheltered environment of the EMU (1999–2008). Indeed, both the SGP and the Lisbon Strategy were insufficient to force the necessary policy reforms that would have addressed Portugal's history of fiscal mismanagement. The recent global financial crisis has renewed market and EU pressures for fiscal and structural reforms.

The Europeanisation of Portugal's Fiscal Policies

Portugal's economic performance was remarkable in the 1990s. Between 1994 and 2000, real GDP growth (export led, but also boosted by private consumption and fixed investment) averaged more than three per cent annually and economic expansion continued for seven years. In 1996, the fifth year of expansion, GDP growth reached almost four per cent. The unemployment rate fell, reaching a record low of around four per cent in 2000 (one of the lowest in Europe), and inflation was brought down to just over two per cent in 1999. Portugal was also able to meet the Maastricht criteria for fiscal deficit following the consolidation efforts prior to 1997, which brought the deficit down to 2.5 per cent of GDP. One of the important factors that contributed to this performance was the transformation of the financial sector, largely spurred by EU directives in interest rate deregulation, liberalisation of the regulatory framework, privatisation, and freeing of international capital movements (Organisation for Economic Cooperation and Development [OECD] 1999, p. 13). The privatisation programme, one of the most ambitious in Europe at the time (more than 100 firms were sold), was also a contributing factor because it increased competition, enhanced productivity gains, and generated revenues that averaged more than two per cent of GDP per year.

However, starting in 1998, this performance started to deteriorate. The disinflation process was halted and inflation increased 2.8 per cent by the end of that year; the trade deficit deteriorated from 5.4 per cent of GDP in 1997 to 6.6 per cent in 1999. The harmonised consumer price index (CPI) reached over four per cent in early 2001 (above the EU average), pushed by higher oil prices and a weaker euro. Furthermore, economic growth also started to slow, dragged down by the ending of major infrastructure projects and Expo 98. The outset of EMU membership led to a progressive easing of monetary conditions and a sharp decline of interest rates. This happened at a time of high consumer demand in which domestic credit was also booming and the current account deficit was widening (it remained at around ten per cent of GDP up to 2002). EMU entry in 1999 did not alleviate the situation because Portugal was in a more advanced position in the cycle than the other EMU member states (the country was experiencing a credit boom and signs of overheating were starting to emerge), but now monetary policy was in the hands of the ECB and it was making decisions based on developments in the entire EMU area, hence the cut in interest rates in April 1999 (OECD 1999, pp. 10–11). Yet, the tightening of monetary policy, when the ECB started to gradually raise rates from November 1999 on, led to a change of conditions.

Furthermore, the end of the decade, which coincided with the country's accession to the EMU (meaning the pressure to fulfil the Maastricht criteria was no longer a powerful incentive), also witnessed a slowdown in the fiscal consolidation efforts, which led to the successful reduction of the fiscal deficit between 1994 and 1997. (There was an annual reduction of almost 1.2 percentage points and the deficit was reduced to 2.5 per cent of GDP by 1997.) Yet, about half of this fiscal adjustment was the result of the reduction of the public debt burden facilitated by the lower interest rates and non-recurring receipts. As a matter of fact, the primary surplus increased half a point per year between 1994 and 1997. In contrast, there was no increase in taxes or revenue as the result of improvements in the collection of taxes or social security contributions. Moreover, current expenditures on education, health, and social protection increased steadily (OECD 1999, p. 11). This pro-cyclical policy stance did not bode well for the subsequent slowdown of the economy because Portugal was left with little fiscal leeway to apply counter-cyclical measures once the crisis hit. In order to improve the margin of manoeuvre, Portugal should have reduced the weight of the public sector and also implemented structural reforms to check the growth of current expenditures, which would have allowed for a reduction in tax pressure. The country would have needed a significant surplus to ensure the balancing of the budget over the cycle, but unfortunately this did not happen.

Indeed, in the context of the EMU, fiscal policy was the main instrument available to the government to dampen demand pressures and bring down the current account deficit (eight per cent of GDP in 2002) and inflation (over 3.8 per cent). Yet, while the general government deficit continued to decline in accordance with the SGP and fell below three per cent of GDP in 2000, the pace of fiscal consolidation was slow and the gains from lower debt payments and higher revenues were used to increase primary current spending. Given the inflationary pressures and the advanced stage of the economic cycle, fiscal consolidation would have helped to control demand pressures. Increasing taxes was not an attractive option because, although the overall tax burden (at 34 per cent of GDP in 2000) was comparatively low, it would have been difficult politically and also risked eroding the export-oriented growth and harming the country's competitive position. Therefore, in order to meet budget deficit targets, the government became accustomed to implementing spending freezes and resorting to non-recurring receipts (such as the sale of mobile concessions in 2000). But it failed to address the structural causes of spending overruns: the public sector payroll bill (spending per employee had been growing rapidly due to high wage increases and pension benefits) and pressures in the social security system caused by population ageing. On the contrary, it continued to rely on increases in current revenue, as opposed to significant progress in spending control, and when these did not materialise, it adopted contingency measures to reduce expenditures, which revealed fundamental weaknesses in the budget process (OECD 2001, p. 12). This would prove to be a major Achilles heel for the sustainability of economic growth.

The failure to meet the conditions of the SGP led the European Commission, as part of the EDP, to issue a recommendation in October of 2002 for a Council decision on the existence of an excessive deficit. In response, in November, the Council issued a decision on the existence of a deficit and asked the Portuguese government 'to put an end to the present excessive deficit situation and to make the necessary budgetary plans for 2002' with the objective 'to reduce the deficit in 2002 to 2.8 per cent of GDP'; it gave a deadline of 31 December 2002 for the Portuguese government 'to take all necessary measures to bring the excessive deficit to an end', and asked that it 'adopt and implement the necessary budgetary measures to ensure that the government deficit in 2003 is further reduced clearly below three per cent of GDP and that the government debt ratio is kept below the 60 per cent of GDP reference value' (EU 2002). As a result, the deficit was brought down to 2.8 per cent in 2003. Unfortunately, the improvement proved to be temporary.

Indeed, the main problem was poor growth performance (Torres 2009, p. 58). Economic performance started to deteriorate markedly after 2000 and real GDP growth averaged less than one per cent between 2000 and 2005 (in 2003, the economy contracted 0.8 per cent) and annual growth remained fragile until 2006. In 2005, the Portuguese economy grew a meagre 0.91 per cent of GDP, and in 2006 1.3 per cent as a result of the depression of demand, and in particular of private demand given the few incentives for consumption. In addition, growth was further hampered because investment, was pushed down as a consequence of the restrictions on public spending and the increase of taxes to bring down the deficit. The accumulated output gap since the recession was one of the largest in the euro area; productivity growth in the business sector fell to around one per cent between 2004 and 2005 (it was three per cent in the 1990s). Unemployment also increased sharply, reaching 7.6 per cent in 2005 and eight per cent in 2007, the highest rate in 20 years (it had been only 3.8 per cent in 2000) (International Monetary Fund [IMF] 2009).

The recession was far longer and more intensive than anyone anticipated, with a dramatic impact on the government accounts; the fiscal deficit reached unsustainably high levels (see Table 2) pushed by the €4 billon bill for organising the European Championship Cup in 2004, which left no room to stimulate demand and thereby contributed to the length of the crisis. The government attempted to reduce the fiscal deficit by raising indirect taxes and establishing emergency spending cuts or freezes and one-off decisions, such as measures to control the wage bill over the short term. However, while these measures helped to reduce the deficit in the short term (it was brought down to 2.8 per cent in 2003), they proved insufficient because of the lower revenues at a time of a depressed economic environment. Thus, in 2005, the deficit went up again to 6.1 per cent. Public debt also deteriorated, growing from 53 per cent of GDP in 2000 to 65.9 per cent in 2005 and then decreasing to 60 per cent in 2006. Fixed capital formation fell 2.9 per cent in 2005 and 0.7 per cent in 2006 and then grew 2.8 per cent in 2007.

The country also suffered a decline in investment and savings. The investment rate fell from a peak of 28.1 per cent of GDP in 2000 to 20.6 per cent in 2006, while the gross savings rate fell from 17 per cent in 2000 to a pale 12.3 per cent in 2006, bouncing back a bit in 2007 to 15.1 per cent (OECD 2006).

Table 2 Economic summary Portugal (2000–10)

Subject descriptor	Units	2000	2001	2002	2003	2004	2005	2006	2007	2008	2009	2010
GDP, constant prices	Per cent change	3.9	1.9	0.7	−0.9	1.5	0.7	1.4	2.3	−0.0	−2.7	1.3
Inflation, average consumer prices	Per cent change	2.8	4.4	3.6	3.2	2.5	2.1	3.0	2.4	2.6	−0.9	1.3
Unemployment rate	Per cent of total labour force	4.4	4.5	5.6	7.1	7.5	8.5	8.5	8.9	8.5	10.6	12.0
General government structural balance	Per cent of potential GDP	−4.0	−4.8	−4.4	−4.7	−5.1	−5.6	−3.8	−3.2	−3.8	−9.0	−9.3
General government net debt	Per cent of GDP	48.4	51.1	53.8	55.8	57.6	62.7	63.9	68.2	71.5	83.0	92.9
Current account balance	Per cent of GDP	−10.3	−10.3	−8.2	−6.4	−8.3	−10.3	−10.7	−10.1	−12.6	−10.9	−9.8

Source: IMF, *World Economic Outlook Database*, September 2011.

In the end, the reliance on one-off measures failed to address the structural causes of the deficit and also reduced the necessary sense of urgency to tackle structural reforms. For instance, once the deficit was below three per cent, the government decided to lower taxes rapidly, despite the fact that the situation had not improved much. Three of the fundamental challenges were: first, the reform of the civil servants' pension system and the need to bring it into line with the general pension system; second, the reform of the health system; and, finally, the reform of the public administration to align the legal condition of employment and remuneration with the private sector and restructure the central administration (OECD 2006).

Portugal had continued violating the SGP (see Table 2), remaining above the maximum three per cent deficit. The country was therefore submitted once again to the EDP in 2005, which further hindered confidence and dampened expectations. In July 2005, the Commission issued another recommendation for a Council decision on the existence of an excessive deficit. In response, that September, the Council issued a decision on the existence of a deficit and asked the Portuguese government again 'to put an end to the present excessive deficit situation as rapidly as possible' and to 'bring the general government deficit below three per cent of GDP in a credible and sustainable manner by 2008'. The Council established 'the deadline of 19 March 2006 for the Portuguese government to take effective action' and asked the Portuguese authorities to 'ensure that the government gross debt ratio is brought onto a firm downward path and approaches the reference value at a satisfactory pace' (EU 2005).

The victory of the Socialist Party (Partido Socialista [PS]) in the 2005 election brought in a new government with an absolute parliamentary majority, committed to implementing the structural reforms needed to bring the deficit below three per cent by 2008. Indeed, the new government pushed for important structural reforms and implemented tough decisions. This shift was based on the perceived need to adapt to new European initiatives (the Lisbon Treaty) as well as strong fiscal and structural reform pressures (SGP and Lisbon Strategy) (Torres 2009, p. 67). Indeed, upon taking office in March 2005, Prime Minister José Sócrates announced an immediate increase of two per cent in VAT, breaking his electoral commitment not to increase taxes, in order to cope with the budget deficit. Moreover, in the face of strident opposition from labour unions and organised interests, his government pushed for the reform of the public sector and the civil servants, and an extensive restructuring of Portugal's state bureaucracy. The government also approved a comprehensive pension reform plan in the summer of 2005 and carried through an ambitious privatisation plan that sought to raise €2.4 billion from the sale of public enterprises between 2006 and 2009.

In the end, the combination of fiscal consolidation (the ratio of public spending to GDP fell from an excessive 47.7 per cent of GDP in 2005 to 45 per cent in 2008), structural reforms, and increasing revenues from stronger economic growth all helped Portugal to bring the deficit back under control. The Sócrates government, which inherited a deficit of 5.6 per cent of GDP from the previous administration, was able to bring its budget deficit back down after achieving a larger cut than forecasted in 2006. The deficit fell to 3.9 per cent of GDP in 2006, 0.7 percentage points lower than the 4.6

per cent target agreed with the European Commission as part of the plan to avoid the sanctions hanging over the country for breaching the SGP. In 2007, one year ahead of schedule, the deficit fell to 2.5 per cent, below three per cent (well down from the initial goal of 3.7 per cent), and the lowest level since 2000. More importantly, this reduction was achieved not only through ad hoc cuts—although the government applied severe cuts in public spending and investment—but also and largely through structural reforms and a sharp increase in tax revenues, which was expected to make it easier to consolidate the gains.

Stronger economic growth resumed: in 2006, the economy grew by 1.3 per cent, and in 2007 by 1.8 per cent, the highest rate in six years. This sudden and unexpected turnaround since 2006 took many economists by surprise. Yet, this improvement proved to be short-lived. Growth was negative again in 2008 at—0.045 per cent, led by the effects of the global economic crisis, which forced the government to adopt new measures to address it (Royo 2011, pp. 9–14).

The Global Crisis Hits Portugal

When the global financial crisis hit Portugal, starting in the winter of 2008, the country was just coming out of a recent recession and still struggling with its fiscal problems (see Table 2). The intensity of the global crisis has been such that it has had devastating consequences for the country and has brought to the fore the imbalances and shortcomings of its economy. Indeed, by the time the global crisis hit its worst point (in 2009), Portugal was already encumbered with high debt (83.01 per cent of GDP) and deficit (9.05 per cent), weak competitiveness, high unemployment (10.63 per cent), stagnant growth (it contracted by 2.5 per cent), and low savings rates (7.5 per cent of GDP). Low savings rates are a better proxy to measure a country's ability to pay down its debt than the debt-to-GDP ratio. While Portugal avoided the property market collapse that Ireland and Spain faced, the country was still suffering from the poor management of public finances. For instance, public sector employees were still virtually guaranteed a job for life regardless of performance, which made it hard for young people to find jobs in the public sector or gain promotion.

The combined effect of increasing spending to address the effects of the crisis and failing tax revenue saw the budget deficit increase again from 3.8 per cent in 2008 to a record 9.4 per cent in 2010. Indeed, despite the structural reforms that Portugal had undertaken in recent years to reduce the size of the public sector, raise the retirement age, and change the social security system, the global crisis precipitated a serious new financial crisis. The increasing cost of financing the debt and the mounting difficulties in generating tax revenues (intensified by fears of a Greek debt default with a contagion effect on Portugal) made it difficult to meet the country's fiscal obligations, thus forcing the government to implement tough austerity measures (Relea 2010). However, despite these tough measures, the country could not avoid having its debt downgraded by ratings agencies (Fitch and Standard & Poor's) over doubts about its ability to cut its deficit, and over comparisons with Greece's situation. Consequently the country's borrowing costs soared and Portugal was forced to negotiate a €78 billion bailout package with the EU and IMF in May 2011. The Socialist government's failure to pass an austerity package in spring 2011, due to the joint opposition of all the opposition parties, led to its collapse and new elections on 5 June 2011, which ushered in a new Social Democratic Party (PSD) government led by Passos Coelho, and the implementation of unprecedented austerity measures to reduce the deficit to three per cent of GDP by 2013. In September 2011, the PSD government announced additional austerity measures to cut its budget deficit to almost zero in five years, promising the biggest cuts in government spending for more than 50 years (to 43.5 per cent of GDP), and introducing the country's harshest budget in living memory for 2012.

Paradoxically, the crisis may provide the impetus that had been lacking so far. The lack of credit and the recession will encourage savings and may help the country 'kick its debt habit'. Moreover, it has already intensified pressures for reforms and fiscal consolidation, which are now inescapable.

The Limits of Fiscal Convergence

Portugal's experience shows that EU and EMU membership, prior to the global financial crisis, did not lead to the implementation of the necessary structural reforms needed to address the country's historical fiscal imbalances, which were severely aggravated by the impact of the global financial crisis (Franco 2008). It illustrates the limits of convergence in light of any pressure in the sheltered environment of the EMU. Indeed, both the SGP and the Lisbon Strategy were insufficient to force the necessary reforms to address Portugal's historical problems of fiscal mismanagement.

In the run-up to the launch of the euro in 1999, the advantages of EMU membership were clear as Portugal benefited from low interest rates and low inflation, which encouraged economic growth. Portuguese businesses benefited, as well, from the increase in cross-border trade, lower transactions costs, and the stability of using a global currency (Atkins 2010). However, as in other Eurozone countries, membership may have offered too much protection by shielding the country against attacks (financial markets failed to distinguish among Eurozone countries). This allowed successive Portuguese governments to avoid the necessary reforms that would have fostered the country's productivity and competitiveness, while making it possible to postpone the necessary measures to reduce fiscal imbalances.[1] This eventually led to poor economic performance, particularly during the decade starting in 2000. This outcome, however, is a problem not of European institutions, but of national policies. Indeed, the process of economic reform has to be a domestic process led by domestic actors willing to carry it out. Structural reforms are crucial to remove the rigidities and bottlenecks behind the country's decade-long growth stagnation. Unfortunately, in Portugal (as in many other countries) 'reform' has become an abused term, which, more often than not, refers to cosmetic measures to maintain the status quo.

At the same time, it is important to stress that Portugal has had a growth problem; real GDP growth over the decade since it joined the euro has been the slowest in the

Eurozone, which reflects the country's loss of competitiveness. In order to improve its external competitiveness, Portugal still needs to implement structural reforms to change the existing economic model. It lagged well behind in the implementation of the Lisbon agenda (Tilford & Whyte 2010) and it is at the bottom of the ranking of competitiveness indicators within the euro area because of its geographical situation, technological disadvantages, and the high entry costs in new economic sectors (Mauro & Forster 2008, pp. 37–38). As indicated throughout this article, the lack of deep reforms has been a major factor in accounting for the lack of competitiveness and stagnant growth (Torres 2009, p. 58). How do we account for the insufficient fiscal and structural reforms in Portugal prior to the 2008 crisis?

Tracing the Role of Institutions, Ideas, and Interests

The experience of Portugal in the EU demonstrates the limits of external pressure and the ability of the *acquis communautaire* to force change. After decades of economic growth, Portugal has experienced an appalling performance for the last decade, struggled with the SGP, and violated its fiscal deficit rules. Institutions, ideas, and interests are crucial to understanding these outcomes.

Institutions, defined as the set of rules, formal and informal, that actors generally follow, are crucial to understanding the behaviour of economic actors and policy outcomes. From an institutionalist standpoint, there have been a number of factors that help to account for the limits of convergence.

First, there has been a problem of temporal inconsistency, which has been a key factor to account for the fiscal problems examined in the previous section. Indeed, in Portugal prior to 2005, political instability was the pattern; there were four prime ministers between 1995 and 2005 and the previous three prime ministers resigned before their terms were over, for various reasons. Furthermore, prior to 2005, the position of minister of finance was a revolving door, bringing instability to the economic policy portfolio, ministers often resigning in protest at their inability to reign over their colleagues and control fiscal policies and expenditures. Between 1990 and 2005, there were ten ministers of finance and on average they served less than two years in the position.

Indeed, the credibility of economic policies (and fiscal policies, in particular) was undermined in Portugal by the relative political instability that prevailed in Portugal before 2005. It is not surprising, therefore, that once there was some stability in the post (held by Fernando Teixeira dos Santos from 2005 to 2011, the longest tenure since 1990), the government was able to implement substantive reforms and pursue fiscal consolidation. The fact that PS had an absolute majority in parliament from 2005 until the September 2009 election was also an important factor in facilitating the implementation of reforms during most of that first term. Unfortunately, the 2009 election led to an expansionary and unsustainable policy stance in that year. Fiscal consolidation only really began again in 2011.

In addition, fiscal problems were compounded by the finance minister's limited powers over the budget. Indeed, according to a study of all the EU-15 finance ministers, it is the Portuguese minister who has the least control over the formulation, approval, and implementation of the budget (Hallerberg, Strauch & von Hagen 2004). In Portugal, the strategic dominance of the minister of finance was associated with strong majority governments between 1985 and 1995 and was maintained through 1998 to sustain the clear preference for credibility until the country had achieved qualification for the euro. Yet, between 1998 and 2002, the minority governments removed the responsibility for public administration from the Ministry of Finance to the office of the prime minister, thus weakening the strategic dominance of the Ministry of Finance and making it more difficult to resist the deficit bias (Macedo 2003a, pp. 190–191).

A third factor has been the fiscal constitution, which has exacerbated the deficit bias. The fiscal constitution includes the institutions enforcing the social contract and incorporates exchange rate regimes, monetary standards, and state revenues. It determines who has the power and under what procedures to legislate on tax issues. In Portugal, it has remained largely unchanged through the years due to vested interests of interest groups (see '*interests*' below). As noted by a former Portuguese finance minister, 'by itself, the euro cannot change the fiscal constitution. Different policy areas need specific reform efforts' (Macedo 2003a, p. 193; 2007). Portugal shows that institutional reforms require active policies from governments that are willing to pay the short-term political price for unpopular policies.

Furthermore, the establishment of semi-rigid institutional mechanisms (as Portugal tried to do with EMU membership in the 1990s) is not a viable solution to impose austerity on its own either. On the contrary, the credibility of monetary and economic authorities must be earned through the adequate management of existing discretionary powers. Portugal also showed that the reform of financial institutions does not necessarily bring about institutional changes in other areas (e.g. the labour market and fiscal policies).

In the end, Portugal's experience shows the crucial importance of an institutional design that generates incentives to develop and implement optimal policies. The problem of temporal inconsistency in policy development and implementation is a problem of institutional design and incentives (Macedo 2003a). Indeed, since Portugal joined the EU, the country's institutions have attempted to cope with the new demands from European policies in an increasingly complex context. There have been changes in the forms of governance driven by economic imperatives; socio-economic modernisation; internationalisation (e.g. EU networking, liberalisation of the economy); lack of convergence; decentralisation; economic globalisation and Europeanisation (e.g. new role for city regions); and new policy changes (e.g. addition of welfare responsibilities and new policy areas, rising demand, and falling political participation) that have led to de-statisation (for instance, in the decades following the country's accession to the EU the role of the state as regulator of the economy has been the subject of significant reforms that have sought, with limited success, to streamline it, decentralise it, and make it more responsive to citizens' needs). Yet, while there has been a shift to complex multilevel governance, the pattern has been that of path-dependent institutional evolution, and the state remains the leading actor.

Ideas, in the form of 'causal beliefs', have not been able to counter Portugal's history of 'fiscal misbehaviour'. Ideas define goals and strategies and they shape the understanding of political problems. Indeed, the national discourses that generate and legitimise change in policies remain distinct in Portugal and they still matter as primary sources of political behaviour. Some of this distinctiveness may be explained by sociological changes. One of the consequences of combined processes of Europeanisation and modernisation has been what sociologists refer to as the increasingly flexible attitudes of Portuguese citizens and groups towards norms and social relations as a whole, and the crisis of great ideologies. In the political field, this has been translated into new cleavages, values, and patterns of behaviour. In the past, to side with the left or the right defined patterns of behaviour and also affected individuals' ethics, religion, and way of life. Nowadays, there has been an internalisation of the value of 'tolerance' and options have become more diverse and pragmatic. The result has been the predominance of the "made to fit" over the "made to think", an "affirmation of new craftsmanship of ideas" (Ferreira de Almeida 1998, pp. 161–162). The polarity of social networks and lifestyles that was integral to the ideological divisions of the past has softened, and Portuguese citizens now manage symbols and ideas with much greater 'autonomy'.

Differences in national discourses extended to the EMU project itself. Indeed, part of the business community led by the CIP (Confederação da Indústria Portuguesa, the Portuguese Industry Confederation) and the ABP (Associação Portuguesa de Bancos, the Portuguese Bank Association), as well as the PCP (Partido Comunista Portigûes, the Portuguese Communist Party), the CGTP-IN [Confederação Geral dos Trabalhadores Portugueses, the General Confederation of Portuguese Workers), even the President's economic counsel, and many independents closer to the PS and members of its Eurosceptic wing, publicly criticised the convergence criteria in the early 1990s, because they considered them to be harmful to the real convergence process. One party, the CDS-PP (Centro Democrático Social-Partido Popular, the Centre Democratic Social-Popular Party) became anti-European. Even the actors more supportive of EMU membership, like AIP (Associação Industrial Portuguesa, the Portuguese Industrial Association) and the UGT (União Geral de Trabahaldores, the General Union of Workers), called attention to the possible negative effects of EMU membership on employment and growth (Torres 2007, pp. 104, 113; Torres & Fraga 2004, pp. 100–101). In other words, there has been no 'strong political cleavage on EU affairs in Portugal' and public opinion has no strong views on Europe (Torres & Fraga 2004, pp. 97–98).

In the absence of strong consensus on EU and EMU membership, it is not surprising that there has been even less consensus on the necessary policies to succeed in Europe. Therefore, in this context the sound public policy paradigm has never been dominant in Portugal and no major group or political party has strongly supported it. At a time when in other countries, like Germany or Spain, there was growing (and rare) agreement among the conservative and socialist parties regarding fiscal consolidation, as well as the need to hold firm on the application of restrictive fiscal policies and the achievement of budgetary surpluses,[2] this did not happen in Portugal. Governments tried to spread the sound public finance paradigm, but political elites lacked political incentives and/or sufficient external pressures to enforce it.

Indeed, there is widespread consensus that Portugal's biggest mistake was its 'chronic fiscal misbehaviour' (Wolf 2008). Vítor Constancio, Governor of the Bank of Portugal, has acknowledged that 'when in 2001 we had these big shocks to growth, tax revenues dropped and suddenly we were in a situation of an excessive deficit ... The sudden emergence of budget problems led to a big revision of expectations about the future' (Atkins 2008). According to Constancio, one of the main lessons from Portugal's experience is that 'countries used previously to high inflation and high interest rates are likely to experience an explosion in consumer spending and borrowing' upon joining a monetary union. This spurt will make a downturn inevitable, particularly in cases such as Portugal, which are vulnerable to higher oil prices and increasing competition from developing countries like India and China. In Portugal, the strong demand stemmed from the sharp fall in interest rates and was further fuelled by expansive fiscal policies. Demand, however, was not followed by a parallel increase in supply, as it was hindered by low productivity growth, which led to a significant increase in imports and high external deficits and debts. External indebtedness, in turn, has led to lower available income domestically.

Finally, the role of *interests* is also essential to understand the fiscal outcomes described in the previous section. Interest groups attempt to influence policy. However, until the global crisis hit Portugal in 2008 and the country faced the risk of default, there was limited change in domestic incentives or external pressures, and the supporters of sound fiscal policies, like the Bank of Portugal and the Ministry of Finance, were not sufficiently empowered. On the contrary, entrenched interest groups, like the civil servants or the unions, including the teachers' unions, were able to exercise effective veto power over any attempt to impose fiscal discipline. Workers' rights are enshrined in the Constitution, one of the legacies of the revolutionary transition to democracy. The Constitution safeguards job security (Article 53), the right to work (Article 58), workers' rights (Article 59), and trade union rights (Articles 55–57). This situation has made any attempt at reforms very problematic for any government, and has further empowered the interest groups that have resisted reforms and supported fiscal profligacy.

Another manifestation of institutional immobility, as noted before, has been the rigidity of the fiscal constitution, which prevented the balancing of political responsiveness and economic interdependence. This is explained, as Jorge Braga de Macedo (2003a, pp. 186–187) points out, by the entrenched and vested interest of groups and the lack of cooperation among them:

> public and private interest groups seeking transfers from the state and thereby holding on to the tax base took advantage of European structural funds. The whole

> process reinforced some of the interests vested in state intervention ... In fact the resistance of public and private interest groups to broadening the tax base or to tightening the link between taxpayers and transfer recipients has been so remarkable that the fiscal constitution could be described as 'get out of my tax!'

Hence, public administration remained largely incapable of reforming itself until the mid-2000s in areas such as justice, social welfare, education, and home affairs. In the end, the competitive forces unleashed by EMU membership were not sufficient to bring about the public sector reform that had been expected for decades (Macedo 2003b, pp. 88–89). In sum, the unwillingness of powerful interest groups to cooperate raised the political transaction costs of inter-temporal cooperation, and made it very difficult to implement reforms and change the fiscal constitution, which thus remained largely unchanged.

While political, civic, and social participation increased considerably following the establishment of democracy, some forms of civic and social participation have been in recession. Indeed, a marked decline can be detected, not only at the level of trade unions and professional associations, but at the level of other social and cultural associations (Barreto 2003). Attempts to break with the country's paternalistic and corporatist past, such as Compromisso Portugal, an initiative that mobilised more than 300 of the country's top businesspeople, economists, and academics to transform Portugal, have not been very successful.[3] A strategy of reforms thus demands a reactivation of civil society (Macedo 2007, pp. 25–26).

In sum, ideas, interests, and institutions help explain why the opportunity for sustained structural reform and improvement in fiscal discipline afforded by the euro was largely lost, which made Portugal a victim of the 'euro holdup'. Table 3 summarises these findings.

Conclusion: Lessons from Portugal

Since Portugal became a founding member of the EMU, monetary policies have no longer been in the hands of its national governments. Yet, differences in fiscal policies, within the constraints imposed by the SGP, have played a central role in economic performance within the EMU (European Commission 2008). It is now widely accepted that increases in government consumption adversely affect long-term growth, and also that while fiscal consolidation may have short-term costs in terms of activity, they can be minimised if consolidation is credible by implementing consistent decisions that deliver solid results.

The Portuguese economy experienced a boom in the second half of the 1990s, boosted by the considerable fall in interest rates, when nominal short-term interest rates converged to those set by the ECB. This growth, however, required a concomitant prudent fiscal policy, which in the case of Portugal did not take place. On the contrary, the cyclically adjusted primary balance fell from 1.2 per cent of GDP in 1994–96 to −0.6 per cent in 1999–2001. Furthermore, the elimination of the exchange rate risk and the easing of constraints in regard to external financing allowed for a sharp

Table 3 A Summary of the main findings

Policy domain	Independent variable: EU	Intervening variable 1: institutions	Intervening variable 2: interests	Intervening variable 3: Ideas	Dependent variable: domestic outcome
Fiscal policy	Prior to 1999: TEU, fiscal convergence criteria	Domestic institutional change (1990s onwards)	Limited change in domestic political incentives or external pressure (1990s onwards)	Limited change of fiscal policy paradigm domestically (1990s onwards)	Accommodation
	After 1999: SGP	Limit: institutionalisation of 'chronic fiscal misbehaviour'	Insufficient empowerment of sound fiscal policy supporters (i.e. Bank of Portugal and Ministry of Finance)	Spread of the sound public finance paradigm, but fiscal and political elites lacked incentives or external pressures to enforce it	Fiscal adjustment in the run-up to EMU (1999); looser policy afterwards until 2005; severe fiscal adjustment after 2008 Opening of protocol for violation of SGP

increase of indebtedness of households and financial enterprises in the late 1990s (Torres 2009, p. 67).

At the same time, the combination of expansionary fiscal policies and insufficient structural reforms did not prepare the country for the economic downturn that started in 2000. Consequently, Portugal performed poorly in the following decade. There were many causes for this performance, including increasing competition for exports with emerging economies; record levels of public and private indebtedness; rigid nominal wages and energy price shocks. However, this paper argues that one of the fundamental reasons for the poor performance of the Portuguese economy prior to the current crisis (2008 onwards) was the lack of fiscal discipline and the failure of ad hoc measures to control the deficit. This development can be traced to the role of institutions, ideas, and interests.

The Portuguese experience shows that countries wishing to join the Eurozone need to have a 'comfortable budget position because that will give for manoeuvre once inside' (Atkins 2008). Not surprisingly, among the countries that qualified for EU cohesion funds, the ones that did better in the decade prior to the global financial crisis were those which maintained fiscal discipline: Ireland and Spain. Both countries maintained a budget surplus or reduced their budget deficits to comply with the SGP, while reducing their total expenditures vis-à-vis GDP.

Portugal's experience within the EMU also shows that lower interest rates and the loosening of credit is likely to lead to a credit boom, driven by potentially over-optimistic expectations of future permanent income. In turn, this may increase housing demand and household indebtedness and lead to overestimates of potential output and to expansionary fiscal policies (Abreu 2006, p. 5). The boom will also lead to higher wage increases, caused by the tightening of the labour market, higher inflation, and losses in external competitiveness, together with a shift from the tradable to the non-tradable sector of the economy, which will have a negative impact on productivity.

In order to avoid these risks, countries should tighten budgetary policies in the event of a boom in demand and/or strong credit expansion. At the same time, they should guard against potential overestimation of GDP, and measure carefully the weight of consumption on GDP, because they may inflate revenues in the short term and create an unrealistic perception of the budgetary accounts. Furthermore, to avoid unsustainable external imbalances, countries should also carry out the necessary structural reforms to increase flexibility and productivity in order to allow their productive sectors to respond to the increasing demand and to ensure that their economies can withstand the pressures of membership. They should also set wages based on Eurozone conditions to ensure wage moderation, and not unrealistic domestic expectations (Abreu 2006, pp. 5–6). In addition, new EMU members should take the opportunity presented by the boom to move into higher value-added and faster-growth sectors and towards a more outward-oriented production structure. Finally, the current global crisis has illustrated the need for tight financial supervision to avoid excessive lending and misallocation of resources.

Notes

[1] Other analysts have blamed the lack of reforms on the country's conciliatory approach and its tendency to back away from radical solutions and to solve problems only partially (Wise 2010).

[2] The balanced budget objective had been established by law in Spain, and in Germany a coalition government had amended the German Basic Law to include it.

[3] They drafted proposals to create pressure for change and force a radical shift in government policies, including a proposal to limit public expenditure to 40 per cent of GDP from 2008.

References

Abreu, O. (2006) 'Portugal's boom and bust: lessons for euro newcomers', *ECFIN Country Focus*, vol. 3, no. 16http://ec.europa.eu/economy_finance/publications/publication1274_en.pdf

Atkins, R. (2008) 'Concerns about divergence "overlook ability to change"', *Financial Times*, 16 May.

Atkins, R. (2010) 'The economy: the gain, then the pain, of life in Euroland", *Financial Times*, 13 July.

Balkir, C., Bolukbasi, H. T. & Ertugal, E. (2013) 'Europeanisation and dynamics of continuity and change in domestic political economies in the "Southern Periphery"', *South European Society and Politics*, vol. 18, no. 2, pp. 121–137.

Barreto, A. (2003) 'Social Change in Portugal: 1960–2000', in *Contemporary Portugal*, ed. A. Costa Pinto, New York, Columbia University Press, pp. 159–181.

Barros, P. P. & Garoupa, N. (1996) 'Portugal–European Union convergence: some evidence', *European Journal of Political Economy*, vol. 12, no. 3, pp. 545–553.

EU (2002) 'Council recommendation with a view to bringing an end to the situation of an excessive government deficit in Portugal – application of Article 104(7) of the Treaty establishing the European Community', available online at: http://ec.europa.eu/economy_finance/economic_governance/sgp/pdf/30_edps/104-07_council/2002-11-05_pt_104-7_council_en.pdf

EU (2005) 'Council recommendation with a view to bringing an end to the situation of an excessive government deficit in Portugal', available online at: http://ec.europa.eu/economy_finance/economic_governance/sgp/pdf/30_edps/104-07_council/2005-09-20_pt_104-7_council_en.pdf

European Commission (2008) 'Emu@10: successes and challenges after 10 year of Economic and Monetary Union', available online at: http://ec.europa.eu/economy_finance/emu10/emu10report_en.pdf

Ferreira de Almeida, J. (1998) 'Society and Values', in *Modern Portugal*, ed. A. Costa Pinto, SPOSS, Palo Alto, CA, pp. 146–161.

Franco, F. (ed.) (2008) *Challenges for the Portuguese Economy*, Instituto Ciencias Sociais, Lisbon.

Hallerberg, M., Strauch, R. & von Hagen, J. (2004) 'The design of fiscal rules and forms of governance in European Union countries', ECB Working Paper, no. 419.

IMF (2009) *World Economic Outlook*, Washington.

Lains, P. (2003) 'Catching up to the European core: Portuguese economic growth, 1910–1990'. Instituto de Ciências Sociais Universidade de Lisboa, Working Paper 1–03, February.

Lobo, M. C. & Lains, P. (eds) (2007) *Em Nome da Europa. Portugal em Mudança, 1986–2006*, Principia, Cascais.

Loureiro, J. (ed.) (1995) *Portugal e a integração monetária europeia*, Universidade do Porto Editora, Porto.

de Macedo, J. B. (2003a) 'Portugal's European integration: the good student with a bad fiscal institution', in *Spain and Portugal in the European Union: The First Fifteen Years*, eds S. Royo & P. Manuel, Frank Cass, Portland, pp. 162–193.

de Macedo, J. B. (2003b) 'Portugal's European integration: the limits of external pressure', in *Portugal: Strategic Options in a European Context*, eds F. Monteiro, J. A. Tavares, M. Glatzer & Angelo Cardoso, Lexington Books, Lanham, MD, pp. 61–97.

de Macedo, J. B. (2007) 'A Mudança do Regime Cambial Português: Um Balanço 15 anos Depois de Maastricht', *UNL WP*, no. 502.

Mauro, F. & Forster, K. (2008) *Globalisation and the Competitiveness of the Euro Area*, ECB, Frankfurt.

OECD (1999, 2001, 2006) *OECD Economic Surveys: Portugal*, Paris.

Relea, F. (2010) 'Portugal se suma al ajuste con una subida general de impuestos', *El Pais*, 14 May.

Royo, S. (2003) 'The 2004 enlargement: Iberian lessons for post-communist Europe', in *Spain and Portugal in the European Union: The First Fifteen Years*, eds S. Royo & P. Manuel, Frank Cass, Portland, pp. 287–313.

Royo, S. (2004) 'From authoritarianism to the European Union: the Europeanization of Portugal', *Mediterranean Quarterly*, vol. 15, no. 3, pp. 95–129.

Royo, S. (2011) *Portugal in the Twenty First Century*, Lexington, New York.

Royo, S. & Manuel, P. C. (2003) *Spain and Portugal in the European Union: The First Fifteen Years*, Frank Cass, Portland.

Tilford, S. & Whyte, P. (2010) *The Lisbon Scorecard X. The Road to 2020*, Centre for European Reform, Brussels.

Torres, F. (2007) 'A Convergência para a Uniáo Económica e Monetária', in *Em Nome da Europa. Portugal em Mudança, 1986–2006*, eds M. C. Lobo & P. Lains, Principia, Cascais, pp. 97–120.

Torres, F. (2009) 'Back to external pressure: policy responses to the financial crisis in Portugal', *South European Society and Politics*, vol. 14, no. 1, pp. 55–70.

Torres, F. & Fraga, A. (2004) 'What "Europe"? Portugal's reactive adaptation to European institutional changes', *South European Society & Politics*, vol. 9, no. 1, pp. 97–120.

Wise, P. (2010) 'Aversion to social unrest is a double-edged sword', *Financial Times*, 14 July, p. 2 (special section on Portugal)

Wolf, M. (2008) 'Struggling to tackle bad fiscal behaviour', *Financial Times*, 8 April.

Spain's Catch up with the EU Core: The Implausible Quest of a 'Flying Pig'?

Luis Moreno

In contemporary times, Spain offers a good example of a very compressed transition to post-industrial socioeconomic structures, passing from peripheral to core status within the European Union (EU) and the international economic order. The present article reviews developments and outcomes in Spain since 2000 by paying attention to the impact of the EU on Spain's welfare political economy. The adoption of EU recommendations in labour activation policies and the increase in female participation in the formal labour market are singled out as highly relevant for policy change. The explanatory account of welfare development focuses on continuity and change by considering the analytical constellation of ideas, interests and institutions.

The impact of Europe and Europeanisation on Spain's domestic political economy and public polices has been paramount. Decades of international isolation and ideological and economic autarchy led the Spaniards to believe that complete modernity was unattainable. Becoming a developed European country was regarded as a necessary condition for political and institutional modernisation. For most of the twentieth century, Europe had been perceived as everything that Spain was not. Spaniards are among the most optimistic about the future of the European Union (EU).[1]

After a long hyper-centralist dictatorship (1939–75), a peaceful transition to democracy (1975–79) and an active involvement in Europe after its accession to the European Economic Community (EEC) (1986), Spain has undergone deep and far-reaching social transformations. A cross-party and cross-sectional common aspiration to become a core European country was put into motion. Such a political drive meant striving for a democratic status away from the shameful memories of a tawdry despotic dictatorship. Culturally, the desire to return to mother Europe was articulated to reverse the anti-European sentiment of 'let them invent!'[2]

Europeanisation has been particularly meaningful given the Spanish historical context, something that has involved incorporating objectives, indicators and procedures defined by European institutions. There has also been a tendency to look to Europe in order to legitimate or de-legitimate certain policies or political proposals. The general framework of analysis of this article concerns the influence of the EU on Spain's welfare political economy through the examination of changes in the constellation of ideas, interests and institutions. The main area of observation relates to the development of the welfare state. Following the framework set out by Balkir, Bolukbasi and Ertugal (2013), this article also considers the extent to which the ideas promoted by the EU (labour activation) have contributed to far-reaching transformations in the particular domain of female employment.

The consolidation in contemporary times of a fully fledged European welfare state can be considered to be the main challenge Spain has had to accomplish in order to rub shoulders with other large EU member states. The examination in this article of reforms in the social policy area seeks to contrast matrices of the recent past concerning Spain's 'catch-up' with EU core countries (Moreno 2009). As a member of the so-called 'Southern European Periphery' (Featherstone & Kazamias 2001), Spain has been regarded as part of the 'Achilles heel' in the European integration project (Verney 2009). Contrary to this view, the fact that Spain was successful in improving economic and welfare developments during 2000–10 can provide a useful case in point to other new-entry EU countries.

Spain's welfare has come close to European medium figures in socioeconomic indicators in parallel with a general convergence of social spending in all EU countries (Adelantado & Calderón 2006). Since 1986, and according to Eurostat time-series data, public social spending—the simplest economic indicator—has grown at a faster pace than in any other EU member state. As in other European countries, the effects of the 2007 global financial crisis have cast doubts on whether Spain can sustain its previous expansion of welfare expenditure. The broadening of social entitlements as a result of welfare policy innovation in the 2000s seems to have stopped. Shifts in the general direction of the country's political economy concerning the regulation of the labour market and the 'pay-as-you-go' pension system follow similar patterns of reforms as in other matured European welfare systems. All these developments seem to foretell a phase of further welfare recasting in line with a closer coordination and economic fine-tuning with other EU member states.

In the second section of this article, a review of Spain's economic performance aims to illustrate the catching-up effort deployed by Spanish society in recent decades. It is contended that the case of Spain validates general 'benchmarking' claims for the achievement of a level of convergent economic development in the EU. Subsequently, the characterisation of the Spanish welfare state as a *via media* seeks to identify the main sets of values, institutional procedures and power arrangements with relation to other European welfare regimes. The very nature of policy arrangements and transformations regarding Spain's welfare reflect the aspiration to adapt a pre-democratic system of social protection to a syncretic version of the various types of European welfare states.

The third section reports the outcomes of this continuity and change. Under the auspices of the EU and other international institutions such as the Organisation for Economic Cooperation and Development (OECD), the paradigm of labour activation has been fully embraced by Spanish authorities. As a result of this, the quantum-leap increase in the participation of women in the formal labour market is singled out as the great transformation in Spanish society during 2000–10. A brief examination of the evolution of the labour market helps explain the degree of Europeanisation in a policy area with important implications for the future evolution of the Bismarckian component of the Spanish welfare state (Guillén 2010). Outcomes concerning welfare and social policy are summarised in Table 1.

The fourth section discusses the processes of continuity and change by paying attention to the interaction of 'ideas', 'interests' and 'institutions' at both supranational (global and EU) and domestic levels in the main areas of analysis. A further look at the international situation, after the 2007 financial crisis, is carried out in order to advance future scenarios. Concluding remarks emphasise the crucial impact that Europe will continue to have in a 'pro-EU' country that has greatly counted on European institutions since its accession to the EEC in 1986.

EU, the Quest to Catch up and Welfare Development

At the time of the approval of the 1978 Constitution, Europe appeared to the Spanish democratic forces to be the 'point of arrival' the country needed to aim for. Europe had become a 'master symbol' (Turner 1997), together with the semiotic meanings of 'civilisation' and 'modernisation' (Moreno & Serrano-Pascual 2011). Spain's main political and social actors had already internalised EEC inputs and practices as the general framework of reference and the institutional source of 'good practice' to comply with. Ideologically, the appeal to Europe had been profusely used by political, social and economic actors as an important rhetorical recourse to convey their interests and demand social justice and/or economic prosperity.

Spain's aspiration to catch up with core European countries implied the formidable material challenge of making up for lost time. Since 1986, Spain's economic growth has accelerated further in order for it to join a select group of the world's large economies. According to the International Monetary Fund (IMF) and World Bank datasets, Spain ranked twelfth in the list of countries by total gross domestic product (GDP) in 2010. Since 2008, Spain has participated in the meetings of the G-20 group of major economies.

Evidence has lent no support to the 'social dumping' explanation for Spain's economic achievements (Guillén & Matsaganis 2000). If anything, Spain offers a good example of a pattern of 'leapfrogging', or a very compressed transition from pre-industrial to post-industrial socioeconomic structures (Espina 2007; Ferrera 2007).

From the end of World War II to 2009, the per capita income in purchasing power parity of the Spaniards went from 49.5 per cent to 95.2 per cent in relation to the EU-15 average. The corresponding figure for EU-27 was 103 per cent (González-Temprano 2003; Moreno 2004; Eurostat).

In the reference period of 1945–2009, Spain passed from peripheral to core status within the international economic order. Since the 1960s, the country has followed a pattern of 'mixed market economy', a variant of the 'coordinated mixed economy' variety of contemporary capitalism (Hall & Soskice 2001). Spain, together with other Mediterranean market economies (Italy, Portugal and Greece), is in a cluster that incorporates market, non-market and mixed forms of economic coordination (Amable 2003; Royo 2008).[3] This categorisation is in line with the polyvalent nature of their welfare systems: at times Bismarckian or liberal, at times even social-democratic (Moreno 2008).

On the initiative of some influential Anglo-Saxon media opinion leaders (e.g. *Financial Times, The Economist*, BBC, *Wall Street Journal*), it has been argued that the economies of the Mediterranean countries grouped under the acronym PIGS (Portugal, Italy, Greece and Spain) were unable to perform economically as successfully as other European states in Central and Northern Europe. This inability was to render those countries hopeless after the crisis triggered by the sub-prime mortgage failure in the US housing market in 2007 and the consequential global financial meltdown. In caustic words, the task for the PIGS countries was impossible to achieve or one that, following the British saying, [4] would only be accomplished 'when pigs fly'.

A distinctive indicator characterising a PIGS country was said to be their high level of external debt and sovereign public debt. This claim is controversial in light of the existing evidence. According to Eurostat figures, the disparities among the PIGS countries concerning public debt as a percentage of GDP were wide at the end of 2009: Italy, 116 per cent; Greece, 115 per cent; Portugal, 77 per cent; and Spain, 53 per cent. Other large EU countries had similar needs for public borrowing, if not higher ones, compared with Spain: Germany, 73 per cent; France, 78 per cent; and the UK, 68 per cent.[5]

All things considered, Spain's economic performance since the transition to democracy in the late 1970s validates the general claim that Europeanisation has acted as a general benchmark for achieving a closer convergence at a faster pace compared with longstanding EU member states (Risse, Cowles & Caporaso 2001). The financial assistance provided by EU structural and cohesion funds has been an additional incentive to catch up. As a result, Spain has been highly successful in articulating the overriding desire to reach an economic level similar to that of other large EU countries. Spain, with a population of 45 million and a GDP per capita that was 103 per cent of the EU27 average in 2010, compared favourably with Germany (82 million, GDP per capita 116 per cent), France (64 million, GDP per capita 108 per cent), the UK (61 million, GDP per capita 112 per cent) and Italy (60 million, GDP per capita 104 per cent) (Eurostat).

During its phase of expansion (1975–95), the Spanish welfare state witnessed a sharp increase in social spending on social insurance benefits and a widening of public health coverage. By the early 1990s, Spain's welfare development had already appeared to be a *via media* between the Bismarckian Continental and liberal Anglo-Saxon worlds of welfare capitalism (Esping-Andersen 1990; 1999; Moreno 2001), and it also incorporated inputs and traits of the Nordic welfare typology (Moreno & Sarasa 1992; Moreno 2008). Later, while Spain became more liberal in its macroeconomic policies, social policymaking followed a pattern of generalisation and universalisation of welfare entitlements and provisions (Rodríguez-Cabrero 2004). As a consequence, there has gradually been a detachment from the Bismarckian principle of income maintenance[6] in parallel with an expansion of the social assistance realm financed by general taxation. Furthermore, the welfare state enjoys a high level of legitimacy and public support (Arriba, Calzada & del Pino 2006).

As a Mediterranean country, Spain belongs to the Southern European welfare typology. Social-demographic trends, institutional peculiarities, political resources, socioeconomic backgrounds, patterns of public policy and value systems are rather similar in southern EU states (Sarasa & Moreno 1995; Ferrera 1996; Moreno 2006).[7] South European welfare is shaped in a differential manner from other regimes by the role played by the family and its interpenetration in all areas of welfare production and distribution, particularly as regards income and services. The self-perception of different needs and lifestyles conditions the strategic configurations of interests by actors and advocacy coalitions. In the Western world, there are countries where families and family ties are relatively strong, whereas in others they are weak. Central and Northern Europe, together with the US, have been characterised by weak family links, and the Mediterranean region by strong family ties. According to this view, differences have deep historical roots and they are not diminishing in contemporary times in any fundamental way (Reher 1998; Naldini 2003). However, recent developments have brought into question some of these familistic assumptions. There have been increases in the rates of informal cohabitation, out-of-wedlock births, divorce and single parenthood in line with the situation in other European countries. These developments require further analysis in the light of recent empirical evidence (Iglesias et al. 2010; Marí-Klose et al. 2010).

The social protection provided by the Spanish welfare state is relatively extensive in coverage (health, pensions, unemployment protection and, to a lesser degree, personal services), but with a relatively low protection intensity. There is a noticeable participation of the market and a growing Third Sector involvement, which in many cases implies shifting the costs of welfare provision to individuals and households. In summary, the Spanish welfare state can be regarded as an incomplete universal system, of an institutionally mixed nature, relatively fragmented in several levels of social protection and with spending levels close to the EU-27 average. The financial effects of the financial crisis have brought about a sharp increase in social spending, particularly on unemployment benefits, coupled with a fall and subsequent stagnation of GDP growth (Adelantado 2000; González-Temprano 2003; Moreno & Rodríguez-Cabrero 2007; Navarro 2009; Rodríguez-Cabrero 2010).

Continuity and Change in Welfare Outcomes

Welfare state studies have paid little attention to EU inputs. The EU has been generally absent because, apparently, it has seemed not to be part of the welfare state 'problem', because it has lacked power and resources and because it has been incompetent and unable to impose any uniform solution to reforming national welfare states. If it is true that the dimensions of social protection, such as the health care system or family policies, show a degree of dissimilarity between EU countries, the same cannot be said of the old age pension or employment policies, where common approaches have been progressively adopted by most member states facing reforms with a similar range of options and little degree of variance. The undisputed moral authority of 'Europe' was reinforced, as with the European Employment Strategy, despite the lack of a tradition for labour activation in some EU countries (Graziano 2009). Other areas that seem to be 'peripheral' in the development of the welfare state, such as equal opportunities, health and safety regulations or poverty and social inclusion programmes, have been progressively harmonised with the initiatives proposed by European institutions by putting into practice the Open Method of Coordination (OMC) (Moreno & Palier 2005).

Welfare is said to be a policy domain of the sovereign competence of the member states. EU inputs were nevertheless important in Spain during 2000–10. Table 1 summarises the outcomes in terms of continuity and change according to a combination of classifications already available in the literature and discussed in the introduction to this monographic issue: Transformation, Accommodation, Absorption, Inertia and Retrenchment (Radaelli 2003; Börzel & Risse 2003; Bache 2008).

Among the outcomes summarised in Table 1, one deserves a special attention because of its knock-on effects in Spain's political economy: the increasing participation of Spanish women in the formal labour market. This development is of particular relevance because it cuts across all areas of welfare and thus it can be singled out as the most important factor in continuity and change during 2000–10. Spain championed the EU's strategy of activation, particularly as regards greater female participation in the formal labour market. If Europeanisation can be regarded as the most important exogenous factor in the increase of female activity rates, improvements in the levels of female education can be identified as the crucial endogenous variable.[8] The following analyses of the longer period 1976–2010 aim to provide the reader with a broad picture of the deep changes in Spain's labour market, in particular those concerning female participation.

Table 1 A summary of the main outcomes in welfare development (2000–10)

Policy domain	EU input	Domestic input	Category of outcomes	Degree of change
Education	Encouragement for permanent training and vocational education	Full management of educational system by Comunidades Autónomas (compulsory coverage 6–16 years)	Accommodation (EU inputs incorporated without modifications in essential features)	Medium
		Opening to private management Law on Education (2006)		
Health	Encouragement for financial sustainability	Full management of the health system by Comunidades Autónomas (universal coverage)	Accommodation (EU inputs incorporated without modifications in essential features)	Medium
		Opening to private management Law on Cohesion and Quality of the National Health System (2003)		
Income transfers	Encouragement for the cost containment of the pension system	Regional programmes of income support (IMI)	Accommodation (EU inputs incorporated without modifications in essential features)	Medium
	2000 Lisbon, 2002 Copenhagen and 2003 Nice (NAPIncls) (OMC)	National Action Plans for Social Inclusion (2001, 2003, 2005, 2006, 2008) Assistance policies for the closure of safety nets		
Social services and care	Encouragement of long-term care policies and family–work conciliation	Universalisation of long-term care (subjective right)	Transformation (new policies, practices and organisation)	High
		Measures for gender parity in the public sector Pre-schooling programmes by region		

(continued)

Table 1 – *Continued*

Policy domain	EU input	Domestic input	Category of outcomes	Degree of change
		Legislation on conciliation and equality (e.g. parental leave)		
Labour market	European Employment Strategy (OMC) Adoption of activation principles	National Action Plans for Employment (2000, 2001, 2002, 2003) National Reform Programmes (2005, 2006, 2008) Employment Laws 45/2002 and 56/2003 Law on Effective Male and Female Equality (2007) (positive discrimination for female employment) Politics of employability, flexibilisation and individualisation	Transformation (new policies, practices and organisation)	High

In 1977, Spain's female activity rate was lower than half that of their male counterparts. In 2010, Spain's female activity rate equalled the male employment rate. During the whole period 1976–2010, the female activity rate nearly trebled in the central ages of women's life cycle (25–49 years). This process has had far-reaching repercussions and has affected women at a stage in their life cycle when they confronted not only demanding job careers but also greater household involvement related to reproduction and childcare activities. In 2010, almost three out every four Spanish women aged 25–54 years were active in the formal labour market. Furthermore, and contrary to the patterns in Central and Northern Europe, Spanish women participated primarily in the labour market on a full-time basis,[9] something that made the reconciliation of domestic and paid work all the more difficult (Salido & Moreno 2009).

In fact, sorting out the apparent conflict between society's expectations of women's role as both mothers and active workers remains a crucial dilemma in familistic Spain. The challenge is both to increase labour productivity growth and to preserve social cohesion (Salido & Moreno 2007). Within families, the role of women has traditionally been pivotal, as they have often cared for children or older relatives at the expense of erratic careers or full withdrawal from the labour market. However, as the hyperactivity of cohorts of 'superwomen'[10] has gradually vanished, there is a serious vacuum emerging in welfare provision that will have enduring effects on social care. The increasing externalisation of personal care services traditionally provided by the family has taken a particular turn in Spain, as it has in other South European countries. Such services are often purchased from immigrants at low cost (sometimes in the underground economy), particularly as regards care for the elderly (Da Roit, González-Ferrer & Moreno-Fuentes 2008; Moreno-Fuentes & Bruquetas-Callejo 2011). Concerning childcare, a mixed family strategy has developed by means of the greater use of formal and informal crèches as well as extracurricular activities for schoolchildren (Marí-Klose et al. 2010). These processes grew increasingly widespread during 2000–10, paralleling the preferences of Southern European neighbours for adopting similar contingent solutions.

EU inputs for the various governmental reforms affecting the Spanish labour market resulted in a high degree of change. Social services and care was the other policy domain in which both EU and domestic impacts induced a high degree of change during 2000–10. EU institutions pointed out the need for member states to secure long-term care policies and family–work conciliation, two areas closely linked to the prioritisation of labour activation. The Law for the Effective Equality between Women and Men (Ley 3/2007 para la Igualdad Efectiva entre Mujeres y Hombres) incorporated measures of positive discrimination in order to avoid discrimination between men and women in the labour market. It also extended parental and family leave. Regional governments were also active in providing pre-schooling programmes for children, as the proportion of children under three years in childcare centres (both public and private) increased from five per cent in 2000 to 37.5 per cent in 2008 (OECD 2011).

The most important policy outcome in Spain regarding care and social services was the legislative approval of the universalisation of long-term care. The Law on Dependency and Long-Term Care (Ley 39/2006 de Promoción de la Autonomía Personal y Atención a las Personas en Situación de Dependencia) established a universal and legally enforceable entitlement for care, not only for the frail, but also for all citizens who lack personal autonomy. The Law created a 'dependency system' (Sistema Nacional de Dependencia) that provides services to dependent citizens (day care, household help or residential homes) and benefits to main care providers. However, the future development of the 'dependency system' for long-term care seems to be uncertain because of the extra financing required from both central and regional governments (Marbán 2009).

Concerning income transfer, EU policy recommendations insisted on the adoption of further measures of cost containment by member states in order to secure financial viability. In the case of Spain, the public contributory system ('pay-as-you-go') did not face the kind of sustainability problem found in other Mediterranean countries, as happened with the 'generous' pension provisions in Greece and Italy (Ramos & del Pino 2009). But Spain was facing rising costs for the provision of income support, mainly for jobless people. Taking into consideration all contributory benefits and those others provided by the social assistance financed by general taxation, safety net programmes allowed 4.5 million beneficiaries to receive income support (around ten per cent of the total population) (Arriba 2010).[11]

Health and education areas accommodated policies based on the general EU recommendations for encouraging permanent training and vocational education and for securing the financial stability of both systems, which are decentralised and managed by the regions (Comunidades Autónomas). State-wide legislation on territorial cohesion was passed in 2003 so that financial inefficiencies in the National Health System could be avoided. Once again, the EU's warnings on cost containment were very present in political debates at the regional level to reduce the level of sub-national public borrowing, something that worsened with the unleashing of the 2007 crisis (Moreno-Fuentes 2009).

Unpacking Change: The Role of Ideas, Interests and Institutions (2000–10)

The changes in outcomes during 2000–10 were mainly induced by the generally accepted 'benchmarking' idea that Spain's policies ought to be in line with those promoted by EU institutions. Following the analytical framework put forward in the introductory chapter of this volume relevant transformations in Spain's political economy can be explained using the triad of 'ideas', 'interests' and 'institutions' (Heclo 1993; Hall 1997; Palier & Surel 2005; Bache 2008; Blyth 2009; Jenson & Mérand 2010). The purpose of this section is to identify not only the interaction between the supranational (global and EU) and domestic levels, but also the 'co-determination' among these three 'I's in order to make sense of paradigm shifts and policy changes. Analytical explanations and interpretations have adopted the following criteria: (a) relevance to welfare state development; (b) expected impacts on future developments; and (c) parsimony and general explanatory power. Modifications to these ideas are thus related to institutional processes and intervening interests in the process of continuity and change concerning Spain's welfare political economy.

Paradigm Shifts: Neoliberalism and Labour Activation

In the 1980s, neoliberal ideas first gained prominence in the Anglo-Saxon world (Australia, Canada, Ireland, New Zealand, the UK and the US). Subsequently, such ideas spread out gradually to other European countries and EU institutions. The whole process resulted in changes in programme design and policymaking based on the following tenets: (a) deregulated labour markets; (b) the individualisation of life-course expectations; (c) financial control of the productive economy; and (d) the unrestrictive movement of speculative capital (financial investments and derivatives).

Most advanced welfare democracies came to share the same strategic aims and an overriding concern for the maximisation of human capital in national markets in order to gain positions of comparative advantage in the global market (Jessop 1994). Anglo-American capitalism (Albert 1993) became not only synonymous with the liberal variant of contemporary capitalism but, most significantly, the very proponent for the 'canonical' political economic guidelines in First World countries. A paradigm shift occurred by which welfare arrangements correlated with changes in economic policies—most notably from Keynesianism to monetarism. Arguably, welfare development became a mere surrogate of economic ideas, interests and institutions (Moreno & Palier 2005).

The incorporation into Spain's political debate of the key concepts and proposals of EU institutions—mainly activation—turned a system of beliefs into assumptions, such as: (a) the alleged disincentive function of 'passive' social protection policies and (b) the proposals that the unemployed should become 'active' in order to avoid social exclusion. A certain epistemic consensus had been reached among academics and policymakers. As in other EU member states, the fight against unemployment was to be replaced by a fight against low employment rates (Salais 2006; Serrano-Pascual 2007). The trend in Spain to take onboard the principles of activation (individualisation, employment-centred schemes or contractual insertion) was reinforced in the employment reforms of 2002 (Law 45/2002). With the transformation of the political concept of security, unemployment protection was conceived more in line with an employee's own self-insurance and responsibility. The European Employment Strategy fitted well and reinforced the long-term traditions of labour activation in the Anglo-Saxon and Nordic member states (Jacobsson 2004). However, this strategy also had an impact on countries traditionally alien to these policy concepts and with different historical traditions, such as Spain (Moreno & Serrano-Pascual 2011).

The 2002 and 2003 labour reforms coincided with a new drive from EU institutions to encourage member states to comply with the promotion of active labour market policies, the extension of an entrepreneurial spirit, the flexibilisation of labour relations and the adaptation to new changing scenarios in the global economic order. With the internalisation of these normative views, the new interpretative framework aimed at establishing a linear causality between unemployment and tax revenue, unemployment rate and economic growth and unemployment benefits and activity rate. Not surprisingly, the introductory statement of the Spanish Employment Law (56/2003) reads, 'globalisation and the process of European integration [with] the co-ordination of EU's policies make it imperative to Spain'. Thus, the EU seemed to be the leader championing these changes vis-à-vis member states. The latter were happy to accept a secondary role and thus they intensified their blame avoidance devices (Guillén & Álvarez 2004).

Institutional Path Dependency and Policy Innovation

During the 1990s and 2000s, Spain's welfare avoided retrenchment so that its catch-up aspirations with Europe were maintained. During 2000–10, the single most important institutional outcome of the efforts to expand Spain's welfare state in line with those of other large EU countries was the approval of the 2006 Law for the Promotion of Autonomous Living and Help for Dependent Individuals (Ley de Promoción de la Autonomía Personal y Atención de las Personas Dependientes). The Law established a new subjective and universal right that entitled dependent persons to coverage for long-term care.

Path dependency and policy innovation can be seen as two sides of the same coin for welfare outcomes (Ebbinghaus 2005). In some instances, the intensity of change in Spain during recent decades has prevailed over institutional inertia. The modernisation of the Bismarckian social insurance system and the extension of those services and benefits funded by the general tax revenue have allowed for the extension of social rights (health, education, non-contributory pensions and new social services) vis-à-vis contributory entitlements. However, the Bismarckian component of the Spanish welfare state continued to play a decisive institutional role during 2000–10 because it carried the bulk of welfare expenditure (Rodríguez-Cabrero 2011).

The constitutional decentralisation of powers and competencies allowed the regions substantial autonomy to manage important domains such as education, health and social services. With the reforms implemented in 2000–10, contributory pensions and unemployment benefit systems remained state responsibilities, but other social policies and services continued to be run by Comunidades Autónomas. In matters of social assistance and services, the central layer of government can be regarded as playing a 'subsidiary' role compared with the regions (Arriba & Moreno 2005).

Other than the proximity rationale claimed by the regions as the criterion of efficiency and democracy in the provision of social policies, the 'home-rule-all-round' decentralisation process in Spain has spurred policy innovation by meso-governments. Most initiatives in regional welfare have been carried out by means of emulation and credit-claiming practices. As a result, innovations in the policy design, production and management of social services have encouraged policy learning and improvements by means of the imitation of regional best practices. The rationale was that no region wanted to be left behind in Spain's political life. Such a pattern of regional mobilisation resulted in de facto policy equalisation as well as an incentive to 'catch up' for those Spanish regions that traditionally lagged behind 'modernised' ones. However, some of them were seen to be spendthrift spenders that increased the level of public debt to unsustainable levels.

After the outbreak of the 2007 financial crisis, the trajectory of the expansion and innovation of Spain's welfare policy came to an end. The further implementation of the long-term and dependency legislation will test in the years to come not only the limits of welfare development in Spain but, most importantly, the shared rule capacity of the Estado de las Autonomías (central, regional, local) to meet the new challenges for multilevel governance.

Actors: The Battle of Ideas and Interests

Consensual politics have been crucial during Spain's main political developments since the death of Franco in 1975. Such a climate for social dialogue (*diálogo social*) was highly successful in the process of democratisation but it came under strain in 2000–10. Debates on the flexibilisation of industrial relations illustrate such a change.

With the outbreak of the global financial crisis in 2007, the discussion on labour market regulations intensified. A battle of ideas took place between epistemic communities of different orientations (Jessop 2004; Schmidt 2008). Illustrative of the growing role played by ideas and think-tanks in Spain was the confrontation between social scientists analysing the effects of the economic crisis on the Spanish labour market. During 2009–10, a group of economists (the G-100) claimed that the introduction of 'flexibilisation' measures was a necessary reform in Spain's labour relations. Claims made by this informal network of economists were widely amplified by large sections of the media favourable to both the flexibility and deregulation of the labour market in Spain. An alternative forum of 700 experts in labour relations (mainly economists, lawyers and sociologists) offered a distinctly different view. As the authority of such analyses is usually based upon the alleged legitimacy of 'rational and apolitical science', the debates between these networks centred on the very definition of and monopoly claims to 'scientificity'. But the technical prescriptions of an economic nature were challenged and they have increasingly become politicised in light of the financial turbulence provoked by the crisis.

Indeed, the concepts, methodologies and indicators disseminated by EU institutions have been of utmost importance in such epistemic debates as well as for the role played by the coalitions of actors and institutions involved in subsequent policymaking. As in other EU countries, the selection of the 'problems' requiring political action was the result of confrontations articulated ideologically by social actors that had the capacity to preserve their views or interests (Jørgensen 2002; del

Pino & Ramos 2009). In the case of 'pro-EU' views, there has been an extensive strategic use of Europe by Spanish social actors in order not only to legitimate their positions and claims but also to create hegemonic or influential positions in political debates. During 2000–10, references to Europe continued to be an important authoritative recourse in order to attain symbolic gains and thereby to articulate organised interests (Moreno & Serrano-Pascual 2011).

All things considered, the pro-EU stance shared by most representative political parties and organised interests in Spain (parties, trade unions, business organisations) has begun to show internal differences, particularly as regards policy options to overcome the effects of the 2007 financial crisis. Despite the fierce electoral competition, the consensus on major constitutional issues between the two main parliamentary parties (centre-right PP [Popular Party] and centre-left PSOE [Socialist Party]) was renewed in establishing spending limits on public borrowing. Such a decision needed a modification to the 1977 Constitution, which was finally implemented in 2011 without the consent of the rest of the parliamentary parties. Trade unions and business associations have also engaged in tough negotiations on industrial and labour reforms. In general terms, advocacy coalitions and interest groups have adopted a wait-and-see strategy on how the economic crisis in the Eurozone could be sorted out. Significantly enough, signs of discontent with the socioeconomic situation were already being voiced loudly in the streets and major squares of Spain. The *indignados* movement, which initiated in Madrid on 15 May 2011 and spread afterwards to other European and American cities, was a manifestation of such discontent that was voiced spontaneously outside mainstream ideas, interests and institutions.

Concluding Remarks

Prior to the 2007 financial crisis, Spain's economy had flown high and had successfully accomplished its longstanding goal of achieving status as a core European and world economy. Whether a PIGS country such as Spain can keep on 'flying' in the medium term remains doubtful. Much of this uncertainty is shared not only by fellow Mediterranean countries but also by other large EU economies. In fact, the very model of the post-1945 European welfare state, as we have known it until now, has become highly questioned by the ongoing realignments in the world economy and the shortcomings in EU governance mechanisms.

During the period analysed (2000–10), Spain's welfare political economy reformed in line with the country's aspirations to develop a mature welfare state like other large EU countries. To this end, reforms were implemented in all pillars of the welfare edifice (education, health, income transfers, social services and labour market). The most important transformation concerned the establishment of a national system for long-term care (according to the 2006 Law for the Promotion of Autonomous Living and Help for Dependent Individuals). The full implementation of this reform, due in 2015, will test the capacity of both central and regional governments for welfare recalibration.

Certainly, the effects of the ongoing economic crisis on Spain's welfare development have put further pressure on governmental decisions for the cost containment of social spending.[12] It remains to be seen how the needs of family and social care can be adjusted with the maintenance of a high female activity rate. As a familistic country, Spain is already facing the huge stumbling block of either favouring deeply seated cultural arrangements within households or promoting women's aspirations to be formally active.

Spain will continue to pay attention to developments in the EU as the main points of reference for its welfare political economy. In attempting to achieve EU welfare standards and economic indicators, the case of Spain can provide useful experiences for new and peripheral member states. The catch-up effort of recent decades was sustained until the outbreak of the financial crisis in 2007. Despite a lack of the further institutionalisation of the EU, the case of Spain still validates the general claims that 'benchmarking' and 'best practices' can induce socioeconomic convergence towards the middle.

Acknowledgments

The author is grateful to comments on an earlier version of this paper made by participants at the international workshop held at the Dokuz Eylul University, Izmir during 14–16 October 2010. I am also grateful to comments and data provided by José Adelantado, Ana Arriba, Eloísa del Pino, María Gómez-Garrido, Antonio González-Temprano, Ana Marta Guillén, Pau Marí-Klose, Francisco Javier Moreno-Fuentes, Olga Salido, Amparo Serrano-Pascual and Gregorio Rodríguez-Cabrero. Responsibility for interpretations remains solely with the author. This article was prepared during the workings of the research projects 'Welfare Attitudes in a Changing Europe' (European Science Foundation Eurocores/HumVib and MICIIN, CSO2008-02874-E/SOCI) and 'New Social Risks, Economic Crisis, and Mediterranean Welfare' (Spanish Ministry of Education, Mobility Programme, PR2010-0095).

Notes

[1] According to Eurobarometer figures, in autumn 2009 (no. 72) three out of every four Spaniards felt optimistic about the future of the EU compared with an average of two out of every three Europeans in EU-27. Among the six most populous countries in EU-27, Spain was the most 'optimistic' with 75 per cent, followed by Poland (74 per cent), Italy (69 per cent), Germany (68 per cent), France (58 per cent) and the UK (50 per cent). For the perception of the EU by political and economic elites in Spain, see Jerez-Mir, Real Dato and Vázquez-García (2010).

[2] This famous sentence was articulated by the Spanish philosopher Miguel de Unamuno in a longstanding dispute with his colleague, José Ortega y Gasset, on the issue of the 'Europeanisation of Spain' (or the Hispanisation of Europe). European 'practicality' was to be confronted with Spanish 'spirituality'. Later, this expression has often been used to criticise the lack of scientific interest in Spain.

[3] Using data on France and Italy, it has been contended that there is no such consistent distinction between Continental and Mediterranean market economies (Geffen & Kenyon 2006). For much of their political economic arrangements, France and Italy could well qualify as Continental European countries of a 'genuine' Bismarckian type. This could apply, at least partially, to other Southern European countries. However, the degree of internal variation within the PIGS countries does not reach that within the group of Continental European

countries. Other studies grouping all four Southern European countries clearly confirm that Greece, Italy, Portugal and Spain cluster robustly in a distinctive group (Vasconcelos-Ferreira & Figueiredo 2005).

[4] According to a traditional Scottish proverb (first written in 1586), if 'pigs fly in the air with their tails forward, flying backwards would seem a small extra feat'.

[5] A more comprehensive picture of the general level of indebtedness must also take into account private borrowing. It comes as no surprise that countries such as Spain, with a total external debt of around 140 per cent, are expected to face hard times during the 2010s along the lines of other core European countries. At the end of 2010, the figures of total indebtedness (as a percentage of GDP) were of a similar range, if not higher, in France (130 per cent), Germany (135 per cent), Italy (155 per cent) and the UK (170 per cent).

[6] This is shown in the higher equalisation of Spanish pension payments (Sarasa 2007).

[7] If there is analytical agreement to include Greece, Italy, Portugal and Spain in a Southern European typology (Giner 1986; Gunther, Diamandouros & Puhle 1995; Malefakis 1992; Morlino 1998), the boundary limits of the Mediterranean mode of social protection remain a debatable issue (Ferrera 1997). Questions in this respect relate, for instance, to whether France should be included as a Mediterranean welfare country, or whether new (Cyprus, Malta, Slovenia) or prospective (Croatia, Turkey) EU member states share analogous welfare characteristics with countries located to the west of the Mediterranean Sea.

[8] The percentage of women that have higher tertiary education went from 12.6 per cent in 1985 to 22.7 per cent and 31 per cent in 1995 and 2005, respectively.

[9] In 2000, just eight per cent of Spanish working couples with children had the woman working part-time, compared with 53 per cent in the Netherlands, 40 per cent in the UK and 33 per cent in Germany (Moreno 2004).

[10] Cohorts of women, now aged between 40 and 64, who could only undertake demanding professional activities in the labour market if they were prepared to combine them with traditional unpaid caring work in households typify Spanish 'superwomen' across all Spanish social groups, classes and geographical areas (Moreno 2004).

[11] According to data produced by the Spanish National Statistics Institute, some 80 per cent of all jobless residents in Spain had some kind of income support in 2010, although this figure did not take into account first-time jobseekers and those not registered as unemployed.

[12] An instance of this financial concern was the cancellation of the 'baby cheque' benefit (*cheque bebé*), which had been introduced as an electoral promise by the PSOE government in July 2007. Mothers were granted €2,500 for birth or adoption. The programme was phased out at the end of 2010.

References

Adelantado, J. (ed.) (2000) *Cambios en el Estado del Bienestar: políticas sociales y desigualdades en España*, Icaria/Universitat Autònoma de Barcelona, Barcelona.

Adelantado, J. & Calderón, E. (2006) 'Globalization and the welfare state: the same strategies for similar problems?', *Journal of European Social Policy*, vol. 16, no. 4, pp. 374–386.

Albert, M. (1993) *Capitalism vs. Capitalism: How America's Obsession with Individual Achievement and Short-Term Profit Has Led It to the Brink of Collapse*, Whurr, London.

Amable, B. (2003) *The Diversity of Modern Capitalism*, Oxford University Press, Oxford.

Arriba, A. (2010) 'Labour market and social protection in Spain', paper presented at the Workshop on Social Protection and Labour Markets: Latin America and Southern Europe Compared, Collegio Carlo Alberto, Montecalieri, Turin, 20–21 May

Arriba, A., Calzada, I. & del Pino, E. (2006) *Las actitudes de los españoles hacia el Estado del Bienestar (1985–2005)*, CIS (Opiniones y Actitudes), Madrid.

Arriba, A. & Moreno, L. (2005) 'Spain: poverty, social exclusion and safety nets', in *Welfare State Reform in Southern Europe. Fighting Poverty and Social Exclusion in Italy, Spain, Portugal and Greece*, ed. M. Ferrera, Routledge, London, pp. 141–203.

Bache, I. (2008) *Europeanization and Multi-level Governance: Cohesion Policy in the European Union and Britain*, Rowman & Littlefield, Lanham, MD.

Balkir, C., Bolukbasi, H. T. & Ertugal, E. (2013) 'Europeanisation and dynamics of continuity and change in domestic political economies in the "Southern Periphery"', *South European Society and Politics*, vol. 18, no. 2, pp. 121–137.

Blyth, M. (2009) 'An approach to comparative analysis, or a sub-discipline within a sub-field? Political economy', in *Comparative Politics. Rationality, Culture and Structure*, eds M. Lichbach & A. Zuckerman,, 2nd edn, Cambridge University Press, Cambridge, pp. 193–219.

Börzel, T. & Risse, T. (2003) 'Conceptualising the domestic impact of Europe', in *The Politics of Europeanisation*, eds K. Featherstone & C. M. Radaelli, Oxford University Press, Oxford, pp. 57–80.

Da Roit, B., González-Ferrer, A. & Moreno-Fuentes, F. J. (2008) 'The new risk of dependency in old age and (missed) employment opportunities', paper presented at the ESPANET-Italia Conference, Ancona, 7 November

Del Pino, E. & Ramos, J. A. (2009) 'Las reformas de las políticas de bienestar en España: una visión de conjunto', in *Reformas de las políticas del bienestar en España*, ed. L. Moreno, Siglo XXI, Madrid, pp. 337–361.

Ebbinghaus, B. (2005) 'Can path dependence explain institutional change? Two approaches applied to welfare state reform', Max Planck Institute for the Study of Societies, Discussion Paper 05/2, available online at: http://www.mpi-fg-koeln.mpg.de/pu/mpifg_dp/dp05-2.pdf

Espina, A. (2007) *Modernización y Estado del Bienestar en España*, Fundación Carolina/Siglo XXI, Madrid.

Esping-Andersen, G. (1990) *The Three Worlds of Welfare Capitalism*, Polity Press, Cambridge.

Esping-Andersen, G. (1999) *Social Foundations of Postindustrial Economies*, Oxford University Press, Oxford.

Featherstone, K. & Kazamias, G. (2001) 'Introduction: Southern Europe and the process of "Europeanization"', in *Europeanization and the Southern Periphery*, eds Kevin Featherstone & Georgios Kazamias, Frank Cass, London, pp. 1–22.

Ferrera, M. (1996) 'The "Southern Model" of welfare in social Europe', *Journal of European Social Policy*, vol. 6, no. 1, pp. 17–37.

Ferrera, M. (1997) 'General Introduction', in *Comparing Social Welfare Systems in Southern Europe*, Mission Recherche et Expérimentation, Paris, pp. 13–24.

Ferrera, M. (2007) *Democratization and Social Policy in Southern Europe. From Expansion to "Recalibration"*, rev. edn, United Nations Research Institute for Social Development (UNISRID), Geneva.

Geffen, D. & Kenyon, T. (2006) 'Heinz capitalism: how many varieties are there? An empirical reexamination of coordination mechanisms in advanced market economies', SSRN, available online at: http://ssrn.com/abstract=1005407

Giner, S. (1986) 'Political economy, legitimation and the state in Southern Europe', in *Transitions from Authoritarian Rule: Prospects for Democracy*, eds G. O'Donnell & P. Schmitter, John Hopkins University Press, Baltimore, pp. 11–44.

González-Temprano, A. (ed.) (2003) *La consolidación del Estado del Bienestar en España (1993–2000)*, CES (Colección Estudios), Madrid.

Graziano, P. R. (2009) 'Bringing the actors back in: Europeanization and domestic policy change: the case of the European Employment Strategy in Italy and France', Cahier de recherché/Working Paper No. 10, *Pacte*, available online at: www.pacte.cnrs.fr

Guillén, A. M. (2010) 'Defrosting the Spanish welfare state: the weight of conservative components', in *A Long Good Bye to Bismarck. The Politics of Welfare Reforms in Continental Europe*, ed. B. Palier, Amsterdam University Press, Amsterdam, pp. 183–206.

Guillén, A. M. & Álvarez, Santiago (2004) 'The EU's impact on the Spanish welfare state: Europeanization on paper?', *Journal of European Social Policy*, vol. 14, no. 3, pp. 285–299.

Guillén, A. M. & Matsaganis, M. (2000) 'Testing the "social dumping" hypothesis in Southern Europe: welfare policies in Greece and Spain during the last 20 years', *Journal of European Social Policy*, vol. 10, no. 2, pp. 120–145.

Gunther, R., Diamandouros, N. & Puhle, H. -J. (eds) (1995) *The Politics of Democratic Consolidation. Southern Europe in Comparative Perspective*, Johns Hopkins University Press, Baltimore.

Hall, P. (1997) 'Institutions, interests and ideas in the comparative political economy of the industrialized nations', in *Comparative Politics: Rationality, Culture and Structure*, eds M. Lichbach & A. Zuckerman, Cambridge University Press, Cambridge, pp. 174–207.

Hall, P. & Soskice, D. (eds) (2001) *Varieties of Capitalism. The Institutional Foundations of Comparative Advantage*, Oxford University Press, Oxford.

Heclo, H. (1993) 'The role of ideas, interests and institutions', in *The Dynamics of American Politics: Approaches and Interpretations*, eds Lawrence C. Dodd & Calvin Jillson, Westview Press, Boulder, CO, pp. 366–392.

Iglesias, J., Marí-Klose, P. & González Blasco, P. (2010) *Matrimonios y parejas jóvenes. España 2009*, Fundación SM, Madrid.

Jacobsson, K. (2004) 'A European politics for employability: the political discourse on employability of the EU and the OECD', in *Learning to Be Employable. New Agendas on Work, Responsibility and Learning in a Globalising World*, eds C. Garsten & K. Jacobsson, Palgrave, Basingstoke, pp. 42–62.

Jenson, J. & Mérand, F. (2010) 'Sociology, institutionalism and the European Union', *Comparative European Politics*, vol. 8, no. 1, pp. 74–92.

Jerez-Mir, M., Real-Dato, J. & Vázquez-García, R. (2010) 'The perception of the European Union by political and economic elites in Spain', *South European Society and Politics*, vol. 15, no. 1, pp. 35–56.

Jessop, B. (1994) 'The transition to post-Fordism and the Schumpeterian workfare state', in *Towards a Post-Fordist Welfare State?* eds R. Burrows & B. Loader, Routledge, London, pp. 13–37.

Jessop, B. (2004) 'Critical semiotic analysis and cultural political economy', *Critical Discourse Studies*, vol. 1, no. 2, pp. 159–174.

Jørgensen, H. (2002) *Consensus, Cooperation and Conflict. The Policy Making Process in Denmark*, Edward Elgar, Cheltenham.

Marbán, V. (2009) 'Atención a la dependencia', in *Reformas de las políticas del bienestar en España*, ed. L. Moreno, Siglo XXI, Madrid, pp. 207–237.

Marí-Klose, P., Marí-Klose, M., Vaquera, E. & Argeseanu Cunningham, S. (2010) *Infancia y futuro. Nuevas realidades, nuevos retos*, Fundación La Caixa, Barcelona.

Malefakis, E. (1992) 'Southern Europe in the 19th and 20th centuries: an historical overview', Working Paper 35, Centro de Estudios Avanzados en Ciencias Sociales, Instituto Juan March, Madrid, available online at: http://www.march.es/ceacs/publicaciones/working/archivos/1992_35_en.pdf

Moreno, L. (2001) 'Spain, *a via media* of welfare development', in *Welfare States under Pressure*, ed. Peter Taylor-Gooby, Sage, London, pp. 100–122.

Moreno, L. (2004) 'Spain's transition to new risks: a farewell to "superwomen"', in *New Risks, New Welfare. The Transformation of the European Welfare State*, ed. Peter Taylor-Gooby, Oxford University Press, Oxford, pp. 133–157.

Moreno, L. (2006) 'The model of social protection in Southern Europe: enduring characteristics?', *Revue française des Affaires sociales*, no. 1–2006, pp. 73–95.

Moreno, L. (2008) 'The Nordic path of Spain's Mediterranean welfare', Center for European Studies Working Paper Series #163, Harvard University, available online at: http://www.ces.fas.harvard.edu/publications/docs/pdfs/CES_163.pdf

Moreno, L. (ed.) (2009) *Reformas de las políticas de Bienestar en España*, Siglo XXI, Madrid.

Moreno, L. & Palier, B. (2005) 'The Europeanization of welfare: paradigm shifts and social policy reforms', in *Ideas and Welfare State Reform in Western Europe*, ed. Peter Taylor-Gooby, Palgrave Macmillan, Basingstoke, pp. 145–175.

Moreno, L. & Rodríguez-Cabrero, G. (2007) 'Política social y Estado del Bienestar', in *Sociología en España*, ed. M. Pérez Yruela, Centro de Investigaciones Sociológicas/Federación Española de Sociología, Madrid, pp. 645–666.

Moreno, L. & Sarasa, S. (1992) 'The Spanish "via media" to the development of the welfare state', Working Paper 92-13, Instituto de Estudios Sociales Avanzados (IESA), Madrid

Moreno, L. & Serrano-Pascual, A. (2011) 'Europeanization and Spanish welfare: the case of employment policy', in *The Spanish Welfare State in the European Context*, eds Ana Guillén & Margarita León, Ashgate, Farnham, pp. 39–58.

Moreno-Fuentes, F. J. (2009) 'Del sistema sanitario de la Seguridad Social al sistema nacional de salud descentralizado', in *Reformas de las Políticas de Bienestar en España*, ed. L. Moreno, Ariel, Barcelona, pp. 73–92.

Moreno-Fuentes, F. J. & Bruquetas-Callejo, M. (2011) *Immigration and the Welfare State in Spain*, La Caixa, Barcelona, available online at: http://obrasocial.lacaixa.es/StaticFiles/StaticFiles/670e2a8ee75bf210VgnVCM1000000e8cf10aRCRD/es/vol31_en.pdf

Morlino, L. (1998) *Democracy between Consolidation and Crisis. Parties, Groups, and Citizens in Southern Europe*, Oxford University Press, Oxford.

Naldini, M. (2003) *The Family in the Mediterranean Welfare States*, Frank Cass/Routledge, London.

Navarro, V. (ed.) (2009) *La situación social en España III*, Fundación Largo Caballero – Editorial Biblioteca Nueva, Madrid.

OECD (2011) *OECD Family Database*, Paris, available online at: www.oecd.org/social/family/database

Palier, B. & Surel, Y. (2005) 'Les "trois I" et l'analyse de l'Etat en action', *Revue Française de Science Politique*, vol. 55, no. 1, pp. 7–32.

Radaelli, C. M. (2003) 'The Europeanization of public policy', in *The Politics of Europeanization*, eds K. Featherstone & C. M. Radaelli, Oxford University Press, Oxford, pp. 27–56.

Ramos, J. A. & del Pino, E. (2009) 'Un análisis político del cambio en el sistema de pensiones en España', in *Reformas de las Políticas del Bienestar en España*, ed. Luis Moreno, Siglo XXI, Madrid, pp. 67–100.

Reher, D. (1998) 'Family ties in Western Europe: persistent contrasts', *Population and Development Review*, vol. 24, no. 2, pp. 203–234.

Risse, T., Cowles, M. G. & Caporaso, J. (2001) 'Europeanization and domestic change: introduction', in *Transforming Europe. Europeanization and domestic change*, eds M. G. Cowles, J. Caporaso & T. Risse, Cornell University Press, Ithaca, NY, pp. 1–20.

Rodríguez-Cabrero, G. (2004) *Estado del Bienestar en España: Debates, Desarrollo y Retos*, Fundamentos, Madrid.

Rodríguez-Cabrero, G. (2010) 'Gasto público social', *Economistas*, no. 123, pp. 193–201.

Rodríguez-Cabrero, G. (2011) 'The consolidation of the Spanish welfare state (1975–2010)', in *The Spanish Welfare State in the European Context*, eds Ana Guillén & Margarita León, Ashgate, Farnham, pp. 17–38.

Royo, S. (2008) *Varieties of Capitalism in Spain. Remaking the Spanish Economy for the New Century*, Palgrave Macmillan, New York.

Salais, R. (2006) 'Reforming the European social model and the politics of indicators: from the unemployment rate to the employment rate in the European Employment Strategy', in *Uwwrapping the European Social Model*, eds M. Jepsen & A. Serrano-Pascual, Polity Press, Bristol, pp. 189–212.

Salido, O. & Moreno, L. (2007) 'Bienestar y políticas familiares en España', *Política y Sociedad*, vol. 44, no. 2, pp. 31–44.

Salido, O. & Moreno, L. (2009) 'Familia y género', in *Reformas de las Políticas de Bienestar en España*, ed. Luis Moreno, Ariel, Barcelona, pp. 281–303.

Sarasa, S. & Moreno, L. (eds) (1995) *El Estado del Bienestar en la Europa del Sur*, CSIC (Politeya), Madrid.

Sarasa, S. (2007) 'Pensiones de jubilación en España: reformas recientes y algunas consecuencias sobre el riesgo de pobreza', *Política y Sociedad*, vol. 44, no. 2, pp. 87–99.

Schmidt, V. A. (2008) 'Discursive institutionalism: the explanatory power of ideas and discourse', *Annual Review of Political Science*, vol. 11, pp. 303–326.

Serrano-Pascual, A. (2007) 'Reshaping welfare states: activation regimes in Europe', in *Reshaping Welfare States and Activation Regimes in Europe*, eds A. Serrano-Pascual & L. Magnusson, PIE Peter Lang, Brussels, pp. 11–35.

Turner, V. (1997) *The Forest of Symbols: Aspects of Ndembu Ritual*, Cornell University Press, Ithaca, NY.

Vasconcelos-Ferreira, L. & Figueiredo, A. (2005) 'Welfare regime in the EU 15 and in the enlarged Europe: an exploratory analysis', FEP Working Papers, University of Porto, Faculty of Economy, available online at: http://www.fep.up.pt/investigacao/workingpapers/2005.htm

Verney, S. (2009) 'Flaky fringe? Southern Europe facing the financial crisis', in *Southern Europe and the Financial Earthquake: Coping with the First Phase of the International Financial Crisis*, eds S. Verney, A. Bosco & M. Costa Lobo, *South European Society & Politics*, vol. 14, no. 1, pp. 1–6.

Europeanisation of Employment Policy in Turkey: Tracing Domestic Change through Institutions, Ideas and Interests

H. Tolga Bolukbasi and Ebru Ertugal

This article examines the impact of the European Union (EU) on Turkish political economy through an analysis of employment policy. Through tracing 'institutions', 'ideas' and 'interests' representing this policy area, it analyses the extent to which the accession process, which started with the granting of candidate status at the Helsinki Summit in December 1999, has prompted a transformation in this policy area. It draws on empirical evidence based on semi-structured interviews and other primary sources. The main finding is that domestic change occurs, however limited and variegated across sub-policy areas, through policy learning. Moreover, the policy ideas transplanted from the EU gain importance only in interaction with preferences of the coalition of dominant actors.

This article, following the framework set out in Balkir, Bolukbasi and Ertugal (2013), examines the impact of the European Union (EU) on Turkish political economy on the road to EU accession through an analysis of employment policy.[1] It analyses the extent to which the accession process, which started with the granting of candidate status at the Helsinki Summit in December 1999, has prompted a transformation in this policy area through tracing the 'institutions', 'ideas' and 'interests' representing Turkish political economy in general and employment policy and governance in particular. It focuses on employment policy to examine the changes in the political economy for several reasons. First, an examination of changes in employment policy promises to reflect the general pattern of change underway in Turkey en route to becoming a 'fully functional market economy'. Second, it is widely claimed that employment policy is *the* policy area that constitutes the greatest 'degree of misfit' between the EU and

Turkey (Çelik 2006), given Turkey's underperformance in comparison with the targets of the European Employment Strategy (EES) and the relatively weaker institutional structure of employment policymaking which, according to the Europeanisation research programme, would invite powerful adaptational pressures stemming from the EU level. Third, Turkish employment policy at the time of writing was undergoing change with the launching of Turkey's first employment strategy. Finally, the issue of unemployment features as the most important problem for citizens in Turkey, more so than any other issue, according to recent public opinion surveys.

In investigating domestic change in employment policy in Turkey, the Europeanisation research programme expects a low degree or no domestic adaptation to EU norms, rules and principles.[2] Given the soft-law (not legally binding) character of the main policy tool of the EU in this policy area (EES), the literature does not expect to find significant substantive change in candidate countries that are not participating in the governance mechanisms of the EES, the Open Method of Coordination (OMC). At the same time, the existence of a high degree of misfit between the EES and policy performance and structure in this area in Turkey is indicative of strong adaptational pressures, which may lead to domestic change only in the long run. Reinforcing the expectation of weak domestic change in the period under study is the extremely low credibility of the prospect of EU membership for Turkey, ruling out altogether the possibility of rapid change motivated by an otherwise strong incentive of EU accession.

Relying on case study methods, the article draws on empirical evidence based on primary sources. These sources include official programming documents such as national development plans, ministerial operational programmes, medium-term and annual economic programmes and 24 semi-structured interviews the authors have conducted with policymakers, representatives of social partners, EU officials and academic experts, on their perceptions of changes in employment policy in Turkey and the main drivers of change in that area. These semi-structured, in-depth interviews were conducted between September 2010 and May 2012. Throughout the article we refer to interviews by their interview numbers as listed in the Appendix.

This article argues that there were varying degrees of change in the form of transformation, absorption and accommodation across different components of Turkish employment policy with no incidence of inertia and retrenchment. Such changes, even limited and differentiated across policy components, are puzzling for several reasons. First, employment policy for the EU is a policy area characterised by soft law, which, by nature, is not expected to have a strong impact at the national level. Second, despite wide elite consensus on Turkey's EU vocation, given the low credibility of the prospect of EU membership (and hence weaker incentives for compliance) for Turkey, domestic actors were not expected to comply with the EU membership conditionality.[3] Third, this is a policy area representing a very high degree of misfit between the EU model and the domestic policy structure, leading to the expectation that any domestic change is likely to be painful and would materialise only over a long timescale.

The article addresses this puzzle in several stages. Following this introduction, the second section provides an overview of the defining features of the EES. The third section summarises the main findings of the Europeanisation research programme in this policy area and extrapolates expectations for the case of Turkey. The fourth section traces changes and continuities in the four main dimensions of the employment policy regime in Turkey. The fifth section explains the direction and content of change in such employment policy through examining the interaction of 'institutions', 'ideas' and 'interests'. The article concludes with the overall finding that there are varying degrees of change across different components of employment policy in Turkey in response to EU pressures. The findings also confirm those of existing research on member states, in that where the EES exerts influence it is largely as a result of ideational change yet only in interaction with preferences of the dominant actor coalition and the institutional context.

Europeanisation of National Employment Policies through the EES

The insertion of an employment chapter into the Amsterdam Treaty in 1997 to form the legal basis of the EES introduced in the same year was followed by the introduction of the OMC as a new instrument of EU governance for employment policy at the March 2000 Lisbon Summit. The EES represents an EU-wide agreement on a cognitive framework and a policy discourse about particular ways of defining problems concerning employment based on a new policy paradigm centring on competitiveness as reflected in the Lisbon Strategy.

The defining features of the EES can be analysed by means of the 'policy structure approach' used to unpack the key features of a given policy (Graziano 2011): principles, objectives, procedures and instruments. The principles embodied in the EES are informed by the concept of 'flexicurity', which summarises the EU's approach to labour markets. It has four dimensions (Commission of the European Communities (CEC) 2006): (i) contractual arrangements providing sufficient flexibility to both workers and employers; (ii) effective active labour market policies (ALMPs) supporting transitions between jobs and from unemployment and inactivity to employment; (iii) lifelong learning systems helping workers to cope with rapid change, unemployment spells and transition to new jobs, and enabling them to remain employable throughout their careers; and (iv) modern social security systems facilitating labour market mobility and transitions with adequate income support during absences from the labour market.

In terms of the *objectives*, rather than aiming to reduce unemployment, the EES aims to activate the labour market outsiders and promote high rates of employment. The priorities of the EES include achieving 'full employment', improving quality and productivity at work, strengthening social and territorial cohesion, promoting a lifecycle approach to work, inclusive labour markets, matching of labour market needs, investment in human capital, employment-friendly wages and the promotion of flexibility combined with employment security.

As far as the *procedures* in the policymaking process are concerned, the EES emphasises the significance of the participation of social partners in policymaking processes at both the domestic and EU level. At the EU level, coordination is secured among member states through the OMC in employment policy through benchmarking and the promotion of best practices. For candidate countries, the EU co-drafts a Joint Assessment Paper (JAP) on Employment Policy Priorities[4] outlining national employment priorities.

Finally, the *instruments* of the EES are twofold. The financial instruments of the EES are additional to national financial instruments. At the EU level, the instrument is the European Social Fund (ESF) aimed at implementing employment policies in member states. The instrument in candidate countries is the human resources development component of the Instrument for Pre-accession Assistance (IPA). The second instrument is the modernised public employment services institutions in member states and candidate countries.

Europeanisation Research Programme, EES and Candidate Countries

The findings of Europeanisation research on member states suggest that the EES through the OMC may (or may not) exert an influence at the domestic level in three main ways: by facilitating 'transnational learning', by encountering 'path-dependent dynamics of national institutions' or by changing the 'domestic constellation of actors' (Heidenreich & Zeitlin 2009, p. 2). These three possible mechanisms of EU (non-)influence emphasise the primacy of ideas, institutions and interests, respectively. Research has shown that due to the soft-law nature of the EES, the EES exerts influence at the domestic level mostly through facilitating policy learning (e.g. Jacobsson 2004; Trubek & Trubek 2005; Heidenreich 2009).

While the literature on the impact of the EES on national employment policies focuses almost exclusively on old member states, there is little research on accession countries (e.g. de la Porte 2009) and hardly any research on candidate countries. This article aims to fill this gap by examining the impact of the EES on a candidate country – Turkey. While candidate countries do not formally participate in the OMC process, they are subject to EU conditionality and a process of adaptation to norms, rules and principles emanating from the EU (Grabbe 2003). Given that the EES constitutes a type of soft law, the literature would not expect a high degree of EU adaptational pressure leading to domestic change.

Although the EES is not enforceable through sanctions, rendering EU conditionality in social and employment policy *acquis* inherently weak, the EU specifies a set of expectations for candidate countries through the Accession Partnership documents and regular progress reports. In the case of Turkey, for example, the EU provides a certain framework and direction for reform by requiring the promotion of social dialogue, ensuring full trade union rights, designing a national employment strategy, drafting of a JAP,[5] and improving the functioning and increasing the financial resources of the Turkish Employment Agency (Türkiye İş Kurumu – İŞKUR) in elaborating active labour market initiatives and concern about the informal economy (CEC 2008a; 2008b; 2009).

Given the nature of EU conditionality defined as such, it is possible to identify three potential ways in which EU conditionality in employment policy may lead to

Europeanisation in a candidate country. First, conditionality involves financial support provided to candidate countries under the human resources component of the Instrument for Pre-accession Assistance (IPA). In Turkey, for example, the Human Resources Development Operational Programme (HRDOP) designed under IPA for 2007–13 identifies four strategic priorities in Turkey: employment (increasing employment and especially the labour force participation of women), education (investing in human capital and improving the linkage between education and labour market), increasing the adaptability of workers by promoting lifelong learning, and social inclusion. Therefore the candidate country has an incentive to promote policy change in the direction desired by the EU in order to receive financial aid.

Second, the preparation of the JAP and the implementation of IPA in the candidate country and contact among policymakers and civil society actors with counterparts in the EU may facilitate transnational learning of those policy ideas embedded in the EES. Through 'socialisation' processes, domestic actors may believe that the direction indicated by the EES may be the best way forward for solving domestic problems.

Third, domestic actors may voluntarily decide for strategic purposes to adopt *some* of the ideas embodied in the EES. In this case they act not so much because they have gone through a 'normative and/or cognitive reassessment' (Weishaupt 2009); they rather pick and choose some (or part) of these ideas which best suit their pre-determined preferences.

Turkish Employment Policy: Changes in the Policy Structure

Any discussion on labour market flexibility and security in Turkey should start with the duality that characterises Turkish labour markets: the Turkish labour market is deeply segmented into primary and secondary segments. The adverse consequences of such duality are further aggravated by the pervasiveness of informality in the labour market. The primary segment (accounting for 25 per cent of total employment) includes public-manufacturing-sector employment, some part of the formal—generally unionised—private sector, and high-end finance and service occupations. Employees in the narrow primary segment have formal contracts granting them well-paid, highly secure jobs. In between the primary and secondary segments lie employees in the agricultural sector, constituting 27 per cent of total employment. The vast secondary segment (accounting for 48 per cent of total employment) encompasses self-employed workers in both agricultural and non-agricultural sectors and waged workers in the services and construction sectors. Engaged almost entirely in unregistered activity, labour market participants in this segment move from one precarious job to another. As they remain unprotected by labour laws or social security system, they enjoy no job security (ETF 2011; Ercan & Tansel 2007).

This section analyses the structure of Turkish employment policy based on the 'policy structure approach' (Graziano 2011). It traces the changes in the principles that characterise the employment policy regime, the policy *objectives* in governments' approach to questions of employment, *procedures* in governance and policy *instruments* employed in addressing the problem of (un)employment in Turkey. The discussion below aims to show whether there has been any change in each of these dimensions and, if so, to what extent these approximate the priorities of the EES.

Principles Governing Employment Policy

This sub-section analyses the changes in the principles of Turkish employment policies in terms of the four dimensions of flexicurity.

Flexibility in labour law. During the period under study, the government introduced a new Labour Act, in 2003 (Act No. 4857), regulating working life and industrial relations. The new act embodied two components of the principle of flexibility in labour law. First, flexible modes of employment were introduced in the formal sector, which allowed for atypical forms of employment for the first time, including part-time work, on-call work, fixed-term contracts and temporary employment. Second, the new act allowed for flexible working, encompassing flexitime, compensatory work and a temporary reduction in working time.

The act also incorporated a Job Security Act (Act No. 4773) that had already been passed in parliament in 2002. This act changed employment termination rules without expanding the coverage of the regulation. Employees who are covered by the new act (who are employed in formal, large private-sector establishments) were already covered through their union contracts. The act incorporated a new unemployment insurance scheme whose legal basis had been established in 1999 (see below).

It is important to emphasise that Act No. 4857 applies only to the part of the formal labour force that is not covered under other pieces of legislation (such as white-collar public-sector employees, self-employed and agricultural workers). It categorically excludes employees in the informal sector where de facto flexibility tout court applies. Although the applicability of de jure flexibility is limited to the primary segment and a smaller portion of the secondary segment, the existence of de facto flexibility in the informal sector that includes most of the secondary segment makes Turkish labour markets highly flexible. Thus the changes in labour law aiming at securing a higher degree of flexibility in line with the core dimension of the EU's flexicurity principle have left Turkish labour markets even more flexible, given the wide incidence of informality.

ALMPs. While the public officials interviewed reported that they had been inspired by the activation strategies of the Organisation for Economic Cooperation and Development (OECD) in designing employment measures back in the 1990s (interview 8), these measures were introduced on a piecemeal, project-by-project basis (ETF 2011, p. 61). It was only after İŞKUR was restructured in 2003 that ALMPs were implemented somewhat more systematically. Among the ALMPs, İŞKUR has been implementing labour force training programmes, job and vocational counselling services, occupational research and development, training services to establishments, and support for alleviating the consequences of privatisation. All these suggest that İŞKUR, whose institutional capacity has been strengthened through EU-funded projects, intervenes with a larger set of policy instruments. Although the coverage of ALMPs has been expanded with rising numbers of beneficiaries of these programmes, their scale, financial resources and coverage still remain very limited (ETF 2011, pp. 65–66). These policies, which are relatively new, still remain inadequate to support the mobility of labour market participants between jobs and to facilitate workers' transitions from inactivity and unemployment to employment.

Lifelong learning systems. This dimension of flexicurity is the least developed, as training opportunities after formal education remain limited. Most of the training programmes are provided by the Ministry of National Education (MoNE) through its Vocational Training Centres and Public Education Centres alongside İŞKUR. The only available way to alleviate skill deficiencies in the Turkish labour force is to channel the youth into vocational schools, since no other instrument exists that aims to provide lifelong learning. Although Turkey has an extensive system of vocational training schools, there remain serious problems in terms of their effective operation. Due to the weak supply of, and demand for, these schools, the system remains inefficient in responding to labour market requirements. Turkey has reformed its vocational training system through an EU-funded project implemented in 2002–06. After establishing the Vocational Training Authority in 2006, it adopted the 'Lifelong Learning Policy Strategy' in 2009 through the same project. Although the Strategy lacks necessary resources and effective means, it was a significant step, as it highlighted the link between education level and employment and labour force participation rates (ETF 2011, pp. 37–40). Despite these steps, however, the country still lacks an integrated and comprehensive approach to lifelong learning which would keep workers employable throughout their careers.

Modernised social security systems. The Turkish social protection system rests upon two pillars. While the social insurance pillar insures labour market participants and their dependents against risks, mainly through healthcare, unemployment and pension schemes, the social assistance pillar aims to alleviate poverty. Turkey's social security system as a whole features characteristics typical of the Southern European model, albeit with lower levels of total public spending, benefits and entitlements. Although social security reforms had been on successive governments' agenda, the reform process was launched only during the late 1990s, through the social security reform bill of 1999 (Law No. 4447). Through new legislation, an unemployment insurance scheme was introduced for the first time in the history of the Turkish social protection system. However, the eligibility criteria for receiving benefits are extremely stringent and the replacement ratios in this scheme remain abysmally low, despite some amelioration recently. The reform process continued with the establishment of the Social Security Institution (SSI) unifying the existing three main social security institutions in 2008. Although the SSI covers 81 per cent of the population, only 27 per cent of its membership is actively working and the rest mostly comprises pensioners and dependents (ETF 2011, p. 68). The new system has failed to increase incentives for mobility in the labour market, as it is organised to cover only full-time employees with indefinite labour contracts. The social assistance system still remains institutionally fragmented and this is reflected in patchy and low coverage.

The Turkish social security system encourages maximum job tenure rather than encouraging mobility in the labour market. Although the new labour law allowed for atypical forms of employment, these forms continue to be the blind spots of the social security system and the unemployment scheme. These schemes exclude employees working in the informal sector altogether. Low replacement ratios, stringent entitlement rules and narrow and patchy coverage fail to provide income security even for the working masses where the burden of adjustment falls disproportionately on the supply side through flexibilised labour contracts. The social security system also fails to provide positive feedback to ALMPs, as the passive benefits (such as unemployment insurance), however meagre, are not conditional on activation. Moreover, the system cannot cover employees in the informal sector, which is de facto flexible. Thus, the Turkish social security system is not designed to facilitate labour market mobility/transitions nor does it provide adequate income support in the event of absence from the labour market.

National Policy Objectives in the Approach to Employment

A review of official documents shows that promoting employment—the defining objectives of employment policy—was never declared as a strategic policy objective of successive governments until the 2000s. The overall development strategy was based on indicative (sectoral) planning in the 1960s and 1970s. This strategy relied on job creation in the public sector which facilitated the operation of the economy at close to full employment levels. In this period, the level of employment was taken as a 'dependent' variable or a 'by-product' (interviews 8, 12, 24)—an automatic outcome of 'economic growth' (State Planning Organisation [SPO] 1967) or 'industrialisation' (SPO 1973; 1979; Gündoğan & Biçerli 2003, p. 227).

In 1980, Turkey underwent a transition from a plan-based to a market-based model of development. During this period, the only change in terms of policymakers' perception of employment was that it was seen to depend more on international competitiveness than on economic growth and/or industrialisation. Although the SPO[6] continued to prepare development plans after the transition, the restructuring meant that governments, which had never been proactive in designing and implementing a national employment policy, distanced themselves even further from 'sensitive questions of employment and unemployment' (interview 1), as labour markets, in the eyes of policymakers, did not require any intervention in the form of employment policy (Gündoğan & Biçerli 2003, p. 228). Therefore, the tradition of not relying on a national employment strategy, programme or policy remained intact until recently, despite record-high unemployment and the 'jobless' nature of economic growth in the 2000s.

There are signs that the absence of an employment policy may have been changing since 2007 when the government took an initiative to draft a national employment strategy for the first time. First, there were references to the need for an employment strategy, which would streamline the content of the EES (read, flexicurity) into Turkey's policy objectives (İŞKUR 2009). Second, the multi-annual Eighth and Ninth National Development Plans (corresponding to the periods 2001–05 and 2007–13, respectively) announced the need for Turkey's harmonisation in this field. Third, during the period 2009–10 a draft strategy document was circulated to social partners, but the strategy never took off. However, some of the measures were incorporated into an omnibus bill passed in 2011. The draft was revised and presented in February 2012. These developments suggest that there are some changes in the direction of adopting measures similar to those in the EES.

Procedures in governance and policymaking

Reflecting the general policymaking tradition in Turkey, processes in employment policymaking can be characterised as centralised and hierarchical, with heavy government presence and direction against a background of adversarial industrial relations. Significant legislative steps were taken in the area of social partnership, the Economic and Social Council becoming permanent with Law No. 4641 of 2001, the establishment of the Tripartite Advisory Board with the new Labour Act (Law No. 4857) of 2003. The extent to which these bodies facilitate consultative decision-making based on negotiation and deliberation divides the different groups of actors interviewed. While public officials (interviews 1, 2, 3, 4, 5, 6, 7) were of the opinion that the new tripartite structures represented novel instruments ensuring participatory decision-making, representatives of employers and especially employees (interviews 16, 17, 18) thought that they did not bring about any major change in governance and policymaking.

In particular, the representatives of employees referred to many instances where their opposition to a proposal was only registered as an annotation in the consultation process, the proposal being adopted in any case without further deliberation. The employee representatives reported that they often disagreed with government proposals, as in the most recent case of the formulation of the National Employment Strategy during 2009–11. They added that the 'government circulated only a series of slides' in the consultation workshops and that when they attempted to discuss certain issues they were 'simply shut off' (interviews 17 and 18). The representative of the Confederation of Progressive Trade Unions of Turkey (Devrimci İşçi Sendikaları Konfederasyonu – DİSK) in particular stated that they had 'no influence on the outcome whatsoever' in any such decision-making process (interview 17). One mid-level bureaucrat corroborated these claims by stating that, 'in one occasion, I remember that the DİSK representative had left the workshop protesting the procedures. Such move has no impact on the outcome', as 'when, for example, one confederation that is close to the government makes a comment that is close to what the Ministry thinks, we take *that* into consideration. In the workshop reports, we rationalise our proposal by adding that "this is what the social partners had demanded anyway"' (interview 3). Another mid-level bureaucrat made similar statements: 'In fact, in all consultative meetings, what happens is, confederation representatives talk and talk and talk, and we respond by saying "OK, we noted these" and then pick and choose what is close to our position from those statements' (interview 4).

Instruments

The major financial instrument for implementing the principles and priorities of the EES in Turkey came from the EU during Turkey's candidacy initially under the Pre-accession Instrument for Turkey (2001–06) and later under the Instrument for Pre-accession Assistance (IPA) (2007–13).[7] In fact, a former senior official of İŞKUR stated that 'the Pre-Accession Instrument for Turkey started with the revamping of İŞKUR back in the early 2000s', which, he believed, 'showed how important this project was for the EU Delegation' (interview 21). More recently, the amount of funds under IPA for human resources development for the period 2007–11 was almost €300 million.

The EU's large-scale grant programme has supported an Active Labour Market Strategy managed by İŞKUR. The EU supported two major projects in particular aimed at institution-building to implement policies for increasing the employability of the unemployed. All of the public officials interviewed were in agreement that EU-funded projects made a significant contribution to the institutional capacity of İŞKUR in the implementation of active labour market measures (interviews 1–13).

In addition to EU funds, national financial instruments have been mobilised, particularly in response to the recent global economic crisis, triggering a number of stimulus packages. These have involved active labour market measures such as short-term working payments, public workfare programmes, vocational training and social security premium incentives for the employment of young people, women and the disabled (International Labour Office [ILO] 2010). As a ratio of GDP, the stimulus packages represented 0.83 per cent in 2008, 2.17 per cent in 2009 and 2.15 per cent in 2010 (ILO 2010, p. 1). The packages include financial resources for training programmes run by İŞKUR. While almost €16.5 million was spent in 2008 on training courses, more than €224 million was allocated for this in 2009 (ETF 2011, p. 63). This massive increase in the amount of resources from 2008 to 2009 to utilise public employment services to implement active labour market measures embedded in the EES enhances the impact of the EU.

Unpacking Varying Domestic Change through Institutions, Ideas and Interests

After reviewing the evidence for domestic change in employment policies in Turkey, this section provides an explanation of the direction and content of such change by analysing the interplay of ideas, interests and institutions.

Domestic Institutions

Key features of the political system in a country are critical for domestic reform (or the lack thereof), since they shape the power and strategy of actors in initiating or obstructing change. They do so by structuring the content and sequence of policymaking and differential allocation of power (Molina & Rhodes 2007). The Turkish political system is characterised by a 'simple polity' and majoritarian system, whereby authority and power are largely concentrated in the government (Schmidt 2006, p. 51). This implies that there is a greater executive capacity for reform should the government so choose in comparison with consensual systems and 'compound' polities where authority is diffused at multiple levels (Schmidt 2006, p. 51). In simple polities and majoritarian systems, the direction and extent of domestic change becomes largely a function of government preferences.

In the case of Turkey, the fact that the same political party has held a parliamentary majority over the past decade reinforces executive capacity. Moreover, the president and the Constitutional Court, which would otherwise constitute veto-points, no longer do so, as the Turkish parliament elected a longstanding senior member of the ruling party as president in 2007 and the majority of the Court's membership leans towards the ruling party's preferences. These recent developments have further reinforced the institutional characteristics of the Turkish political system.

Another important institutional feature of Turkey's political system concerns weak bureaucratic autonomy. Top-level bureaucrats (i.e. undersecretaries, deputy undersecretaries and general directors) are politically appointed and such practice is becoming more common under the current government. Policies, including strategies and decisions on priorities and financial resources, are formulated at the top under the direction of ministers. Mid-level bureaucrats (i.e. experts) play a role in so far as their expertise is required in the direction of policy change so decided (interviews 2, 3, 4, 5, 7).

This does not, however, mean that there are no learning effects. In particular, interviews show that EU financial assistance focuses on capacity-building through training and twinning projects involving mid-level experts (interviews 1–13). Exposure to paradigms and policy ideas in the EU and individual member states in an environment of persistent high unemployment and paucity of alternative paradigms at home engenders socialisation effects over time. One manifestation of such learning was the striking consensus among bureaucrats on the 'competitiveness imperative' and the common opinion that flexicurity was 'the only means' to fight unemployment (interviews 1–13). Moreover, Turkey's accession process has intensified the learning process not least through the EU's programming requirement whereby IPA funds can only be disbursed after an operational programme for human resources development has been put in place.

In the words of an interviewee, 'this was the Ministry of Labour and Social Security's first experience in formulating a policy. For the first time we had to decide which priorities we should have and how to support these priorities before dispensing any funds' (interview 5). All the bureaucrats interviewed shared the view that the EU has a significant impact on policymaking capacity, despite modest financial resources (interviews 1–13). As the bureaucracy does not have autonomy from politicians, the decisions to comply with the programming requirements of the EU and adopt the priorities of the EES point to the need to understand the preferences of the government.

The adversarial industrial relations system, which is typical of the South European model, amplifies employers' interests. The main features of this system include a 'paternalistic state' that has always been the largest employer and heavy reliance on legislation to resolve industrial disputes (Blanpain 2006; Çelik & Koray 2008). Given the majoritarian character of the political system, trade unions have 'less opportunity to gain access to decision-making and exercise "positive veto powers"' (Molina & Rhodes 2007, p. 233). Furthermore, their ability to exert 'negative veto power' (Molina & Rhodes 2007, p. 233) is constrained by the ideological polarisation, competition and fragmentation among the confederations and the successful cooptation attempts by the government (interviews 14, 15, 17, 18). All trade unions, whose membership is limited to the registered sector, are structurally powerless, mainly as a result of the reluctance of successive centre-right governments (especially since the 1980s) to grant full trade union rights.

Powerful Ideas

As demonstrated above, Turkey has not had a legacy of policymaking on employment, as policymakers saw employment as a derivative of economic growth during the 1960s and of industrialisation during the 1970s. Conceptualised within the context of development planning, such a linkage was informed by the then dominant Keynesian policy paradigm in which policymakers could 'stimulate the demand-side' through 'expansionary macroeconomic policies'. After the conservative revolution of the 1980s, however, Turkish policymakers began to think that the (un)employment problem could only be solved through a new paradigm of 'supply-side policies' (interview 21 and also interviews 8 and 12). Policymakers operating within this emerging policy paradigm began to emphasise international competitiveness as the primary goal for which other secondary goals (such as employment) could be sacrificed. This supply-side policy paradigm with its attendant policy idea of competitiveness gained ground in Turkish policymaking circles through the process of economic liberalisation that began in the 1980s and the completion of the Customs Union with the EU in 1996. It is in this context that the term 'flexibility' entered the lexicon of Turkish policymakers for the first time during the 1990s through the influence of the OECD (interview 8). Thus, there emerged a consensus among policymakers in employment policy that competitiveness could be achieved through labour market flexibility (interviews 8 and 21).

From the late 1990s onwards, however, after the granting of candidacy status to Turkey, policymakers were increasingly under the influence of the normative and cognitive policy idea of 'labour market flexicurity' propagated by the EU through the EES. Such policy transfer is not only a result of EU financial assistance, which has been increasing since Turkey's candidacy to the EU, but also of policy learning in which top-level bureaucracy and ministers themselves 'follow developments in the developed world' (interview 8). Such learning has not always translated into policy change, since ministers are exposed to electoral pressures. Moreover, there were limits on the institutional capacity of the bureaucracy to initiate reform (interviews 6 and 8), which means that new policy ideas, rather than being home-grown, are generally transferred, mostly from the West.

As a result, 'flexicurity', as part of everyday common policy discourse, is so deeply engrained in the Turkish policymaking apparatus that it features as a *referentielle* overwhelmingly in all the interviews conducted, and systematically in all official programming documents reviewed. In an earlier academic paper, one former director general of İŞKUR succinctly summarises this process of adoption of a new approach to employment policymaking as 'mind change' (Biçerli 2005, p. 13). Interestingly, however, all stakeholders in the area of employment policy view flexicurity from the same angle—policymakers, employers and unions alike, either with exultation or anxiety, categorically take it as flexibility. Whereas policymakers and employers discursively use this EU policy invention (reading it as flexibility) as a universal solution to the competitiveness imperative, union representatives stand against it, for they also read it as what dominant actors make of it (see the next section).

Dominant Interests

Given the political institutions described above, the government emerges as the most powerful actor likely to bring about policy reform, its preferences being shaped by competitive electoral pressures. Some of these pressures are of a general nature, such as delivering high rates of economic growth and reducing unemployment rates. Recent public opinion surveys demonstrate clearly that unemployment features as the top concern for the great majority (*Akşam* 2010; Çarkoğlu & Kalaycıoğlu 2007, p. 51). Interviews with bureaucrats corroborate the 'highly politically salient nature of the issue of unemployment' (interview 1).

The government is also subject to particularistic pressures stemming from the preferences of its strong constituencies. Small merchant and industrialist communities organised in the form of small and medium-sized enterprises (SMEs) across Anatolia comprises one such strong constituency (Çarkoğlu & Kalaycıoğlu 2007, p. 27). Predominantly based on family ownership, the majority of the SMEs are engaged largely in unregistered activity, relying on an informal (and hence de facto flexible) workforce. Although these conditions seem to have helped in responding to the current economic crisis, they become a trap, slowing down economic modernisation and productivity growth (OECD 2010).

The interviews show that the preference of the SME sector (represented by the Union of Chambers and Commodity Exchanges of Turkey [TOBB]) is to continue with informality (involving unregistered activity and informal, hence insecure, forms of work) rather than undergoing a (painful) process of restructuring involving organisational change (interviews 16, 17, 18). In the words of a representative from a trade union confederation, during the negotiations for the Labour Act of 2003 'TOBB tried to do everything in its power to dispense with rules [guaranteeing security] altogether that would otherwise regulate the labour market—a clear indication of a preference for maximum flexibility' (interview 17). A senior representative of TOBB, however, contested this claim by adding that they have always supported 'registered forms of work' (interview 24).

The concerns of the large registered sector also play a role in shaping government preferences, as interviews with top bureaucrats indicate (interviews 1, 6, 9). In an interview one bureaucrat said, 'We need to relieve the pressure on big businesses to increase their competitiveness' (interview 1). These remarks resonate with those from the representatives of big businesses who complained about 'excessive labour market regulation' concerning, for example, 'taxes', 'non-wage costs' and 'regulations for employing the disadvantaged'. The main interest of the big businesses is thus perceived to reside in 'securing competitiveness through flexibility' (interviews 16 and 23).

The foregoing analysis suggests that there is a convergence of preferences of the government and employers on exclusively emphasising the flexibility dimension of flexicurity. The crisis hitting the Turkish economy in 2001 strengthened the hands of the government and employers in introducing flexibility reforms. This period coincided with the accession process, in which Turkey has been effectively exposed to EU policy paradigms (represented in the EES in particular) through EU conditionality and IPA (Prime Ministry of the Turkish Republic 2003).

In contrast to the SME sector and the big businesses, trade unions remain politically and institutionally weak. Unions represent a very small portion of the workforce in the registered sector and become even weaker in times of economic crisis, such as in 2001 and 2008. Union representatives have come to agree with employers and the government on the structural necessity of maintaining competitiveness. They demand, however, that the existing labour law (which they see as imposing more flexibility than security) be 'implemented in full', covering workers in precarious jobs in the informal sector as well as those in the formal sector (interviews 17 and 18).

Against this domestic political economic constellation, powerful actors cherry-pick flexibility out of the 'flexicurity' promoted by the EES and refer to European norms when they need to justify their efforts to make Turkey's labour market more flexible. Flexibility has been such an overarching discursive narrative that all interviewees, when talking about their understanding of the EES norms and principles, unanimously referred exclusively to the 'flexibility' dimension of flexicurity (interviews 1–12, 16–18). Only when probed about their perceptions of the security dimension did the interviewees comment on this aspect of flexicurity. A mid-level bureaucrat at the Ministry of Labour and Social Security explains why: 'unfortunately, everyone in Turkey perceives [EES or flexicurity] in the way it suits their interest. It is mostly understood as flexibility. Only trade unions try to promote security, but they, too, view the EES as promoting flexibility rather than both' (interview 4). Moreover, in the parliamentary debates concerning the Labour Law of 2003 which brought flexibility to the registered sector of the economy, the members of parliament representing the ruling party made extensive use of 'European norms' in justifying the law against the opposition, as was reflected in the parliamentary minutes (Turkish Grand National Assembly [TGNA] 2003). In fact, every member of parliament speaking in favour of the proposed legislation referred to the policies in European countries as good practices to be replicated and European norms as solutions to domestic problems. It is striking that these practices and norms were referred to as 'flexible' as opposed to 'flexicure'.

In summary, the EES, to which Turkey was expected to streamline through EU conditionality, strengthened the hands of the reform coalition advocating flexibility in Turkey. This discursive tool delegitimised any call whatsoever by trade unions that could be associated with security. Interviewees at the EU Delegation and the Ministry for EU Affairs referred to the principle of flexicurity as involving both flexibility *and* security dimensions, and said that, given the extent of informality in Turkey's economy, the security dimension 'should be prioritised at least as much as the flexibility dimension' (interview 14, and also interviews 13 and 15). The overarching competitiveness paradigm, however, helps legitimise the interests of the dominant coalition, which is pushing for changes in employment policy towards more flexibility, disregarding entirely the security dimension.

The EU and Domestic Change in Employment Policies in Turkey

This section summarises the findings on the dynamics of change and continuity in the Turkish employment policy structure and identifies the role the EU plays. In detecting the degree of change, it relies on the categories of 'transformation', 'accommodation', 'absorption', 'inertia' and 'retrenchment' proposed by Balkir, Bolukbasi and Ertugal (2013). Our conceptualisation and operationalisation of change rest upon comparing the degree of change across different components of employment policy in Turkey.

First, in terms of the *principles* of employment policy, the narrative above on the flexibility dimensions of flexicurity suggests that changes in Turkish labour law in the direction of more flexibility amount to a *transformation*. Two caveats are in order, however. Although such legislative change allowing for atypical employment forms constitutes a radical change in working life, the applicability of legislation is limited to less than half of the entire workforce, given the large size of the informal sector (which, itself, is far from EU norms and practices) and the large number of employee groups covered by other laws governing their contracts. At the same time, although the direction and content of such legislative change is towards flexibility, new policy ideas that seem to be instrumental in bringing about legislative change seem to have started a decade earlier in the 1990s under the influence of the OECD. Nevertheless, the EU played a striking role in the transformation process through its structuring impact on policy programming, by providing a powerful discursive instrument through which policymakers could legitimise their goals as well as deflecting blame and providing a common language for policymakers through twinning and training practices.

Systematic deployment of ALMPs has only begun with the restructuring of the Turkish public employment services. The number of staff at İŞKUR and the coverage of and spending on ALMPs remain significantly lower than EU averages, however. The modesty of changes in coverage and spending notwithstanding, the fact that İŞKUR has adapted its institutional set-up to implement these new policy instruments suggests that there has been an *accommodation* in this dimension of flexicurity. In terms of the EU role in such change, the narrative above shows that ALMPs have effectively entered into the official programming documents, increasing the financial resources allocated to activation policies and policymakers' everyday tasks.

Slower developments in the area of lifelong learning systems, the third dimension of the flexicurity principle, point to *absorption* in which EU policies and practices are gradually incorporated into the Turkish education system without substantially ameliorating the existing rather weak institutional capacity in policymaking and implementation. EU policies and practices, however, seem to have infiltrated the programming process by triggering the adoption of new strategies with additional financial ramifications. Moreover, although it may be too early to pass judgement on their effectiveness, efforts on the part of the MoNE and İŞKUR to cooperate on this front have begun to create a common language across the different units responsible for this cooperation.

In tracing changes in the fourth dimension of flexicurity, the foregoing discussion shows that, although there have been legislative changes in the area of social security, these seem to have been carried out largely independent of any effort to provide more security to labour market participants. Thus, while security may be increasing through some of the legislative changes, these can only amount to *absorption*, as they do not substantially modify the existing domestic policies which are categorically characterised by path-dependent processes. While the recent unemployment insurance scheme and other universalist expansions in healthcare may constitute novelties, the EU does not seem to have played any significant role, for example, through the programming process, as modernisation of social security systems does not feature as a priority axis in the Human Resources Development Operational Programme (HRDOP).

Second, in terms of the changes in the objectives of employment policy, the institutionalisation of an employment policy for the first time can be seen as adaptation to the EU's requirements in policy programming. In this sense, the degree of change is one of *accommodation* involving the launching of a national employment strategy. While policymakers have adapted to the need to formulate a strategy, they have not been actively using the EU as a discursive tool to legitimise their actions. Rather, the need to formulate an employment strategy involving specific targets similar to those found in the EES appears to have been internalised among bureaucrats. Such internalisation, however, is partly a result of the EU's impact through policy programming, training, and twinning programmes. The traditional orientation of policymakers towards looking for policy solutions in the 'developed world' would have brought about such a change sooner or later, given the low levels of employment especially among women, but the EU seems to have accelerated this process. Another reason for not using the EU as a discursive tool is due to the political benefits that come from making an effort, through the formulation of a strategy, for example, to tackle rampant unemployment, the number one item on the electorate's agenda.

Third, in terms of changes in the *procedures* in governance and policymaking, the narrative above shows that recent changes allowing for better participation of social partners can be categorised as *absorption*. Whereas social partners' formal role in policymaking is ensured by law, their ability to influence decisions is severely restricted, especially if these are against the preferences of the government. The EU procedures of social dialogue have acted as a discursive tool, as whenever politicians and bureaucrats take a decision with the participation of those social partners they are in agreement with they claim that they have done so through social dialogue. This helps legitimise the decisions taken, even when they are made without the actual input of trade unions in particular.

Finally, in terms of *instruments*, changes involving increased national financial allocations for active labour market measures can be categorised as *accommodation*. The massive increases in financial allocations from 2008 onwards are a response to domestic economic difficulties triggered by the global economic crisis. However, the EU funds under IPA which have been coming into Turkey since 2002 have both informed the content of measures adopted in the direction of ALMPs and helped expand the institutional capacity to implement such measures.

This analysis of the degree, nature and direction of domestic change in Turkish employment policy and the role that the EU plays therein confirms the findings of existing research on member states in that, where the EES exerts influence, it is mostly as a result of policy learning. However, such learning in this accession country is qualitatively different from practices in member states, as it is facilitated not only by the OMC but also through membership conditionality, involving policy-programming requirements for eligibility for EU funding as well as training and twinning programmes. While this finding points to the significance of ideas in domestic reform, ideas themselves cannot account for the entire story in the absence of an account of how they interact with the preferences of the dominant actor coalition and the institutional context. In the domains characterised by a medium to higher degree of change (i.e. transformation in labour law and *accommodation* in ALMPs, objectives and instruments), it is the framing effects of the flexicurity policy idea and the selective appropriation of ideas by dominant interests that are causally significant. In contrast, the path-dependent institutional context remains causally significant in explaining the lower degree of change (i.e. *absorption*) in lifelong learning and social security systems and procedures in governance. In particular, it is important to note that social security systems and procedures in governance are domains where change encouraged by the EES would lead to a shift in the power balance among domestic actors—wherein lies the difficulty of change.

Acknowledgements

This article benefited from the research project 'Transformation of Turkey's Labour Market and Employment Policies and the European Union' (Project No. 111K108) funded by the Scientific and Technological Research Council of Turkey (TUBITAK).

Notes

[1] Employment policy consists of 'laws and conventions that establish the rights and entitlements of workers and structure the work relationship' and strategies, programmes, policies and measures 'to protect and promote employment more generally' in a systematic manner (Rhodes 2005, p. 280).

[2] Please see Bolukbasi, Ertugal and Ozcurumez (2010) for an overview of the EU's impact on Turkey.

[3] See Bolukbasi and Ozcurumez (2011) for an analysis of the broad-based elite support for Turkey's full membership in the EU.

[4] Upon the formulation of the JAP outlining national employment priorities, the European Commission provides recommendations.

[5] In Turkey's case, even though a draft JAP was prepared, it was not finalised due to a disagreement on how to address employment issues affecting vulnerable groups (CEC 2008b).

[6] The SPO was renamed the Ministry of Development in June 2011.

[7] Turkey has been receiving pre-accession assistance from the EU since 2001 under the Pre-accession Instrument for Turkey. As of 2007 this pre-accession financial instrument for Turkey has been replaced by IPA, which provides funding and support to candidate countries and potential candidates.

References

Akşam. (2010) 'İktidarın Mazbatasını İşsizler Verecek' [It is the unemployed who will determine the government], 1 March. Available at http://aksam.medyator.com/2010/03/01/haber/5492/ekonomi/haber.html

Balkir, C., Bolukbasi, H. T. & Ertugal, E. (2013) 'Europeanisation and dynamics of continuity and change in domestic political economies in the "Southern Periphery"', *South European Society and Politics*, vol. 18, no. 2, pp. 121–137.

Biçerli, M. K. (2005) 'Aktif İstihdam Politikaları İşsizliği Azaltır mı?', [Do active employment policies reduce unemployment?] *Çimento İşverenleri Dergisi*, vol. 19, no. 6, pp. 1–15.

Blanpain, R. (ed.) (2006) 'Flexibilisation and modernisation of the Turkish labour market', *Bulletin of Comparative Labour Relations*, Kluwer Law International BV, The Hague.

Bolukbasi, H. T. & Ozcurumez, S. (2011) 'Of context, interaction and temporality: historical institutionalism and Turkey's approach to the ENP and the UfM', *Comparative European Politics*, vol. 9, no. 4–5, pp. 524–542.

Bolukbasi, H. T., Ertugal, E. & Ozcurumez, S. (2010) 'The impact of the EU on Turkey: toward streamlining Europeanisation as a research programme', *European Political Science*, vol. 9, no. 4, pp. 464–480.

Çarkoğlu, A. & Kalaycıoğlu, E. (2007) *Turkish Democracy Today*, I. B. Tauris, London.

Çelik, A. (2006) *AB Sosyal Politikası: Uyum Sürecinin Uyumsuz Alanı* [EU Social Policy: The Nonaligned Area of the Allignment Process], Kitap Yayınevi, Istanbul.

Çelik, A. & Koray, M. (2008) *Avrupa Birliği ve Türkiye'de Sosyal Diyalog*, Belediye-İs, Ankara.

CEC (2006) *Employment in Europe*, Office for Official Publications of the European Communities, Luxembourg.

CEC (2008a) 'Council decision of 18 February 2008 on the principles, priorities and conditions contained in the Accession Partnership with the Republic of Turkey (2008/157/EC)', *Official Journal of the European Union*, L51, 26 February.

CEC (2008b) 'Turkey 2008 progress report', available online at: http://www.abgs.gov.tr/files/AB_Iliskileri/Tur_En_Realitons/Progress/turkey_progress_report_2008.pdf

CEC (2009) 'Turkey 2009 progress report', available online at: http://www.abgs.gov.tr/files/AB_Iliskileri/Tur_En_Realitons/Progress/turkey_progress_report_2009.pdf

De la Porte, C. (2009) 'The role of the OECD and the EU in the development of labour market policy in the Czech Republic', *Journal of Contemporary European Research*, vol. 5, no. 4, pp. 539–556.

Ercan, H. & Tansel, A. (2007) 'How to approach the challenge of reconciling labour flexibility with job security and social cohesion in Turkey', *Reconciling Labour Flexibility with Social Cohesion*, Trends in Social Cohesion, No. 17, Council of Europe, Strasbourg.

ETF (2011) 'Flexicurity analysis of the Turkish labour market', draft report, European Training Foundation, Turin.

Grabbe, H. (2003) 'Europeanisation goes east: power and uncertainty in the EU accession process', in *The Politics of Europeanisation*, eds K. Featherstone & C. M. Radaelli, Oxford University Press, Oxford, pp. 303–329.

Graziano, P. R. (2011) 'Europeanisation and domestic employment policy change: conceptual and methodological background', *Governance*, vol. 24, no. 3, pp. 583–605.

Gündoğan, N. & Biçerli, M. K. (2003) *Çalışma Ekonomisi*, [Labour Economics], Anadolu Üniversitesi İktisat Fakültesi Yayını, Eskişehir, 2003.

Heidenreich, M. (2009) 'The open method of coordination: a pathway to the gradual transformation of national employment and welfare regimes?', in *Changing European Employment and Welfare Regimes*, eds M. Heidenreich & J. Zeitlin, Routledge, London, pp. 10–36.

Heidenreich, M. & Zeitlin, J. (2009) 'Introduction', in *Changing European Employment and Welfare Regimes*, eds M. Heidenreich & J. Zeitlin, Routledge, London, pp. 1–9.

ILO (2010) *Turkey's Response to the Crisis*, Geneva.

İŞKUR (2009) *Genel Kurul Çalışma Raporu* [Report of the General Assembly], Ankara.

Jacobsson, K. (2004) 'Between deliberation and discipline: soft governance in EU employment policy', in *Soft Law in Governance and Regulation*, eds U. Mörth & Edward Elgar, Cheltenham, pp. 81–101.

Molina, O. & Rhodes, M. (2007) 'The political economy of adjustment in mixed market economies: a study of Spain and Italy', in *Beyond Varieties of Capitalism*, eds B. Hancke, M. Rhodes & M. Thatcher, Oxford University Press, Oxford, pp. 223–252.

OECD (2010) *OECD Economic Surveys: Turkey*, Paris.

Prime Ministry of the Republic of Turkey. (2003) 'Report of the Parliamentary Commission on Health, Family, Work and Social Affairs', available online at: http://www.tbmm.gov.tr/sirasayi/donem22/yil01/ss73m.htm

Rhodes, M. (2005) 'Employment policy: between efficiency and experimentation', in *Policy-Making in the European Union*, eds H. Wallace, W. Wallace & M. Pollack, Oxford University Press, Oxford, pp. 279–304.

Schmidt, V. (2006) *Democracy in Europe*, Oxford University Press, Oxford.

SPO (1967) *İkinci Beş Yıllık Kalkınma Planı 1968–1972* [Second Five Year Development Plan], Ankara.

SPO (1973) *Üçüncü Beş Yıllık Kalkınma Planı 1973–1977* [Third Five Year Development Plan], Ankara.

SPO (1979) *Dördüncü Beş Yıllık Kalkınma Planı 1979–1983* [Fourth Five Year Development Plan], Ankara.

TGNA (2003) *Tutanak Dergisi* [Journal of Assembly Minutes], Session 22, Legislative Year 1, Sittings 45–46, 75–80, 82–83.

Trubek, D. M. & Trubek, L. G. (2005) 'Hard and soft law in the construction of social Europe: the role of the open method of coordination', *European Law Journal*, vol. 11, no. 3, pp. 343–364.

Weishaupt, J. T. (2009) 'Money, votes or "good ideas"? Partisan politics and the effectiveness of the European Employment Strategy in Austria and Ireland', *European Integration Online Papers*, vol. 13, available online at: http://eiop.or.at/eiop/index.php/eiop/article/view/2009_014a

Appendix. List of Interviewees

(1) Senior bureaucrat, Ministry of Labour and Social Security (MoLSS)
(2) Mid-level bureaucrat, MoLSS
(3) Mid-level bureaucrat, MoLSS
(4) Mid-level bureaucrat, MoLSS
(5) Mid-level bureaucrat, MoLSS
(6) Senior bureaucrat (retired), İŞKUR
(7) Mid-level bureaucrat, İŞKUR
(8) Former senior bureaucrat, SPO
(9) Senior bureaucrat, SPO
(10) Mid-level bureaucrat, SPO
(11) Mid-level bureaucrat, SPO
(12) Mid-level bureaucrat, SPO
(13) Mid-level bureaucrat, Ministry for EU Affairs
(14) Senior official, EU Delegation in Ankara
(15) Mid-level official, EU Delegation in Ankara
(16) Senior representative of Turkish Confederation of Employer Associations (Türkiye İşveren Sendikaları Konfederasyonu – TİSK)
(17) Former senior representative of DİSK
(18) Representative of Confederation of Turkish Trade Unions (Türkiye İşçi Sendikaları Konfederasyonu – TÜRK-İŞ)
(19) Expert, Middle East Technical University (METU)
(20) Expert, Bilkent University
(21) Senior bureaucrat (retired), İŞKUR
(22) Senior representative of Turkish Industry and Business Association (Türk Sanayici ve İşadamları Derneği – TÜSİAD)
(23) Senior representative of TOBB
(24) Former senior bureaucrat, SPO

Europeanisation in the 'Southern Periphery': Comparative Research Findings on the EU's Impact on Domestic Political Economies

Canan Balkir, H. Tolga Bolukbasi and Ebru Ertugal

This article presents the comparative findings of six case studies of continuity and change in Southern European political economies which make use of the Europeanisation research programme. It summarises the varied European Union (EU) level inputs, frameworks or agendas in the different policy areas that each case study focuses on. It gauges the magnitude and direction of domestic change at the level of policy and governance in each political economy. In order to show how the case studies unpack the relationship between the EU input and domestic change in public policies, the article explains how the prevalent ideas, dominant interests and structuring institutions co-determine the nature of domestic change in political economies.

This article presents comparative findings based on the six case studies on Greece, Italy, Malta, Portugal, Spain and Turkey included in this volume titled "Europeanisation and the Southern Periphery' in Retrospect: Another Decade of Dynamism, Asymmetry, and Fragmentation?' through an analytical framework drawn up on the basis of the research questions set out by Balkir, Bolukbasi and Ertugal (2013). Its goal is to show how the contributions in this volume aim to follow the most recent research design focusing on f as represented in the equation $Y = f\ (X)$, where X represents the EU input and Y represents domestic change (Radaelli 2012).[1] In focusing on f, contributions in this volume explore the relationship between the EU input and domestic change in different public policy and governance domains. In order to unpack the relationship between the EU input, on the one hand, and domestic change and continuity in public policies and governance arrangements, on the other, the contributions analyse the diverse constellations of ideas, interests and institutions characterising domestic political economies. By analytically reviewing the contributions in this volume, this article demonstrates that in order to focus on *f* a practical research strategy is to capitalise on the three types of Europeanisation research that Radaelli (2012) elucidates by taking them as successive, iterative steps at capturing *f*.

Therefore, this article summarises, first, what the contributions locate as the relevant European Union (EU) level inputs, frameworks or agendas in the policy area they focus on (*X*), which constitute their points of departure for further analysis. It shows how, by doing so, each of the case studies identify the potential 'adaptational pressure' stemming from the EU level. Second, it reviews the narratives presented in each case to gauge the magnitude and direction of domestic change at the level of policy and governance. Third, it shows that once these analytical stages laying the ground for the final research stage are completed, the case studies then continue with their final research stage where they focus on the constellation of ideas, interests and institutions to isolate the exclusive impact of the EU input (identified in the first stage) on domestic change (identified in the second stage).

Readers will notice that the three research stages that the contributors of this volume follow are, in fact, structured so as to answer the research questions set out in the introductory article (Balkir, Bolukbasi & Ertugal 2013). The rest of this article is organised as follows. The following section draws on what the case studies take as 'EU input' in answering the research question 'What are the EU's key formal and informal rules, procedures, frames of reference, mechanisms and governance structures that may potentially bring about change at the domestic level?' The third section traces continuity and change in the outcome variables, i.e. specific public policies and governance arrangements in different political economies. It provides a comparative analytical summary of the contributors' responses to the questions 'How can we portray the direction, extent and dimensions of domestic change (as well as continuity) in Southern European political economies over the course of the last decade?' and, to the extent that the EU constitutes a key driver of change (which will be evaluated below), 'What are the different manifestations of Europeanisation in different public policy areas?', which a leading exponent of the Europeanisation research programme defines as 'Europeanisation as *outcome*' (Radaelli 2012, p. 7).

In doing so, this section relies on the categories deployed in the Europeanisation research programme for conceptualising and operationalising domestic change – transformation, absorption, accommodation, inertia and retrenchment. The fourth section portrays comparatively the diverse constellations of prevalent ideas, powerful interests and structuring institutions representing different policy and governance areas across Southern European political economies. It summarises the findings in each of the case studies related to the questions 'How are the respective constellations of ideas, interests, and institutions representing these domains evolving?', 'How does the EU play a role in the evolution of these constellations over time?' and therefore

'How can one portray the dynamics of Europeanisation' which Radaelli (2012, p. 7) calls 'Europeanisation as *process*'?

Based on the comparative findings obtained through these case studies, the concluding section revisits, more than a decade later, Featherstone and Kazamias' (2000) conclusions characterising the Europeanisation experience of Southern Europe with three key attributes—'dynamism', 'asymmetry' and 'fragmentation'. It does so by reassessing the extent to which processes of Europeanisation in Southern Europe are still characterised by these attributes, through focusing on continuity and change in domestic political economies.

'EU Input': EU-Level Frameworks, Regimes, Models, Policies, Rules

The case studies in this volume focus on a small sample of policy and governance domains in domestic political economies. Even with such a limited sample, they collectively demonstrate that the EU has developed an elaborate, far-reaching catalogue of competences. As a result of successive waves of deepening, the 'EU input' has come to encompass formal and informal rules, procedures, frames of reference, mechanisms and governance structures. Such an extensive catalogue increasingly resembles those of contemporary polities with complex policy structures. In terms of their substantive scope, the sample of public policy and governance domains that are the focus of the case studies in this volume include social and employment policies (Malta, Spain and Turkey), macroeconomic policies (Italy and Portugal), financial regulation (Italy) and regulatory agencies (Greece) and their impact on domestic policies and governance structures. While the case studies take these policy areas as their main focus, they also speak to broad patterns of continuity and change in their respective domestic political economies.

In terms of social and employment policies, the 'EU input' is generally viewed as far from being strong, as the EU lacks both 'power' and 'resources' in these fields (Moreno 2013, p. 222). In the area of social policy, the EU has remained 'incompetent and unable to impose any uniform solution to reforming national welfare states' (Ibid). In time, however, in the specific areas of old age pensions and employment policies, there was a process of progressive adoption of common approaches which went hand in hand with progressive harmonisation in 'peripheral' areas such as equal opportunities, health and safety regulations, and poverty and social inclusion programmes (Ibid).

In their discussions of EU employment policy, the case studies focus on the European Employment Strategy (EES). The EES represents the current consensus across the EU and is informed by a 'policy paradigm centring on competitiveness'. The Strategy rests on the principle of 'flexicurity', which serves its 'cognitive framework' and aims at 'activation of labour market outsiders' (Bolukbasi & Ertugal 2013). It is based on the sharing of best practices and voluntary cooperation among member states to achieve common 'objectives' in relation to the labour market, such as the employment rate and the labour force participation rate. In terms of its governance structure, the EES relies on the 'participation of social partners in policymaking processes' and policy coordination is ensured through its 'governance mechanism'—the Open Method of Coordination (OMC)—in member states and the co-drafting of the Joint Assessment Paper (JAP) in candidate countries.

The Strategy is equipped with financial instruments (the European Social Fund for member states and the Instrument for Pre-Accession for candidate countries). It operates through modernised public employment services in delivering active labour market policies (Bolukbasi & Ertugal 2013). The case studies emphasise the 'soft law' basis of EU employment policy, which, they argue, renders the EES weak (Azzopardi 2013; Bolukbasi & Ertugal 2013). In member states, the 'governance mechanism' of the EES, the OMC, leaves the route to be taken in achieving common objectives open to domestic discretion. Although the EU input is relatively less forceful than in other policy areas that rely on 'hard law', the common approaches in the EES constrain the room for manoeuvre of governments in reform processes by promoting certain routes rather than others.

In terms of how EU inputs generally hinge upon EU-level ideas, the case study on Spain shows how the activation ideas stemming from the EU level (which was also propagated by the Organisation for Economic Cooperation and Development [OECD]) have acted as the 'general framework of reference' and 'the institutional source of "good practice"' stimulating female labour force participation in that country (Moreno 2013, p. 219). The potential impact of the EES on the candidate countries is thought to be through conditionality. Conditionality is accompanied by 'financial support' under the human resources component of the Instrument for Pre-Accession Assistance (IPA), which, as case studies show, acts as a carrot. The formulation of a JAP and the implementation process of IPA facilitate 'socialisation' and 'transnational learning' of EU's 'policy ideas' among policymakers at the domestic level. In terms of how ideas may be causally consequential, the case study on Malta shows that during the EU candidacy of Malta the European Commission's recommendations repeatedly 'resonated with the same message' as those of the EES ideas, which triggered processes of Europeanisation (Azzopardi 2013, p. 192). The case study on Turkey, however, demonstrates that the ideas stemming from the EU, such as flexicurity, can be strategically used by domestic actors who in turn only 'pick and choose' those parts of ideas that 'best suit their pre-determined preferences' (Bolukbasi & Ertugal 2013).

In terms of macroeconomic policies, the EU's ever-evolving, increasingly elaborate macroeconomic policy framework has been shaped by the introduction of the Economic and Monetary Union (EMU) in 1999. The case study on Italy traces the EMU's history and shows how the EMU was inspired by the German macroeconomic model, which was the quintessential model of success over the 1980s on the road to Maastricht. By replicating this model, the EMU has come to institutionalise 'sound money' and 'sound public finance' as central principles governing monetary and fiscal policies (Quaglia 2013, p. 170). The Italian case study also shows that, while the EMU policy framework is most elaborate in central banking, monetary policy and exchange rate policy with direct explicit rules (e.g. central bank independence), there exist 'no hard EU rules on fiscal policy' (Ibid), which may be changing in response to the European sovereign debt crisis. Despite its asymmetric nature with respect to its economic and monetary pillars, the case study shows how the EU input, i.e. the EMU, has effectively constituted the broader framework within which domestic macroeconomic policies have been designed and implemented since the adoption of the euro.

Although the Italian case study emphasises that there are 'no hard EU rules' in the area of fiscal policy, the case study on Portugal shows that the main EU input in the area of fiscal policy has been confined to the specific fiscal rules associated with EMU membership. Both the fiscal convergence criteria included in the Maastricht Treaty and the Stability and Growth Pact (SGP) adopted in 1996 stipulate two concrete measures of budgetary discipline: 'a deficit-to-GDP ratio of three per cent and a debt-to-GDP ratio of 60 per cent'. In particular, the SGP includes an Excessive Deficit Procedure (EDP) to sanction countries that breach budgetary discipline defined as such, rendering fiscal rules legally binding on the member states (Royo 2013, p. 200). Despite these de jure constraints, however, the fiscal rules were de facto breached several times even before the onset of the European sovereign debt crisis by small and large member states alike. The failure on the part of the Council of the EU to implement the EDP gave way to intense criticisms which in turn led to their amendment.

In the area of financial regulation, the case study on Italy, which focuses on the banking and securities sectors, traces how the EU's financial regime was modelled on the British approach to financial regulation. The British model, which was 'uploaded' to the EU, has traditionally been depicted as one based on 'market-making measures and a light touch regulatory philosophy' (Quaglia 2013, p. 170). In the area of banking, the EU regulatory framework rests on EU competition policy (encouraging privatisation of large public financial institutions), pre-EMU constraints (where the fiscal consolidation process required public revenues to be raised by selling off public banks), requirements of economic and monetary integration, including the completion of the single financial market (through unleashing regulatory competition in the financial sector across the EU), and other measures such as the Second Banking Directive issued in 1988 (introducing an 'all-purpose universal bank') and the endorsement of the Financial Services Action Plan by the EU (allowing foreign banks to penetrate the Italian market) (Quaglia 2013, p. 166). In the area of securities, which 'was the sector of most intense activity in the EU in the 2000s' (Quaglia 2013, p. 168), the EU regulatory framework rests on a 'market-making approach' that, through the 'Lamfalussy directives', privileges 'financial market integration', 'competition' and 'market efficiency' through 'opening up national markets' over 'financial stability, consumer protection and in some cases the protection of national operators' (Quaglia 2013, p. 169).

In the area of independent regulatory and oversight bodies, the case study on Greece documents that the EU input is 'quite concrete and prescriptive', effectively leaving no room for flexibility in domestic arrangements (Blavoukos, Caramanis & Dedoulis

2013, p. 140). The case study focuses, in particular, on a specific European Commission Recommendation issued in 2001 and the new Eighth Directive 2006/43/EC, which require member states to establish independent public oversight bodies. Hence, the case study on Greece shows how the 'EU input', which prescribes a very specific institutional template, details the procedures, format and composition of newly introduced institutions such as independent public oversight bodies. The case study, which emphasises the legally binding nature of the EU pressure in this area, discusses the ways in which there is 'a very low "goodness of fit" between EU policies and domestic practices' in the case of Greece (Blavoukos, Caramanis & Dedoulis 2013, p. 144).

Europeanisation 'Outcomes': Continuity and Change in Public Policies and Governance

The case studies in this volume trace the direction, extent and dimensions of domestic change (as well as continuity) in Southern European political economies over the course of the 2000s. In doing so, they analyse the different Europeanisation 'outcomes' in different components or dimensions of a set of public policy areas that this volume takes as 'the domains where the effects of Europeanisation are supposed to materialise' (Radaelli 2003, p. 35). In conceptualising and operationalising domestic change (or the lack thereof) the case studies rely on the categories of transformation, absorption, accommodation, inertia and retrenchment that are widely used in the Europeanisation research programme. This section reviews the findings of the case studies by showing how Europeanisation advances in differentiated forms not only *across* different policy sectors but also *within* the distinctive components of a single policy sector.

The case study on Greece, which traces the establishment of the Greek independent oversight board for accounting and audit practices, demonstrates that, despite the forcefulness of the EU pressure in this particular area of governance, overall domestic change in Greece can be characterised as 'a mere *absorption* of the EU pressures, at best their *accommodation*' (Blavoukos, Caramanis & Dedoulis 2013, p. 150). While the establishment of the independent Accounting and Auditing Oversight Board (ELTE) in 2003 satisfies, at least in façade, the EU prescriptions in this area, having realised formal policy and institutional adaptation, ELTE has not substantially been reformed in accordance with the Directive of 2006 as the traditional practice of political appointment of personnel continues to preclude its independence and effectiveness. The case study shows the overall limits of Europeanisation, by pointing to the Greek state's continuing practices to maintain indirect control through 'the appointment of party-associated experts who influence the operation of these bodies in accordance with the governmental agenda' (Blavoukos, Caramanis & Dedoulis 2013, p. 151–152). Such practices, the authors conclude, are characteristic of the Greek political system. Strikingly, they also contend that their findings on the establishment and the operation of ELTE can conveniently be generalised to the workings of other oversight and independent authorities in other policy areas in Greece. Moreover, the authors also expect to find parallel Europeanisation outcomes in other Southern European countries facing 'similar constraints' (Blavoukos, Caramanis & Dedoulis 2013, p. 152).

In examining the outcomes of Europeanisation, the case study on Italy observes that there exists a differentiation with respect to the degree of Europeanisation between macroeconomic policies (as a case of 'strong' Europeanisation outcome) and financial regulation (which is an example of 'weak' Europeanisation outcome). First, in terms of the macroeconomic policies, although the Italian central bank followed the monetary policy of the Bundesbank prior to the establishment of EMU, the Italian monetary policy constitutes the 'most extreme case of *transformation*' as the policy capacity that had rested at the domestic level was effectively 'transferred to the EU level' with EMU (Quaglia 2013, p. 163). In parallel, the Italian exchange rate policy has undergone a 'major *transformation*' as 'the conduct of exchange-rate policy was transferred to the authorities of the euro area' as of 1999 (Quaglia 2013, p. 163). Fiscal policy, however, remained an exception to this rule as the changes therein amounted to *accommodation* where the 'adaptation of Italian fiscal policy to the requirements imposed by the EU and by EMU remained problematic', despite a 'major adjustment in the 1990s' (Quaglia 2013, p. 165). Second, in terms of financial services regulation, while in the area of banking and insurance the EU framework stumbled on 'domestic *retrenchment*' due to the protectionist intervention of the Governor of Banca d'Italia blocking a foreign takeover bid, this proved temporary, giving way to *transformation* (Quaglia 2013, p. 167). In the area of securities, the transposition of EU directives introduced a 'different set of priorities' into the Italian financial system and resulted in 'institutional adaptation' (Quaglia 2013, p. 169). The Italian case study shows that *transformation* occurs in cases of hard EU rules (such as treaty provisions in the case of monetary policy and exchange rate policy) or when hard EU rules prescribe certain institutional changes (such as in the case of financial regulation). *Accommodation* characterises the outcome when hard EU rules are accompanied by 'not so hard' EU rules (such as in the case of fiscal policy) (Quaglia 2013, p. 172). In fact, *reversals of transformation* take place when EU rules become less hard in time (such as in the case of the weakening of the SGP). *Inertia* occurs when EU rules are either 'only soft' or 'indirect' (as in the case of structural reforms) (Quaglia 2013, p. 171).

The case study on Malta shows that the overall Europeanisation outcomes in both labour market performance and labour market policy have been rather limited. The case study emphasises that there exists a wedge between the formal and informal labour markets in terms of the degree of Europeanisation. With regard to labour market performance in the formal sector, continuity in terms of 'high inactivity rates, untaxed work and resistance by employers to offer workers increased protection and benefits' renders the outcome in this area as *retrenchment* (Azzopardi 2013, p. 193). There was some improvement in employment and labour force participation rates during the 2000s, but this lasted only until about the onset of the Great Recession. Still, Malta continues to score the lowest levels in employment and labour force participation rates compared with EU averages, especially in the categories of women and older workers as well as among the youth (Azzopardi 2013). Moreover, skill shortages continue to remain a major challenge in the context of declining birth rates. With regard to labour market performance in the informal sector, the EU impact has been even less (Azzopardi 2013).

In terms of labour market policies, the EU's minimum requirements have been generally transposed into the Maltese legislative framework, albeit without having any impact on the fundamentals. While official policy documents have adopted the standard EU rhetoric on ideas about flexicurity (which is the EU's approach to labour markets), flexicurity as a 'practice' still has 'a long track to cover' (Azzopardi 2013, p. 191). Similarly, with respect to labour market performance, business establishments continue to find 'loopholes' in the implementation of EU legislation (Ibid). Thus, in the area of labour market policies, the Maltese case points to *absorption* of some of the non-fundamental aspects of the EU policies, rules and preferences without substantially modifying the core domestic practices, policies, rules or preferences.

The case study on Portugal centres on fiscal policies and performance as outcomes of Europeanisation. The forcefulness of the EU pressures stemming from EMU membership has not been sufficient in itself to lead to any transformative change in either fiscal policies or fiscal performance in Portugal. In terms of fiscal policies, the SGP has been 'insufficient to force the necessary policy reforms that would have addressed Portugal's history of fiscal mismanagement' (Royo 2013, p. 201). Thus, limited domestic change in fiscal policy explicitly 'demonstrates the limits of external pressure and the ability of the *acquis communautaire* to force change' (Royo 2013, p. 208). Whereas EMU pressures alone have been insufficient in bringing about reform due to the 'sheltered environment' (i.e. low interest rates and low inflation) created by the EMU, it is only with the onset of the global financial crisis since 2008 that Portugal has been under severe pressure for fiscal reform. The crisis forced the government to implement tough austerity measures. In 2011 the government promised 'the biggest cuts in government spending for more than 50 years' and introduced the 'harshest budget in living memory' (Royo 2013, p. 207). Thus, only with the recent crisis does Portugal seem to have adopted the 'sound public policy paradigm' (Royo 2013, p. 210).

In terms of fiscal performance, Portuguese fiscal balances continued to be represented by fiscal profligacy throughout the 2000s and breached the SGP's fiscal deficit rules. The author argues that this explains the country's poor economic performance during the same decade. Therefore, the change in Portuguese fiscal policy (and by implication performance) throughout the 2000s can be characterised as *accommodation*, as a result of the adaptation of existing domestic practices and policies to those of the EU through 'cosmetic' changes, largely maintaining the status quo without having gone through a change in their essential features (Royo 2013, p. 207).

The case study on Spain explains the changes in Spanish social and employment policies by analysing the surprising 'quantum leap' in the participation of women in formal labour markets, which amounts to a 'great transformation in Spanish society during 2000–10' (Moreno 2013, p. 219). Such an increase in female labour force participation is 'the most important factor' in accounting for continuity and change, not only in all areas of welfare in Spain but also across the Spanish political economy during the 2000s (Moreno 2013, p. 222). As a result of such change, Moreno observes, the Spanish welfare state during the 2000s was characterised by overall 'expansion and innovation' until the onset of the Great Recession (Moreno 2013, p. 229).

In terms of changes in Spanish social and employment policy regime, Moreno summarises the changes in the two key policy areas that have undergone *transformation*. The first is in labour market policies where new employment laws, including the law on positive discrimination for female employment, have been shaped by the National Action Plans for Employment and National Reform Programmes in response to the EES. A second policy area that has undergone a high degree of change is social services and care through the universalisation of long-term care, measures aiming to accomplish gender equality in the public sector, regional pre-school programmes, and other legislation on conciliation and equality. The changes in other policy areas, such as education, health and income transfers, are characterised by *accommodation*, EU inputs being incorporated into the Spanish welfare regime, albeit with modifications in their essential features. What determines the magnitude and direction of change (i.e. *transformation* in some areas versus *accommodation* in others) in the case of Spain, the author concludes, is the extent to which the policy area in question is directly linked with rising female labour force participation.

The case study on Turkey explicitly addresses the variation with respect to the magnitude and direction of change across different components of national employment policy. In terms of the principles of employment policy, the case study focuses on four components: first, changes in Turkish labour law towards more labour market flexibility amount to a *transformation*, whose applicability, however, is limited to less than half of the Turkish labour force. Second, the somewhat unsystematic deployment of active labour market policies is characterised by *accommodation* as these policies have recently entered the official programming documents. This became possible with the restructuring of the Turkish Employment Agency (Türkiye İş Kurumu—İŞKUR). Third, the introduction of lifelong learning systems into the Turkish education system amounts to *absorption*, where EU policies and practices gradually infiltrate without substantially enhancing the policymaking and implementation capacity of the institutions overseeing these policies. Finally, although the social security system has undergone some changes, these can be characterised only as *absorption*, as they fail to modify the existing path-dependent domestic policies and are carried out largely independent of the EU.

In addition to the principles of employment policy, the case study reviews the changes in the objectives of employment policy and shows that the preparations for launching a national employment strategy can be viewed as *accommodation* to the EU's requirements in policy programming. Moreover, with respect to the procedures in governance and policymaking, improvements in the participation of social partners in tripartite mechanisms can only be categorised as *absorption*, as their ability to influence decisions remains severely restricted. In terms of instruments, increases in financial allocations for active labour market measures as a result of EU accession and İŞKUR's expanded capacity (on the road to a modernised public employment service) to deliver these measures can be categorised as *accommodation*.

Ideas, Interests and Institutions in 'Processes' of Europeanisation

The case studies in this volume aim to show *how X* (EU input in the relevant policy area) and *Y* (the magnitude and direction of domestic change) are related in a given political economy. As explained in the introductory article to this volume (Balkir, Bolukbasi & Ertugal 2013), by focusing on the relationship *f* the case studies aim to go beyond following a bottom-up research design. Such a research design helps contributors isolate any extraneous variable that may potentially affect the magnitude and direction of domestic change. In order to unpack the causal processes of Europeanisation in Southern European political economies, the case studies analyse the evolution of distinct configurations of prevalent ideas, powerful interests and structuring institutions representing different policy and governance areas. While the case studies aim to show how the co-dependency among ideas, interests and institutions explain domestic change as well as continuity, this section provides prominent examples of each of these that features in these narratives.

Prevalent Ideas

The case studies in this volume have conceptualised ideas as roadmaps, strategic weapons in the battle for control, and larger frames of reference. As Balkir, Bolukbasi and Ertugal (2013) (based on Schmidt 2008) explain, these ideas can be conceptualised at three different levels ranging from the more specific policy level to the more general philosophical level: policy ideas, programmatic ideas and worldviews.

At the most specific level, the case studies show the centrality of several specific 'policy ideas' or 'policy solutions' that all Southern European policymakers refer to. In the area of labour market and employment policies, policymakers, across the board, emphasised key EU 'policy ideas' of 'labour activation' and 'flexicurity'. The case study on Spain elucidates how these policy ideas are equipped with their distinct 'concepts, methodologies and indicators' (Moreno 2013, p. 229). The case study on Malta shows how these policy ideas have penetrated into the official rhetoric and discourse at the domestic level (Azzopardi 2013). The case study on Turkey demonstrates examples of how the idea of 'flexibility', under false pretences of 'flexicurity', was strategically deployed by policymakers to pursue the policy goals of enhancing 'international competitiveness' as well as legitimising 'economic liberalisation' (Bolukbasi & Ertugal 2013, p. 248). In the area of macroeconomic policies, the case study on Portugal depicts how the 'policy idea' of 'fiscal consolidation', which has taken root in the EU, never took hold in the Portuguese political economy over the course of the

2000s, although this seems to be changing due to the recent global financial crisis (Royo 2013, p. 207)

At a more general level, Southern European case studies point to examples of 'programmatic ideas', 'policy paradigms' and 'frames of reference' that embed more specific policy ideas. The case study on Spain shows that the policy idea of labour activation is embedded in a larger, more general policy paradigm of 'neo-liberalism' (Moreno 2013). In parallel, the case study on Turkey demonstrates that in recent decades there has been a change in thinking on economic policymaking away from the once-dominant 'demand-side' 'Keynesian policy paradigm' towards another paradigm that emphasises the 'supply-side' (Bolukbasi & Ertugal 2013, p. 248). Likewise, the case studies on Portugal and Italy emphasise the ascendance of the programmatic idea of the 'sound public policy paradigm' at the level of the EU. The case study on Italy, for example, demonstrates that the Italian elite used a set of 'programmatic' 'causal ideas' such as the 'stability-oriented paradigm' in legitimising reforms (Quaglia 2013, p. 171). The case study on Portugal shows, however, that this policy paradigm was never dominant in Portugal and that 'no major group or political party' lent support to it (Royo 2013, p. 210).

The Southern European case studies also provide examples of how more general, philosophical-level 'worldviews' generally underlie the more specific policy and programmatic ideas. The case study on Spain provides an example of how the changes in the Spanish welfare regime, whose 'traditional historical structure' was 'alien to [labour activation] concepts', can be represented by a new 'system of belief' (Moreno 2013, p. 227). In Greece, the general worldviews concerning the role of the state in public policymaking shaped the fate of the newly established regulatory institutions (Blavoukos, Caramanis & Dedoulis 2013). In Malta, societal ideas with regard to, for example, the role of women in working life hindered domestic change (Azzopardi 2013).

The case studies also show how different types of ideas (cognitive versus normative) operate in domestic political economies. They provide many examples of cognitive, causal ideas. By providing a 'new interpretive framework' defining policy problems, as well as methods with which to solve them, and around which an 'epistemic consensus' among academics and policymakers emerged, labour activation constituted a key causal idea in Spain (Moreno 2013, p. 227). The policy idea of 'flexicurity', which is used as a 'cognitive' map in Turkey, seems to have taken on a life of its own; it features as the standard *referentielle* in the 'everyday common policy discourse' of policymakers in the area of employment policy (Bolukbasi & Ertugal 2013, p. 249). In Greece, politicians rediscovered 'efficiency' as a 'primary policy goal' and realised the 'strategic importance' of 'policy credibility' rendered by independent agencies (Blavoukos, Caramanis & Dedoulis 2013, p. 140). These cognitive ideas were used by politicians, who were increasingly willing to delegate their power to technocratic bodies, to deflect blame for unpalatable reforms.

The case studies also point to the currency of normative ideas emphasising the appropriateness of policies and providing legitimacy to them by attaching values to political action. In Spain, the idea of labour activation provides a 'normative view' among academics and policymakers (Moreno 2013, p. 228). In parallel, in Turkey, the policy idea of 'flexicurity' is strategically used as a 'normative policy idea' as 'the only means' for fighting unemployment (Bolukbasi & Ertugal 2013, p. 247). In Italy, policymakers have relied on 'normative ideas' such as 'visions of European political order' in seeking legitimacy (Quaglia 2013, p. 161). In Greece, in engineering a cosmetic change in the area of independent regulatory bodies, policymakers used normative ideas imported from the EU centring on the desirability of technocratic empowerment and policy expertise in policymaking at the expense of state control of such processes (Blavoukos, Caramanis & Dedoulis 2013). In Portugal, the normative ideas that circulated widely in Brussels of the 'need to hold firm in the application of restrictive fiscal policies' and the 'achievement of budgetary surpluses' could not be transplanted into the Portuguese policymaking apparatus (Royo 2013, p. 211).

Powerful Interests

The case studies examined the preferences and strategies of dominant actor coalitions whose interests lay either in bringing about reform or in resisting it. The coalitions that feature in episodes of reform are composed of the government (especially in 'simple polities' like Turkey where governing activities are traditionally carried out through the executive), organised functional interests (employers' associations representing big and small and medium-size enterprises and trade unions and their confederations), different political parties (representing different or similar ideological positions in government or in opposition), diverse interests within public bureaucracies (characterised by clashing esprit de corps in different public institutions such as the treasury and the central bank) and epistemic communities (equipped with technocratic know-how).

The pro-reform coalitions in Southern Europe generally include ruling parties in government, employers' associations, epistemic communities and bureaucratic organisations. First, in Greece, the executive (the government in power) and prominent politicians of the ruling party constitute the most powerful interests given the institutional characteristics of the Greek political system (Blavoukos, Caramanis & Dedoulis 2013). In parallel, the case study on Turkey identifies the government as 'the most powerful actor that is likely to bring about policy reform', not only in employment policy, but also in all public policy domains. The government features as *the* protagonist in virtually every account of domestic reform, which is a characteristic feature of 'simple polities' (see below) (Bolukbasi & Ertugal 2013, p. 247).

Second, in addition to the government and ruling parties and their stronghold constituencies, the Italian case shows that bureaucratic actors, too, have led pro-reform coalitions. During the 1990s and 2000s, the Italian political economy was dominated by a 'macroeconomic adjustment coalition' supporting Italy's membership in the EMU (Quaglia 2013, p. 171). This coalition, members of which were 'at the interface between Italy and the EU', was composed of policymakers at the Bank of Italy and the Treasury (Quaglia 2013, p. 171). In particular, in the area of monetary policy, 'policy entrepreneurs' whose hands were strengthened by the Maastricht strictures were successful in bringing about reform, especially until EMU membership was achieved (Quaglia 2013). In Portugal, it is only since 2008, when the country has been faced with the risk of default, that the Bank of Portugal and the Ministry of Finance, traditionally ardent supporters of sound fiscal policies, have been influential in the design of fiscal policies (Royo 2013).

Third, interest groups based on functional representation, especially business interests, join pro-reform coalitions. In Italy, for example in the area of fiscal policy, the Italian industry represented by Confidustria joined the Bank of Italy and led a 'weak constituency that had a stake in budgetary rectitude' (Quaglia 2013, p. 165). In the area of financial regulation, 'an outward-oriented coalition' of 'large financial groups', which stood to gain from further financial integration and opening up of national financial systems, supported domestic change (Quaglia 2013, p. 171). Likewise, in Turkey, the government's preferences towards reform in the direction of increased labour market flexibility are shaped by strong domestic constituencies, composed of small and medium-size enterprises alongside traditionally strong big business (Bolukbasi & Ertugal 2013). Accordingly, there has emerged a 'convergence of preference' between the government and the employers on emphasising exclusively the flexibility dimension in flexicurity (Bolukbasi & Ertugal 2013, p. 250).

Fourth, the 2000s also witnessed epistemic communities composed of thinktanks and professional groups equipping pro-reform coalitions with 'scientific' rationales. In Spain, for example, an informal network of professional economists, G-100, advocated the flexibilisation of Spanish labour markets. The claims by this group were covered heavily by the media, which were in favour of introducing increased levels of flexibility into labour markets. Even after the onset of the most recent economic crisis, this influential network of economists continued to advocate the ongoing process of labour market deregulation and flexibilisation (Moreno 2013). In Malta, despite some resistance to reforms, the participation of social and economic actors, including 'employers, unions, local councils, women's organisations, the self-employed, consultancies', in EU-funded projects related to the labour market led them to advocate labour market reforms (Azzopardi 2013, p. 190).

In cases where public policy reforms have been successfully introduced, the dominant actors have relied on several strategies including 'usages' of the EU. In Spain, the strategies that allowed Spanish policymakers to carry out their reform initiatives in the direction of labour activation in particular and neoliberalism in general included 'blame avoidance devices', 'credit-claiming practices', 'emulation' and 'policy learning'. In doing this, policymakers have extensively used the EU strategically in order not only to 'legitimate their positions and claims' but also to 'create hegemonic or influential positions in political debates' (Moreno 2013, p. 230). Similarly, when the Greek government intended to fix its 'tarnished image' and restore 'public confidence in the stock exchange' following the 1999 Athens Stock Exchange crisis, politicians instrumentally used EU pressures 'to legitimise government action' in creating ELTE. In doing so, however, they have not given up control of the policymaking process (Blavoukos, Caramanis & Dedoulis 2013, p. 150). In parallel, Maltese policymakers have used the EU to justify and legitimise reforms otherwise unpalatable. Reform has been a treacherous enterprise, employers in particular opposing any change unless they were convinced that it stemmed from the EU. The case study also shows that the financial incentives provided by the EU have 'infiltrated material interests' and the government has coopted certain social and economic actors who have benefited from these funds (Azzopardi 2013, p. 190).

In cases where reforms stalled, resistance came from a diverse set of interests including government actors, segments of the business community, trade unions, political parties and epistemic communities. In Greece, the nature of institutional change in response to EU pressures has been rendered 'shallow and a mere façade' by the government actors themselves, who continue to maintain 'control indirectly through the appointment of party-associated experts who influence the operation of these bodies in accordance with the governmental agenda', which is a characteristic feature of the Greek political system (Blavoukos, Caramanis & Dedoulis 2013, pp. 151, 152). In Portugal, given the absence of a strong consensus on EMU membership, policymakers did not have any incentive to enforce the new 'sound money' paradigm underlying EMU (Royo 2013).

The case studies show that anti-reform coalitions encompass diverse interests outside government. In Portugal, for example, a wide coalition composed of part of the business community, led by the Portuguese confederation of industrialists and association of bankers, as well as the Communist Party and its closer trade union confederation, openly stood against the convergence criteria in the 1990s for fear that they would undermine the Portuguese economy. Even the organised actors who were supportive of Portugal's membership in the EMU (such as the association of industrialists and a trade union) articulated serious doubts over the EMU's impact on employment and growth. Moreover, 'entrenched interest groups' composed of civil servants, unions, and professional groups (such as teachers' unions) 'were able to exercise effective veto power over any attempt to impose fiscal discipline' (Royo 2013, p. 211). In Italy, a group of 'inward-oriented', 'less competitive' financial institutions (with the support of the Bank of Italy under Antonio Fazio between 1993 and 2005) were powerful enough to have initially acted as a veto point in processes of financial market integration (Quaglia 2013, p. 171). In Malta, both employers and trade unions have resisted reforms towards flexicurity. Employers have been against these reforms, due to the perceived harm to their interests emanating from the security component of flexicurity. Unions have remained cautious in their approach too, as they have seen that the more the labour market is regulated, the less is their power in collective bargaining schemes (Azzopardi 2013).

Structuring Institutions

The case studies identify different types of institutions that are examples of conventional systems of formal and informal rules that may constrain or enable the behaviour of actors. By representing 'the political dimensions of economic management' (Hall 1986, p. 19), these institutions structure social interactions through allocating power among different actors in a given political economy. As they also structure policymaking, institutions also shape the procedures of how decisions are adopted in a given public policy domain. The institutions that feature in the case studies concern the type of political systems, the nature of bureaucratic traditions with different forms and levels of politicisation, the variety of capitalism (with its distinct production regime, welfare state regime, industrial relations regime, corporate governance and financial system), the nature of territorial governance, the level of political instability and the level of control of the executive over the budget.

First, in terms of the type of political systems in Southern European countries, the majoritarian character of the Greek political system renders any reform attempt to establish independent regulatory agencies unlikely, as the state maintains its control through political appointments of their staff (Blavoukos, Caramanis & Dedoulis 2013). In Turkey, the political system may be characterised as a 'simple polity' where the government enjoys ultimate power and authority in virtually all public policy domains. This means that, especially in the absence of strong veto players (which generally is the case), 'the direction and extent of domestic change become largely a function of government preferences' (Bolukbasi & Ertugal 2013, p. 247).

Second, the nature of bureaucratic traditions with different manifestations of politicisation structure political economic outcomes too. In Turkey, for example, the hierarchical and centralised bureaucratic tradition magnifies the power and authority of the ruling political party in a highly skewed political system. When the top echelons of the bureaucracy are increasingly politicised, as was the case over the decade following the elections of 2002, such a tradition leads to a swift process of designing and implementing public policies (Bolukbasi & Ertugal 2013). While politicisation of the bureaucracy helps explain public policy reform in Turkey, it is a source of inertia in Greece. The case study on Greece shows that the establishment of independent regulatory agencies was impossible given the 'long-established, often institutionalised' bureaucratic tradition of 'extended politicisation' (Blavoukos, Caramanis & Dedoulis 2013, p. 140). This is a case where only cosmetic changes could be introduced, since policymakers did not wish to relinquish their political leverage on regulatory institutions.

Third, the Southern European variety of capitalism has been variously characterised as 'mixed market economies' (Molina & Rhodes 2007), 'Mediterranean capitalism' (Amable 2003) or 'state capitalist' models (Schmidt 2003). The case studies in this special issue provide ample evidence on the institutional pillars of the Southern European political economies which largely confirms the findings of this body of literature. In terms of the production regime, the case study on Malta depicts the

Maltese traditional production units as generally composed of 'small, mainly family owned and family run businesses', which in part explains absence of policy reform in the area of labour market policy (Azzopardi 2013, p. 192). In terms of the welfare state regime, the case study on Spain emphasises the hybrid nature of the Spanish welfare regime, composed of Bismarckian social insurance and Beveridgean tax-financed pillars. The case study shows that, as an overarching institution, the Bismarckian pillar continued to play a 'decisive institutional role' in reform processes during the 2000s in refracting the effects of rising female labour force participation (Moreno 2013, p. 228).

In terms of the industrial relations regime, the case studies on Turkey and Malta exemplify typical Southern European 'adversarial industrial relations' overwhelmed by a state playing a paternalistic role. This regime 'amplifies employers' interests' and undermines the 'positive' and 'negative veto powers' of trade unions (Bolukbasi & Ertugal 2013, p. 248; Azzopardi 2013). The nature of the industrial relations regime, however, produced contrasting outcomes in Turkey and Malta. In Turkey, given the institutional nature of this regime, the original EU idea of flexicurity was translated into policy as flexibility only (Bolukbasi & Ertugal 2013). In Malta, the poor record of social dialogue at the national level led to limited change with respect to labour market policy (Azzopardi 2013). Interestingly, the case study on Spain emphasises the significance of 'consensual politics' in the area of industrial relations. Although social dialogue has enabled reform since the mid-1970s, it has 'come under strain during 2000–10' given the emphasis on the 'flexibilisation of industrial relations' in political debates (Moreno 2013, p. 229).

In terms of corporate governance and the financial system, the case study on Italy shows that the Italian political economy of the 1990s was a typical representative of the Southern European variety of capitalism with an inefficient, 'dysfunctional' state with 'chronic problems with unsustainable fiscal policy' in the macroeconomic realm (Quaglia 2013, pp. 162, 173). In terms of corporate governance, the Italian model has traditionally been characterised by a 'family-type of capitalism created by an underdeveloped capital market' and an 'outdated', 'fragile national regulatory framework' (Quaglia 2013, p. XX). The financial regime, which was under the influence of the 'market-shaping approach' of the Italian state, used to be mainly 'bank oriented' with an underdeveloped securities market (Quaglia 2013, p. 169). Large state-owned banks, which restricted competition, dominated the traditional and highly segmented banking sector. Against this institutional background, the Italian political economy went institutional change over the course of the 1990s and 2000s, the macroeconomic and financial pillars of the domestic political economy converging 'towards an EU model largely informed by a (German-inspired) stability-oriented approach to macroeconomic policies, and (Anglo-Saxon-inspired) market-friendly regulation in financial services' (Quaglia 2013, p. 173).

Fourth, in terms of the nature of territorial governance, the case study on Spain shows that the process of constitutional decentralisation enabled 'policy innovation by meso-governments' whereby different subnational government levels share 'rule capacity' (Moreno 2013, p. 228). In this changing institutional structure, different regions compete in a process of 'policy equalisation as well as an incentive to "catch up" for those Spanish regions that traditionally lag behind "modernised" ones', which has speeded up change (Moreno 2013, p. 229).

Fifth, the case study on Portugal provides examples of how institutionalised forms of political instability account for domestic continuity and change. Political instability has manifested itself in a number of ways. Especially in the first half of the 2000s, the office of prime minister changed hands frequently. It was only between 2005 and 2011, 'the longest tenure' in 18 years, that the government was able to pursue a degree of fiscal consolidation (Royo 2013, p. 208). Likewise, until 2005 the Ministry of Finance had not been powerful enough to control fiscal policies with 'ministers often resigning in protest at their inability to reign over their colleagues' (Royo 2013, p. 208). Additionally, the minister of finance has had limited control over the budget, which also helps explain the absence of reform in the area of fiscal policy and governance in Portugal until the onset of the global financial crisis.

Conclusions

This article, first, summarises the varied EU-level inputs, frameworks or agendas in the different policy areas each case study focuses on. Second, it gauges the magnitude and direction of domestic change at the level of policy and governance in each political economy. Third, it explains how the prevalent ideas, dominant interests and structuring institutions affect the nature of domestic change in political economies. Based on the discussion above, this section provides a set of overall conclusions pointing to the diverse nature of the EU input, the differentiated nature of the EU's impact across different dimensions in a given policy sector and the co-dependency of ideas, interests and institutions in accounting for domestic change as well as continuity.

This volume examines processes of continuity and change in Southern European political economies during the decade following the publication of Featherstone and Kazamias (2000). Although the Great Recession started towards the end of the decade examined by the volume, the case studies mainly focus on the trajectories of Southern European countries until the early period of the crisis. Although the case studies do not exclusively focus on how the Southern European political economies are responding to the crisis, they shed empirical light on the causes of the crisis as well as on the inherited legacies that inevitably have played a role in conditioning these countries' crisis responses.

In terms of the nature of the EU's role, the case studies in this volume attest to the EU's wide-ranging inputs in diverse domains of policy and governance. The case studies demonstrate that these inputs have the potential to run deep throughout a given policy area. They range from more general and highly abstract policy and governance templates to more specific and rather concrete tools. Among the general templates are the broad *approaches* (e.g. the EU's 'approach to labour markets', centring on flexicurity that reconciles labour market flexibility and security; and its 'market-making approach' in the area of financial regulation following the British model), *frameworks of reference* (e.g. activation of the labour force; the EMU delineating a broad macroeconomic framework for domestic policymakers; the EU's regulatory framework in financial regulation centring on EU competition policy, pre-EMU constraints and post-EMU requirements) and comprehensive *strategies* (e.g. the EES coordinating national governments' efforts to create more and better jobs).

At the same time, among the more specific tools, EU inputs may involve very specific *targets* (e.g. the headline goals of the EES aiming to achieve higher labour force participation rates, higher levels of educational attainment and lower school drop-out rates, and to reduce the number of people in or at risk of poverty and social exclusion) and concrete *policy measures* (e.g. measures such as guidelines, declarations and opinions adopted within the context of the workings of the EES and aimed at creating or maintaining employment with different time horizons, targeting all workers or tailored to specific groups; and measures and sanctions for countries breaching fiscal rules defined by the Excessive Deficit Procedure of the Maastricht Treaty which was bolstered by the SGP). With respect to their binding status, these measures may take the form of usually non-binding 'soft law' (e.g. measures associated with the EES such as guidelines, declarations and opinions; the Broad Economic Policy Guidelines aiming to coordinate macroeconomic policy associated with the workings of the EMU), which is, in principle, distinguished from legally binding 'hard law' that is the outcome of the traditional 'Community Method' (e.g. the Second Banking Directive of 1988 and the more recent 'Lamfalussy Directives' governing financial regulation; the European Commission Recommendation of 2001 and the Eighth Directive of 2006 requiring member states to establish independent public oversight bodies).

In terms of the nature of the EU's impact at the domestic level, the case studies collectively show that,despite the complex and elaborate policy and governance structure of the EU, uniformity in 'Europeanisation as outcome' across member states and candidate countries is not a foregone conclusion. In fact, the findings of the more recent waves of the Europeanisation research programme, especially when taken together with those of the literature on 'differentiated integration', suggest that there are neither substantive nor theoretical reasons to expect uniform Europeanisation outcomes across different clusters of states, whose levels and nature of integration with the EU are different, ceteris paribus. As defined in a recent research review, EU rules and policies whereby 'the territorial extension of EU membership and EU rule validity are incongruent' constitute 'cases of differentiated (or flexible) integration' (Holzinger & Schimmelfennig 2012, p. 292). Southern Europe, as depicted by the original special issue that inspired the present volume, is composed of states that are differentiated 'according to the length of EU membership; states inside and outside the EU; the size of state; and historically competing identities and ties' (Featherstone & Kazamias 2000, p. 2). At the same time, there is no intuitive rationale for expecting uniform outcomes across a set of policy and governance areas in a given political economy.

What is perhaps more striking in light of the evidence presented in the case studies in this volume, however, is that there is also no uniformity in Europeanisation outcomes across different components of a given policy and governance sector in a given political economy. The Europeanisation research programme and the 'differentiated integration' literature should take into account the fact that different components in or dimensions of a given a policy sector may become Europeanised at variable speeds. Regardless of the level at which we observe outcomes, our South European case studies show that instances of limited change (such as absorption or accommodation) occur more frequently than other categories of change, including absence of change (i.e. inertia), significant change yet in the opposite direction of EU inputs (retrenchment) and wholesale replacement of domestic practices, policies, rules, etc. (i.e. transformation) due to, or in parallel with, EU pressures.

In terms of how ideas, interests and institutions co-determine outcomes, the case studies in this volume unequivocally suggest that the ideas that played a prominent role in domestic policy change invariably had their sources in the EU.[2] These case studies also suggest that these ideas themselves do not have a direct bearing on the outcome. When they have an impact, they do so only when they are mediated by the dominant interests in respective institutional contexts. Such mediation may take different forms. First, ideas may be used as strategic weapons in the battle for control. Powerful interests may embrace and instrumentally use ideas stemming from the EU. They may even go all the way to champion them in different platforms, as was the case in Spain. Alternatively, dominant actors may cherry-pick only one idea in a given package of ideas and strategically use it partially when they engineer cosmetic change, as the case studies on Greece and Turkey show. Moreover, EU ideas may be welcomed as scapegoats or garbage cans when dominant interests, as in the case of Italy, intend to deflect blame for policies otherwise unpalatable. Second, EU ideas may be resisted altogether by dominant actor coalitions whose interests, as in the cases of Portugal and Malta, would either be hampered or simply not affected by them. Third, certain ideas, which may have been resisted in the first place, may become more attractive in time and only after they are bundled together with additional incentives (such as EU financial assistance under the IPA and the European Social Fund), as in the case of Malta.

At the same time, the case studies show how path-dependent institutional structures strengthen the hands of certain actors. For example the institutional features of macro-political systems that may be characterised as simple polities empower ruling parties, as the case studies on Greece and Turkey demonstrate. A second example is the institutional arrangements represented by certain bureaucratic traditions where politicisation, again as in the cases of Greece and Turkey, renders policy change simply a function of government interests. A third example is the legacy of adversarial industrial relations empowering dominant business actors to pursue their interest in the political realm, as in the cases of Malta, Spain (only after the onset of the Great Recession) and Turkey. A fourth example is the nature of a production regime that strengthens small and medium-size enterprises whose support leads to policy reform as in Turkey, or whose lack of support for reform prevents it coming about. A final example is a type of financial system whose traditional structure, as in the case of Italy, over-determines which interests matter in the game of resisting or bringing about change.

When we review the findings of this volume with respect to 'Europeanisation outcomes' and 'Europeanisation processes', we conclude that the South European experience of Europeanisation is still characterised by the three key attributes observed by Featherstone and Kazamias (2000) more than a decade ago. *Dynamism* continues to prevail as processes of Europeanisation remain an 'interactive, iterative process between actors, domestic and European or both', with contingent evolution of public policies resulting in 'uncertain', and at times 'reversible', outcomes across Southern Europe (Featherstone & Kazamias 2000, p. 12, p. 3). *Asymmetry* is still the norm in Southern European political economies because unfolding Europeanisation processes are 'incremental, irregular and uneven over time and between locations, national and subnational', resulting in profound disparities not only within and without the region, but also among different policy areas and different dimensions of a given policy area (Featherstone & Kazamias 2000, p. 11). As the case studies show, *fragmentation* remains a key Southern European trait as Europeanisation continues to 'create and reinforce domestic cleavages' and restructure 'the power, preferences and interests of sets of actors', setting new constraints, revising opportunities and redefining preferences and interests (Featherstone & Kazamias 2000, p. 13).

Notes

[1] As reviewed in the introductory article of this volume by Balkir, Bolukbasi and Ertugal (2013), Radaelli (2012) differentiates between three types of Europeanisation research. The first type of Europeanisation research focuses on the EU input (*X*) as its point of departure and in search of the 'effects of causes' adopts a top-down research design focusing on the impact of 'adaptational pressure' on domestic change (*Y*). The second type of research starts from analysing domestic change (*Y*) where the potential impact would take place and then in search of the 'causes of effects' adopts a bottom-up research design tracing the possible causes of domestic change, which may or may not include the EU input. The third type of research focuses on *f* in isolating the exclusive impact of the EU input on domestic change, once the relationship between *X* and *Y* has been analytically unpacked.

[2] This may be an indication of the peripheral status of the South European countries within the EU as importers (rather than exporters) of policy ideas, policy paradigms or worldviews.

References

Amable, B. (2003) *The Diversity of Modern Capitalism*, Oxford University Press, Oxford.

Azzopardi, R. M. (2013) 'All hands on deck! How Europeanised is the Maltese labour market?', *South European Society and Politics*, vol. 18, no. 2, pp. 177–196.

Balkir, C., Bolukbasi, H. T. & Ertugal, E. (2013) 'Europeanisation and dynamics of continuity and change in domestic political economies in the "Southern Periphery"', *South European Society and Politics*, vol. 18, no. 2, pp. 121–137.

Blavoukos, S., Caramanis, C. & Dedoulis, E. (2013) 'Europeanisation, independent bodies and the empowerment of technocracy: the case of the Greek auditing oversight body', *South European Society and Politics*, vol. 18, no. 2, pp. 139–157.

Bolukbasi, H. T. & Ertugal, E. (2013) 'Europeanisation of employment policy in Turkey: tracing domestic change through institutions, ideas and interests', *South European Society and Politics*, vol. 18, no. 2, pp. 237–257.

Featherstone, K. & Kazamias, G. (2000) 'Introduction: Southern Europe and the process of "Europeanization"', *South European Society and Politics*, vol. 5, no. 2, pp. 1–24.

Hall, P. A. (1986) *Governing the Economy: The Politics of State Intervention in Britain and France*, Oxford University Press, Oxford.

Holzinger, K. & Schimmelfennig, F. (2012) 'Differentiated integration in the European Union: many concepts, sparse theory, few data', *Journal of European Public Policy*, vol. 19, no. 2, pp. 292–305.

Molina, O. & Rhodes, M. (2007) 'The political economy of adjustment in mixed market economies: a study of Spain and Italy', in *Beyond Varieties of Capitalism*, eds B. Hancke, M. Rhodes & M. Thatcher, Oxford University Press, Oxford, pp. 223–252.

Moreno, L. (2013) 'Spain's catching up with the EU core: the implausible quest of a "flying pig"?', *South European Society and Politics*, vol. 18, no. 2, pp. 217–236.

Quaglia, L. (2013) 'The Europeanisation of macroeconomic policies and financial regulation in Italy', *South European Society and Politics*, vol. 18, no. 2, pp. 159–176.

Radaelli, C. M. (2003) 'The Europeanisation of public policy', in *The Politics of Europeanisation*, eds K. Featherstone & C. M. Radaelli, Oxford University Press, Oxford, pp. 27–56.

Radaelli, C. M. (2012) 'Europeanization: the challenge of establishing causality', in *Research Design in European Studies: Establishing Causality in Europeanization*, eds T. Exadaktylos & C. M. Radaelli, Palgrave Macmillan, Basingstoke, pp. 1–16.

Royo, S. (2013) 'Portugal in the European Union: the limits of convergence', *South European Society and Politics*, vol. 18, no. 2, pp. 197–216.

Schmidt, V. A. (2003) 'French capitalism transformed, yet still a third variety of capitalism', *Economy and Society*, vol. 32, no. 4, pp. 526–554.

Schmidt, V. A. (2008) 'Discursive institutionalism: the explanatory power of ideas and discourse', *Annual Review of Political Science*, vol. 11, pp. 303–326.

Index

Note:
Page numbers in **bold** type refer to figures
Page numbers in *italic* type refer to tables
Page numbers followed by 'n' refer to notes

Abela, A. 64
Accountancy Greece 27
Accounting Standardisation and Auditing Committee *see* ELTE
Accounting Standardisation Committee (SLOT) 23
Active Labour Market Policies (ALMPs) 13, 54, 118–19; examples 55
adaptational pressures: Southern Europe 4
adversarial industrial relations 148, 151
Alfonso, A.: and Papadopoulos, Y. 57–8
Alogoskoufis, G. 24
Amato, G.: and Carli, G. 49n
Anglo-American capitalism 103
Ardy, B.: and Umbach, G. 57
Athens Stock Exchange crisis (1999) 29, 146
auditing: oversight body (Greece) 17–30; policymaking (EU) 19–22, *see also* ELTE
Azzopardi, R.M. 11–12, 53–69

Bache, I. 7
Baldacchino, G. 59
Balkır, C.H.: Bolukbasi, H.T. and Ertugal, E. 1–13, 94, 133–52
Banca Bilbao Vizcaya Argentaria 43
Banca Popolare di Lodi 43
Bank of Portugal 87
banks 42
Barros, P.P.: and Garoupa, N. 75
Basel Committee on Banking Supervision (BCBS) 37–8
Berlusconi, S. 44
Beveridge curve: Malta **60**
Blavoukos, S.: Caramanis, C. and Dedoulis, E. 10, 17–30
Blyth, M. 9
Bolukbasi, H.T.: and Ertugal, E. 12–13; Ertugal, E. and Balkır, C.H. 1–13, 94, 133–52
Borsa Italiana 45
Braga de Macedo, J. 87–8
Bundesbank 39
bureaucratic tradition: Turkey 147, 151

capitalism: Anglo-American 103; Southern Europe 147
Caramanis, C.: Dedoulis, E. and Blavoukos, S. 10, 17–30
Carli, G.: and Amato, G. 49n
Cerami, A. 57
change: domestic (Bache) 7
Christodoulakis, N. 23
Coehlo, P. 83
Commission of the European Communities *see* European Commission (EC)
Compromisso Portugal 88
Conditions of the Employment Regulation Act (CERA, 1952) 67
Confederation of Progressive Trade Unions of Turkey 121
Constancio, V. 87
constitutional decentralisation: Spain 148–9
corporate collapses 20
Council for Economic and Social Development (Malta) 67–8
Czech Republic: EES 57

debt: public 41, 79
decentralisaton: constitutional (Spain) 148–9
Dedoulis, E.: Blavoukos, S. and Caramanis, C. 10, 17–30
Della Sala, V. 38
design types (Radaelli) 5–6
domestic change 7
domestic political economies 133–52; Italy 46–8; Southern Europe 3–5; Spain 93
dynamism 152

Economic and Monetary Union *see* EMU (Economic and Monetary Union)
economic performance: Portugal 77, 79
education: Malta 61–2
EES (European Employment Strategy) 13, 54, 57, 60–4, 98, 135; main aspects 54–5; Turkey 115–16, 116–17
ELTE (Greek Accounting Standardisation and Auditing Committee) 138; Administrative

Council (AC) 23; establishment 22–4; foundation 29; governance 19; ideas 28–9; insights 28–9; institutionalisation of local constraints 24–7; interests 28–9; Law 3148/ 2003 23
employment: National Action Plans (Spain) 141, *see also* EES (European Employment Strategy); İŞKUR (Turkish Employment Agency)
employment policy: Spain 140–1; Turkey 114, 117–22, 127–9
Employment and Training Corporation (ETC) Report (2009) 60–2, *60*
EMU (Economic and Monetary Union) 11, 21, 35, 46, 78, 136; convergence criteria 75; fiscal policies 76–7; Italy 39–42, 47, 136–7; member states policies 41
Ertugal, E.: Balkır, C.H. and Bolukbasi, H.T. 1–13, 94, 133–52; and Bolukbasi, H.T. 12–13
Estrella Report 66
EU15 (1995) 57
EU27 (2007): labour market policies 62
Eurobarometer 107n
Eurofound 59
Europe: corporate collapses 20; labour market Europeanisation 56, *see also* Southern Europe
European Central Bank (ECB) 39
European Championship Cup (2004) 79
European Commission (EC) 20, 62, 68; Italian fiscal policy 41; Recommendation (2001) 20, 23
European Community (EC) 73; and Portugal Preferential Trade Agreement (PTA, 1972) 74
European Economic Community (EEC) 93
European Employment Strategy *see* EES
European Foundation for the Improvement of Living and Working Conditions (Eurofound) 59
European Monitoring Centre on Change (EMCC) 59
European Union (EU): auditing policymaking 19–22; domestic level impact 150; domestic political economies 133–52; Eighth Directive 2006/43/EC 27; financial regime 137; financial services regulation 42–5, 46; frameworks 135–8; ideas 151; inputs 134, 150; integration studies 5; Investment Services Directive (ISD, 1993) 45; key rules 2; Labour Directives 67; Lamfalussy Directives 44; Market Abuse Directive (MAD, 2003) 44, 45; models 135–8; policies 65, 135–8; policy paradigm 37; Portugal's membership and economy 74–90; regimes 135–8; rules 37, 45, 135–8; Spanish catch up quest 93–107
European Values Surveys (EVS) 64
Eurostat 96
Exchange Rate Mechanism (ERM) 39, 75

Featherstone, K.: and Kazamias, G. 2, 3, 149
financial regulation: Italy 35–49, 139
Financial Services Action Plan (FSAP) 43, 137
fiscal constitution: Portugal 85
fiscal convergence: Portugal 83–4
fiscal performance: Portugal 140
fiscal policy: Italy 40, 41; Portugal 77–84, 140, 145
Fleckenstein, T. 57

Garoupa, N.: and Barros, P.P. 75
Germany 40–1, 46
Great Recession 149
Greece 10–11, 58; Athens Stock Exchange crisis (1999) 29, 146; auditing 22–4; auditing oversight body 17–30; bureaucratic tradition 151; efficiency 143; EU pressure 138; extended politicisation 18; independent regulatory agencies 147; institutional change 146; labour market 21; macro-political systems 151; Ministry of Economy 25; normative ideas 144; policymaking 29, 30n; politicians 144, 145–6; Quality Inspections Committee (SPE) 23; reform 147, *see also* ELTE
Greek-European Community/EU relations 20

Hall, P.A. 9
Heclo, H. 10
Human Resources Development Operational Programme (HRDOP) 117

ideas 7–10, 141–9; cognitive 8; conceptualisation 8; Malta 64–8; normative 144; policy 8; Portugal 84–8; Spain 102–6; Turkey 122–7
IMF (International Monetary Fund) 95
Independent Accounting and Auditing Oversight Board *see* ELTE
independent oversight bodies 17–30
independent regulatory agencies: Greece 147
industrial relations 148, 151
institutions 7–10, 141–9; Italy 46–8; Malta 64–8; Portugal 84–8; Spain 102–6; Turkey 122–7
Instrument for Pre-Accession Assistance (IPA) 117, 136
instruments: Turkey 122
interests 7–10, 141–9; Italy 46–8; Malta 64–8; Portugal 84–8; Spain 102–6; Turkey 122–7
Investment Services Directive (ISD, 1993) 45
İŞKUR (Turkish Employment Agency) 116, 118–19, 122, 127–8
Italy 11; banks 42; domestic political economy 46–8; EMU 39–42, 47, 136–7; EU financial regime 137; EU financial services regulation 42–5; financial regulation 35–49, 139; fiscal policy 40, 41; institutions 46–8; interests 46–8; Law on Savings (2005) 43, 44; macroeconomic adjustment coalition 144–5;

macroeconomic policies 35–49, 139; monetary policy 40; normative ideas 144; political economy 47, 49; political economy (1990s) 148; public debt 41; research design 36–8; Second Banking Directive (1992) 42; study findings *49*

Kazamias, G.: and Featherstone, K. 2, 3, 149
Koster, F.: and Van Vilet, O. 57
Kroes, N. 43

labour activation: Spain 103–4, 143
Labour Directives 67
labour market 56; Greece 21, 53–4; Malta 53–69, *63*, 139; Spain 101, 145
labour market policies (LMPs): active (ALMPs) 13, 54, 55, 118–19; EU27 62; interventions 55
labour relations: Spain 105
Lamfalussy Directives 44
lifelong learning systems: Turkey 119, 128
Lisbon Strategy (2000) 54
Lisbon Summit (2000) 115
London Stock Exchange 45
Luxembourg Process *see* EES

Maastricht Treaty (1992) 36, 76, 137
McCreevy, C. 43
macro-political systems 151
macroeconomic adjustment coalition: Italy 144–5
macroeconomic policies: Italy 35–49, 139
Malta 11–12; adversarial industrial relations 148, 151; Beveridge curve **60**; case study 58–68; education 61–2; EES targets *60*; EU policy 65; Europeanisation 56; Foundation for Educational Services 64; ideas 64–8; institutions 64–8; interests 64–8; Joint Assessment of the Employment Policy Priorities 61; labour market 53–69, *63*, 139; maternity leave 66; National Reform Programme (2005–8) 61; policymakers 146; private pension funds 66; reforms 146; traditional production units 147–8
Malta Council for Economic and Social Development (MCESD) 67
Market Abuse Directive (MAD, 2013) 45
Market in Financial Instruments Directive (MiFID, 2004) 44
maternity leave 66
Mediobanca 38, 43
monetary policy: Italy 40
Moreno, L. 12, 93–107, 141

National Action Plans for Employment (Spain) 141
National Reform Programmes (Spain) 141
neoliberalism: Spain 103–4
New Democracy (ND) 24
normative ideas 144

Olympic Airways/Airlines 21
Open Method of Coordination (OMC) 55, 98, 114
Organisation for Economic Cooperation and Development (OECD) 95, 118
outcomes 138–42
oversight bodies: independent 17–30

Pan-Hellenic Socialist Movement (PASOK): ELTE 24; government 30n
Papadopoulos, Y.: and Alfonso, A. 57–8
Papathanasiou, J. 27
PIGS countries (Portugal, Italy, Greece and Spain) 96
policies: economic (Portugal) 84; employment 114, 117–22, 127–9, 140–1; EU 65, 135–8; macroeconomic (Italy) 35–49, 139; Spain 93, 140–1, *see also* labour market policies (LMPs)
policy innovation: Spain 104–5
policymakers 145, 146
policymaking: auditing (EU) 19–22; procedures (Turkey) 121–2, 124
political economy 2, 133–52; definition 3; Italy 47, 49, 148
politicians: Greece 144, 145–6
Portugal 12; Bank of 87; consumer price index (CPI) 77; convergence criteria (1990s) 146; and EC Preferential Trade Agreement (PTA, 1972) 74; economic performance 79; economic performance (1990s) 77; economic policies 84; economic summary *80*; EMU accession 78; EU fiscal policy input 137; EU membership and economy 74–90; expenditures 78; findings summary *89*; fiscal constitution 85; fiscal convergence 83–4; fiscal performance 140; fiscal policy 77–84, 140, 145; fiscal problems 84–5; GDP 77; global crisis 82; ideas 84–8; institutional design and incentives 85; institutionalised political instability 149; institutions 84–8; interests 84–8; Ministry of Finance 87; national discourses 86; normative ideas 144; policy change 86; public administration 88; public debt 79; SGP violations 81; Social Democratic Party (PSD) 83; Socialist Party 81; state intervention 74
Pre-accession Instrument for Turkey (2001–6) 122
Preferential Trade Agreement (PTA, 1972) 74
pressures 20
private pension funds 66
production units: traditional 147–8
Prospective Directive (2003) 44
public debt: Italy 41; Portugal 79

Quaglia, L. 11, 35–49

Quality Inspections Committee (SPE, Greece) 23

Radaelli, C.M. 56, 69, 134; Europeanisation conception 5–6
regulatory agencies: independent 147
research design: Italy 36–8
research programme 1; defining attributes 2; Europeanisation as 5–7
Risse, T.: *et al* 37
Royo, S. 12, 73–90

Sarbanes-Oxley Act (US, 2002) 19
savings 43, 44
SGP (Stability and Growth Pact) 12, 40, 47, 76, 137; Excessive Deficit Procedure (EDP) 137; multilateral surveillance 76
Social Security Institution (SSI) 120
social security systems: Turkey 119–20
Sócrates, J. 81
Sotiropoulos, D.A. 58
South European Society and Politics 1
Southern Europe: asymmetry 152; capitalism 147; domestic political economies 3–5; Europeanisation adaptational pressures 4; pro-reform coalitions 144; worldviews 143
Southern Europe Periphery 1–13, 94; Europeanisation 133–52
Spain 12; adversarial industrial relations 151; constitutional decentralisation 148–9; domestic political economy 93; economic performance since democracy 96; employment policies 140–1; EU catch up quest 93–107; EU-level activation ideas 136; Europeanisation 94; expansion (1975–95) 96; female activity 101; ideas 102–6; institutional path dependency 104–5; institutions 102–6; interests 102–6; labour activation 103–4, 143; labour markets 101, 145; labour relations 105; Law on Dependency and Long-Term Care (2006) 102; Law for Effective Equality Between Women and Men (2007) 101; Law for Promotion of Autonomous Living and Help for Dependent Individuals (2006) 104; National Action Plans for Employment 141; National Reform Programmes 141; National Statistics Institute 108n; neoliberalism 103–4; policy innovation 104–5; policymakers 145; public policies 93; social policies 140–1; Southern European welfare typology 97; welfare 94; welfare development 95–8, *99-100*; welfare outcomes 98–102; women's role 101, *see also* PIGS
Stability and Growth Pact (SGP) *see* SGP
state intervention: Portugal 74

technocracy: empowerment 17–30
Theophanous, A.: *et al* 58
Transformation, Accommodation, Absorption, Inertia and Retrenchment 98
Transparency Directive (2004) 44
Treaty on European Union (TEU) 36, 76, 137
Turkey 12–13; adversarial industrial relations 148, 151; ALMPs 118–19; approach to employment 120–1; big businesses 126; bureaucratic tradition 147, 151; Confederation of Progressive Trade Unions 121; Constitutional Court 123; development model 120; DİSK (Confederation of Progressive Trade Unions) 121–2; Economic and Social Council 121; and EES (European Employment Strategy) 115–16, 116–17; employment policy 114, 117–22, 127–9; Europeanisation 113–29, 115–16, 117; flexibility 142; flexicurity 125, 126–7, 144; governance procedures 121–2; Human Resources Development Operational Programme (HRDOP) 128; ideas 122–7; institutions 122–7; Instrument for Pre-Accession Assistance (IPA) 122; instruments 122; interests 122–7; İŞKUR (Turkish Employment Agency) 116, 118–19, 122, 127–8, 141; Job Security Act (2002) 118; Labour Act (2003) 118, 125–6; labour law flexibility 118; lifelong learning systems 119, 128; macro-political systems 151; Ministry for EU Affairs 127; Ministry of Labour and Social Security 123, 126; Ministry of National Education (MoNE) 119; national employment policy 141; policy reform 144; policymaking procedures 121–2, 124; Pre-accession Instrument (2001–6) 122; production regime 151; social security systems 119–20; TOBB (Union of Chambers and Commodity Exchanges) 125–6; unions 126

Umbach, G.: and Ardy, B. 57
Unipo 43
United States (US): regulatory authority 18

Van Vilet, O.: and Koster, F. 57
Verney, S. 4, 13n

welfare: Spain 95–8, 98–102, *99-100*
welfare state studies 98
women: Spain 101
World Bank 95

Zartaloudis, S. 58

For Product Safety Concerns and Information please contact our EU representative GPSR@taylorandfrancis.com Taylor & Francis Verlag GmbH, Kaufingerstraße 24, 80331 München, Germany